DISCARD

# Creating
# Online Tutorials

# PRACTICAL GUIDES FOR LIBRARIANS

## ⟳ About the Series

This innovative series written and edited for librarians by librarians provides authoritative, practical information and guidance on a wide spectrum of library processes and operations.

Books in the series are focused, describing practical and innovative solutions to a problem facing today's librarian and delivering step-by-step guidance for planning, creating, implementing, managing, and evaluating a wide range of services and programs.

The books are aimed at beginning and intermediate librarians needing basic instruction/guidance in a specific subject and at experienced librarians who need to gain knowledge in a new area or guidance in implementing a new program/service.

## ⟳ About the Series Editor

The **Practical Guides for Librarians** series was conceived by and is edited by M. Sandra Wood, MLS, MBA, AHIP, FMLA, Librarian Emerita, Penn State University Libraries.

M. Sandra Wood was a librarian at the George T. Harrell Library, the Milton S. Hershey Medical Center, College of Medicine, Pennsylvania State University, Hershey, PA, for over thirty-five years, specializing in reference, educational, and database services. Ms. Wood worked for several years as a development editor for Neal-Schuman Publishers.

Ms. Wood received an MLS from Indiana University and an MBA from the University of Maryland. She is a fellow of the Medical Library Association and served as a member of MLA's Board of Directors from 1991 to 1995. Ms. Wood is founding and current editor of *Medical Reference Services Quarterly*, now in its thirty-fifth volume. She also was founding editor of the *Journal of Consumer Health on the Internet* and the *Journal of Electronic Resources in Medical Libraries* and served as editor/coeditor of both journals through 2011.

### Titles in the Series

# Creating
# Online Tutorials
## A Practical Guide
## for Librarians

**Hannah Gascho Rempel**
**Maribeth Slebodnik**

PRACTICAL GUIDES FOR LIBRARIANS, NO. 17

ROWMAN & LITTLEFIELD
*Lanham • Boulder • New York • London*

Published by Rowman & Littlefield
A wholly owned subsidiary of The Rowman & Littlefield Publishing Group, Inc.
4501 Forbes Boulevard, Suite 200, Lanham, Maryland 20706
www.rowman.com

Unit A, Whitacre Mews, 26-34 Stannary Street, London SE11 4AB

British Library Cataloguing in Publication Information Available

**Library of Congress Cataloging-in-Publication Data**

Rempel, Hannah Gascho.
  Creating online tutorials : a practical guide for librarians / Hannah Gascho Rempel, Maribeth Slebodnik.
      pages cm
  Includes bibliographical references and index.
  ISBN 978-0-8108-9326-9 (cloth : alk. paper) – ISBN 978-0-8108-9243-9 (pbk. : alk. paper) – ISBN 978-0-8108-9244-6 (ebook)  1. Library orientation–Web-based instruction. 2. Web-based instruction–Design.  I. Slebodnik, Maribeth, 1957– II. Title.
  Z711.2R37 2015
  025.5'6–dc23

                                                                              2015008317

♾™ The paper used in this publication meets the minimum requirements of American National Standard for Information Sciences—Permanence of Paper for Printed Library Materials, ANSI/NISO Z39.48-1992.

Printed in the United States of America

*To Marc, Madeleine, and Katherine*—Hannah

*To my two best guys: my father, David A. Slebodnik, dearly loved
and daily missed, and Mr. Pearson, who came along at last*—Maribeth

# Contents

# Figures and Tables

## 🌀 Figures

# ⊚ Tables

# Preface

## Why Do You Need to Read a Book on How to Create Tutorials?

Online tutorials are increasingly an expected component of library instruction programs. The ability to reach out to learners wherever they are, whenever is convenient for them through tutorials is a logical extension of librarians' core value of providing equitable access to information. As a result, the ability to create tutorials is becoming an assumed skill set for many librarians. However, librarians come to instruction-related tasks with a wide range of past experiences. Few of us are experts in instructional design, e-learning theory, or sometimes teaching in general. That said—most of us are willing to learn! *Creating Online Tutorials: A Practical Guide for Librarians* focuses on the nuts and bolts of designing and constructing tutorials and strives to provide a framework to help you make informed decisions as you create tutorials.

For librarians who have never created tutorials before, beginning with concrete tasks and a clear strategy will help you feel more confident as you try out a range of new skills and concepts. And because creating tutorials involves a wide range of skills, you will likely realize that you possess some of these skills already. For those who have already had previous experience in creating tutorials but still feel like you are missing some key skills or best practices, embracing an intentional process for creating tutorials will help fill in those gaps and develop a road map for creating more successful tutorials. Regardless of your starting point, *Creating Online Tutorials* will save time and prevent frustration as you move toward the desired end result of creating effective and engaging tutorials for your learners.

## What Will You Take Away from This Book?

*Creating Online Tutorials: A Practical Guide for Librarians* uses the familiar ADDIE (**a**nalysis—**d**esign—**d**evelopment—**i**mplementation—**e**valuation) model for instructional design as a framework for creating tutorials. In particular you can use this framework to:

- Create a learner-centered tutorial based on information relevant to your context
- Design an instructional strategy based on learning goals that clearly link to assessment outcomes

- Develop a tutorial using tools appropriate for the content you want to teach
- Implement a tutorial that will be user friendly for your learners
- Evaluate how effective your tutorial has been in promoting learning

This book is written with the assumption that technologies will continue to change and that the same technology available when this book was written may not be available in exactly the same form when you read this book. As a result, as you read, focus on the key instructional principles that you can use to help evaluate the tools that are available in your context. Technology can be a stumbling block for some librarians considering tutorial design, and the frustrations associated with learning new technologies are not minor obstacles. Make time to increase the skills you need by focusing on the areas in which you are not as proficient. Be willing to practice and ask for help when needed. While this book is not designed to provide all the answers to every technology question that may come up, the knowledge gained from reading this book will help you focus on the instructional principles surrounding your questions so that you will be able to arrive at your own solution.

## How Is This Book Organized?

*Creating Online Tutorials: A Practical Guide for Librarians* is organized using the ADDIE framework. One of the benefits of using the ADDIE framework is that the model is meant to be used recursively. Consequently, you should read through the book in that spirit. Likely you will return to some sections repeatedly as you find yourself redesigning or reevaluating at various points in your own tutorial-creation practice.

Chapters 1 and 2 guide you through the process of preparing and planning how to start your tutorial project. Beginning with a solid plan, gathering the appropriate tools, and figuring out who will be working with you on this project will help you to deliver your final project in a timely manner.

Chapters 3 and 4 walk through best practices for developing a tutorial based on your learners' needs. Analyzing what the learning gaps are and then developing learning objectives based on those gaps will provide you with an instructional strategy for scaffolding the rest of your tutorial-creation project.

Chapters 5 and 6 cover a wide range of tools needed to assemble your tutorial. You will develop an understanding of what tools work best for your content, along with a deeper knowledge of the choices you can make to develop a professional tutorial that is accessible for your learners.

Chapters 7, 8, and 9 help you develop the skills needed to create a tutorial that achieves what you want it to. Focusing on usability, promoting your tutorial to the right stakeholder groups, assessing how well your learners understand the content delivered in the tutorial, and developing a maintenance plan will ensure that your tutorial will be effective for many years.

## Some Key Terminology

Before you begin reading, take a little time to browse through the definitions for a few of the key terms frequently used in this book. Language changes over time, and some of these words may have different meanings in different contexts. Other terms will be defined in the chapters in which they appear. For the purposes of this book, the term *tutorial* is used broadly to include all online instructional learning tools from learning objects to elements of LibGuides or other types of library guides to video demonstrations. The term *learner* is also used broadly and includes students, patrons, or staff who might be the intended audience for a tutorial. Finally, the term *instructional design* is defined as a process that includes analysis of learners' needs and strategic and systematic development of learning materials suited to the learners' context.

## Learning by Doing

The practice of learning by doing links back to another core value of librarians—lifelong learning. Use the best practices, examples, and strategies discussed in *Creating Online Tutorials* to continue your commitment to your own professional development. As with most things in life, your ability to create successful tutorials that meet your learners' needs will grow the more you practice. Adapt the examples provided in *Creating Online Tutorials* to your own context. Start with a small project and progressively increase the number of new elements you add to your tutorial-creation repertoire. And then share your work with others, so that the broader librarian community can profit and learn from your experience!

# Acknowledgments

Thank you to the Oregon State University Libraries' Teaching and Engagement Department for all of the encouragement, insights, and kindness you have provided along the way. You all have helped me to become a better librarian and teacher.

—Hannah

Thanks to all my mentors and colleagues in Missouri and Indiana, whose support and encouragement has shaped my practice as a librarian and educator.

—Maribeth

# Getting Started
# with Online Tutorials

ONLINE TUTORIALS SEEM TO BE EVERYWHERE—on library websites, software websites, web guides to knitting and all manner of crafts, you name it! In this book, tutorials will be defined broadly to include a wide spectrum of possible levels of technological sophistication, as well as a variety of ways that learners may choose to interact with the content. Tutorials created using everything from Microsoft Power-Point to Articulate Storyline will be covered, along with options for creating tutorials with text, images, or videos. You will also learn about tutorials created for learners who are required to take tutorials, as well as those created for learners simply looking for help at a particular point of need.

Throughout this book the focus will be on providing frameworks for you to make informed decisions rather than on suggesting one "best" path or tool for making tutorials. This approach was chosen due to the wide range of skills and previous knowledge that librarians bring to the tutorial-creation process, the constantly changing technological landscape, and the desire to keep pedagogical considerations at the forefront of the tutorial-creation process. To that end, this chapter will start with a discussion of some of the reasons why you should make tutorials, along with some of the barriers to creating tutorials in order to help you decide whether tutorials are right for your instructional program. Next, to keep learners and their needs at the center of the tutorial-creation process, instructional design strategies will be introduced. Last, tips will be provided to help you start creating tutorials.

## ⊚ Building a Case for Making Tutorials

Just because tutorials are apparently everywhere doesn't mean you are automatically comfortable with creating them. Don't worry—many librarians feel the same way. In a nationwide survey conducted in 2010, Anne-Marie Deitering and Hannah Gascho Rempel (2012) found that the two biggest barriers for librarians who wanted to create tutorials were lack of time and a feeling that they didn't have enough technology skills. Most librarians can probably relate to those feelings. The skills needed to create new tutorials don't always seem easy to acquire, and carving out the time to learn those skills or to try out new things can feel daunting. However, the importance and demand for online tutorials isn't diminishing. In fact, tutorials are increasingly necessary as more learners access library tools and content either from a distance or outside of standard classroom times. So if you haven't jumped into learning about creating tutorials yet, now is the time to give it a try!

To help build a case for the value of online tutorials (either for yourself or for your administrators), this chapter begins with a discussion of two major reasons why you should create online tutorials: to help you better connect with your learners and to support your instructional program.

### Learner-Centered Focus

One of the key reasons for developing online tutorials reflects librarians' learner-centered focus—librarians recognize the importance of meeting learners at their point of need. Tutorials help to meet learners at their point of need in a variety of ways (see sidebar). Much of the impetus for creating online tutorials starts with the first learner-centered need—the need to access information at a distance, regardless of where learners are located. Providing online tutorials allows learners to access library concepts and skills regardless of their proximity to campus or the library. The popularity of a wide range of alternative educational delivery models, from massive open online courses (MOOCs) to more traditional online courses to hybrid courses, means that many learners will not attend library instruction programs in person. Even students who live on or near a college campus may prefer to use web-based tutorials rather than try to fit a face-to-face class into their schedule. Providing web-based alternatives ensures that learners both on and off campus, in or out of the library can learn more about how to engage with library resources and information literacy concepts regardless of their location.

Another aspect of point-of-need instruction recognizes that libraries and librarians serve learners of many abilities. Some learners have visual or hearing impairments or need to approach learning at a different pace than what can be accommodated in a typical fifty-minute instruction session. Online tutorials provide learners with the option to use closed-captioning or screen readers. Alternatively, learners can watch the same learning module multiple times at their own pace. Technological advances in accessibility continue to help librarians serve all learners better.

An additional way that tutorials can help librarians to more effectively meet learners at their point of need is by giving learners more control of their own learning environment. Tutorials can be a great strategy for helping to solve the perennial problem that librarians face when attempting to teach relevant content to learners from widely varying educational backgrounds. Not only can learners choose the pace at which they will proceed through a tutorial based on different learning needs, but tutorials can also be constructed with different content levels to allow learners with more experience to choose more challenging or advanced content. In addition, if learners need remedial help, tutorials can provide that branch of instruction as well. The option to simply click a button and get different instructional content based on each individual learner's needs and past learning experiences just isn't an option in an in-person session.

## Supporting Library Instructors and Instruction Programs

Online tutorials can also help library instruction programs more realistically meet their goals and more effectively make use of librarians' skills in an environment where resources are continually shifting. The option to deliver instruction via an asynchronous online tutorial helps resolve some of the scalability issues many libraries struggle with. While a single librarian can't physically be in two classrooms at the same time or provide in-person instruction twenty-four hours a day, an online tutorial that same librarian creates can be viewed by hundreds of classes at the same time. Student learning can even take place via an online tutorial when the librarian is happily asleep, dreaming of new online modules to make!

Online tutorials can enhance a library's instruction program not only by replacing in-person instruction to help deal with issues of scalability but also by supplementing in-person instruction. The e-learning community has continued to adapt sound pedagogical approaches to the online environment. One of these adaptations has been to "flip" the classroom (Educause 2012) by delivering lecture content online ahead of class so that in-class time can be used for more engaging, active-learning activities. Academic librarians have been using the flipped classroom model to explain key concepts in tutorials that students watch prior to class, enabling them to spend in-class time involved in group exercises or in researching topics with targeted advice from librarians (Arnold-Garza 2014; Benjes-Small and Tucker 2013). Another pedagogical strategy that has been adapted to the online-learning context employs active-learning techniques to help learners create meaning and understanding based on their own contexts. Therese Skagen et al. (2009) discuss this type of social-constructivist approach in their development of a term-long online tutorial that involves reflection, tiered learning options, and online discussions. These types of learning activities create more personalized interactions and a higher degree of accountability that may lead to higher retention and hopefully increased learning (Westerveldt 2013).

While this type of intensely interactive approach may not be possible for all tutorial projects, for many librarians, making sure there are viable options for active learning is key to their understanding of themselves as an effective teacher. Creating truly active and interactive learning experiences is a very real goal to keep in mind when making tutorials. It is encouraging that tools are continually becoming available that make it easier to build in interactive elements in order to engage learners in appealing ways. Chapter 4 will introduce you to ways to incorporate these kinds of activities.

Online tutorials can also provide great options for learners with a variety of learning styles. Lori Mestre (2012) documents a range of approaches that tutorial creators can use to engage learners with different learning-style preferences. Some of these pedagogical ideas and best practices will be discussed more in chapter 4, but take heart—in many ways, online tutorials can be used to complement the in-person strategies you have already been using to engage and reach out to learners with different learning styles. Creating tutorials does not mean checking your pedagogical values at the door! If you have been wondering whether or not learners actually learn anything via online tutorials, you are not alone. Library researchers have been asking that same question. For example, when Penny Beile and David Boote (2005) examined the effectiveness of tutorials in comparison to face-to-face sessions for a group of graduate students, they found that students performed similarly on a multiple-choice quiz assessing their learning, regardless of the delivery method. Joanna Burkhardt, Jim Kinnie, and Carina Cournoyer (2008) found that online students actually performed slightly better on the learning assessments in a for-credit course than those who were taking the course in person.

At this point, the literature seems to indicate that for many information literacy concepts, learners are able to acquire the skills they need to begin their information literacy journey by means of online tutorials. However, continued assessments are necessary to make sure that learners are meeting the desired learning outcomes via online delivery platforms, especially at your local institution. Assessment will be discussed in more depth in chapters 4 and 8. In addition, suggestions for assessments that go beyond multiple-choice questions will be provided in those chapters if you want to work toward encouraging deeper engagement with the learning materials in your tutorial.

## Barriers to Creating and Using Tutorials

You should now have a better sense of where tutorials can fit into your instructional program in terms of meeting your learners at their point of need and supporting your

## LEARNER- AND LIBRARIAN-BASED CONCERNS ABOUT USING TUTORIALS

### Learner-Based Concerns

- Creating authentic interactivity takes work
- Can be difficult to create meaningful interpersonal interactions

### Librarian-Based Concerns

- Time consuming to create
- Require maintenance

library's instruction program. However, it is also important to acknowledge some of the difficulties that tutorials pose for both learners and librarians. Learner-centered concerns will be discussed first, followed by hurdles for tutorial creators.

## Learner-Centered Concerns

The importance of including interactive elements in a tutorial in order to support learning was touched on earlier in this chapter. Including interactive elements can take programming time and skills, and interactive elements may be difficult to keep up to date. However, including fancy Adobe Flash–based interactions is not the only way to provide interactivity. And increasingly, because of the incompatibility of most mobile devices with Flash-based products, this type of interactive element is no longer desirable anyway. Simpler methods of providing interactivity are possible. In fact, for many library-based skills, Mestre (2012) found that the opportunity to practice within a realistic context can be more desirable for learners than a complicated gaming scenario. Another interactive option suggested by Rita-Marie Conrad and J. Ana Donaldson (2011) is the use of problem-based learning to "hook" learners into realistic learning scenarios. Without meaningful interactive components in a tutorial, it is difficult for learners to transfer what they have learned to new situations. Chapter 4 will discuss how to design tutorials that provide multiple opportunities for interaction.

Another issue that needs to be addressed when considering how well learners will engage with a tutorial is the difficulty of creating truly personal online experiences. Librarians have long recognized the importance of the "human touch" in library interactions. Ameliorating library anxiety has been a standard affective learning outcome for many in-person library sessions (Onwuegbuzie and Jiao 2004), especially sessions for first-year students (Farkas 2013). However, many learners who take an online tutorial will never meet a librarian in person or perhaps even enter your library building.

The question of how to create a personal connection within a tutorial is not an easy problem to solve. Success in creating meaningful interpersonal interactions has been described for a term-long hybrid course through the use of online discussion boards and group work (Thorpe 2008); however, not as many libraries are involved in creating these types of online learning experiences. For shorter tutorials, the only option for a personal connection may be the inclusion of a library chat box. In some cases, avatars or videos of a real instructor may provide sufficient human connection. And, of course, there will always be those students who may be perfectly content not to have a personal connection with a librarian! For now, recognizing that creating a personal experience is a real concern and continuing to provide online channels for communication, whether in real time, as with chat, or with other methods, such as FAQs or good old-fashioned e-mail, may need to suffice.

## Library Instructor and Instruction Program Concerns

While considering the learners' needs is essential, unfortunately you don't function in a world with endless resources in terms of time, money, or skills, so clearly your needs must be considered as well. One of the great promises of using tutorials is that they will help save time. And this time-saving concept certainly has elements of truth: tutorials created modularly can be recombined and used in a variety of contexts, and they can be shared with others, thus helping to avoid the infamous re-creating of the wheel trap. Tutorials can certainly help extend limited instructors' time, but creating tutorials can also take a substantial amount of time.

Chapter 2 will detail the importance of planning your tutorial project carefully and will provide some illustrations of the amount of time example tutorial projects have taken. Depending on your current level of expertise (or the expertise of those around you that you can borrow from), you may need to acquire some training in storyboarding or graphic design or a few programming skills. And even if you (extremely lucky and rare person) already have all of those skills, inevitably technology, vendor interfaces, and the content you want to teach rapidly changes or goes out of date, and tutorials need to be updated and maintained. The time investment in tutorial maintenance will need to be part of your ongoing routine. However, the payoff in the increased ways that you are able to reach out to your learners should make this investment worth your while.

## Designing Tutorials Based on Knowledge Types

The remainder of this chapter will focus on some of the building blocks of instructional design in order to help organize the process of deciding what type of tutorial to create, how to create your tutorial, and how to measure whether or not your tutorial is effective. Don't feel like you need to incorporate each and every one of these instructional design elements into all of your tutorials. Selectively used, these elements can provide a basic foundation to help you think through the steps of tutorial creation regardless of whether you are considering a simple learning object or a more complex project.

Before you embark on a tutorial project, one of the most important things to think about is whether or not you are choosing the right tool for the job. In other words, before you start drafting your tutorial, ask yourself whether a tutorial is the best instructional strategy for the type of knowledge you want your learners to gain. Online educational content like tutorials have been described as most suitable for "task-based learning," for learning skills or "how to do something" (Raftery 2010, 213–14). Fortunately, a lot of library instruction falls into this category and can be well suited for tutorials. In this next section, we will take Stephen Covey's (2013) advice and "begin with the end in mind." We will think about what it is we want our learners to know and then think backward as to how a tutorial can (or can't) help them gain that knowledge.

One way to think about whether or not a tutorial is the best tool for your instructional job is to consider what type of learning you are trying to communicate, or as instructional designers Patricia Smith and Tillman Ragan (2005) describe it, what kind of knowledge are you trying to teach? Smith and Ragan created a list of different knowledge types that instructors try to convey in instructional settings. The benefit of categorizing learning into various knowledge types is that instructors can then choose the learning strategies that are most effective for each knowledge type. Lesley Farmer (2011) suggested some adaptations to these knowledge types specifically for library instruction. In this book, these knowledge types are further adapted to apply to online library instruction (see table 1.1).

**Table 1.1.** Determining the Appropriateness of Using a Tutorial and Tutorial Strategies by Types of Knowledge.[1]

| | WHAT IS IT? | LIBRARY EXAMPLE | LEVEL OF APPROPRIATENESS FOR TUTORIALS |
|---|---|---|---|
| Declarative Knowledge | Learning baseline facts, memorizing terminology | Learning database names or library vocabulary (e.g., "catalog," "interlibrary loan," "call numbers") that will help learners navigate the library's website | Very High |
| Conceptual Knowledge | The ability to apply knowledge to new situations; the ability to categorize information | The ability to recognize and differentiate different information containers, such as scholarly articles, trade publications, blogs, commercial websites, so that learners can more efficiently navigate the information they encounter | High |
| Procedural Knowledge | Knowing how to do things in a particular order and then applying these procedures to a new situation | Learning how to start with broad keywords, then use facets to narrow a search; or learning how to use a particular tool like Zotero | High |
| Problem-Solving Knowledge | Combining previously learned procedures, concepts, or declarative knowledge to solve a new problem. This type of knowledge contains an element of domain-specific knowledge. | Troubleshooting a search; starting with keywords and iteratively searching based on new knowledge gained from successive searches and reading; using a variety of tools to explore an idea and retrieve the actual sources | Low |
| Cognitive Strategies | Learning to learn, using metacognition and self-reflection. This is not a domain-specific practice. | Note taking; concept mapping; brainstorming | Low |
| Attitude Learning | The predisposition to approach a task in a certain way | Library anxiety; finding sources then forming conclusions; thinking like a researcher | Low to none |
| Psychomotor Skills | Practicing skills that contain a physical element; learning to "perform coordinated muscular movements" | Remedial computer instruction, such as how to use a mouse or keyboarding skills | Low |

[1] Adapted from Smith and Ragan 2005.

This section will discuss the knowledge types best suited for the online environment as well as learning strategies and examples to help you successfully think through designing a tutorial that meets particular instructional needs. The knowledge types that are the best fit for tutorials are discussed first, followed by the knowledge types that are less suited to the tutorial environment.

## Declarative Knowledge

*What is it?*—Declarative knowledge involves memorizing terminology and facts to achieve a basic understanding of a topic or field.

*Library example*—In libraries, becoming oriented to the library's website and learning basic library vocabulary such as "catalog," "interlibrary loan," and "call numbers" falls under the category of declarative knowledge.

*Learning strategies*—The suggested learning strategy for gaining declarative knowledge is basically practice, practice, practice.

*Appropriate for tutorials?*—Yes, the repetition required to acquire declarative knowledge makes tutorials highly appropriate.

*Tutorial activities*—Some suggested tutorial activities to help learn declarative knowledge, such as library lingo, are to include self-checks and quizzes with a variety of multiple-choice, true/false, or drag-and-drop questions that allow learners to try out new terminology several times in a variety of ways. Depending on the assessment tools available to you (a range of assessment options will be covered in chapters 4, 7, and 8), consider including heat maps to allow learners to click on and identify information on a picture of a library website. Finally, link the quiz questions you ask with learners' existing knowledge to help reinforce their skills.

## Conceptual Knowledge

*What is it?*—Conceptual knowledge is the ability to apply knowledge to new situations, as well as the ability to categorize information.

*Library example*—The ability to recognize and differentiate between different information containers, such as scholarly articles, trade publications, blogs, and commercial websites, or the ability to distinguish between citations for a book or an article are examples of conceptual knowledge in a library setting. This knowledge requires learners to see patterns in information to help make sense of the information they find.

*Learning strategies*—To learn how to categorize information, it is helpful to provide learners with a stepwise checklist or dichotomous decision-making tree. These types of learning tools help learners see the process behind how information becomes categorized in different ways. In addition, it is a good idea to use multiple examples and images to help learners apply knowledge to a variety of new contexts.

*Appropriate for tutorials?*—Yes, the types of decision-making tools and visualizations involved in gaining conceptual knowledge translate well to tutorials.

*Tutorial activities*—Suggested tutorial activities to reinforce learning include matching exercises, creating a concept map by dragging and dropping terms from a list of choices, and filling in "if/then" statements about types of source containers such as books or journals. For example, a sample question could ask: "If a citation contains the name of a publisher, the source is a _____."

## Procedural Knowledge

*What is it?*—Procedural knowledge involves knowing how to do things in a particular order and then applying those procedures to a new situation.

*Library example*—In libraries, learners use procedural knowledge when they learn how to iteratively navigate the research process, for example, by starting with broad keywords in a database search, then using facets to narrow the search. Procedural knowledge is also important for learning how to use particular tools, such as a bibliographic manager like Zotero, which requires following a specified set of directions to make the tool work in the desired manner.

*Learning strategies*—It is easier to gain procedural knowledge if each step describes a single action. Break the steps of the process into phases so learners don't have to learn all of the steps at once. Teaching procedural knowledge requires a high degree of clarity on the part of the instructor and the ability to visualize the process at a granular level.

*Appropriate for tutorials?*—Yes, procedural knowledge can be communicated effectively through tutorials. However, applying the knowledge will typically involve using an interface or tool that is not embedded within the tutorial itself, such as Zotero or a subject database. Tutorial-creation tools like Guide on the Side (http://code.library.arizona.edu/) can mitigate that drawback by allowing learners to practice what they are learning in the tutorial directly on a library website without having to leave the tutorial or the library website.

*Tutorial activities*—Learners can demonstrate that they have learned how to do a particular procedure by dragging and dropping actions into a correct sequence order. Depending on the level of feedback you are able to give, learners could upload screenshots of a completed action or demonstrate the end result of having correctly followed an entire procedure. For example, learners could upload a screenshot of their own Zotero library collection or a set of search results that they have narrowed using facets. Another, more high-touch option could involve requiring learners to provide a self-report or journal of the steps they took to perform the assigned procedure.

## Problem-Solving Knowledge

*What is it?*—Problem-solving knowledge requires that learners combine previously learned procedures, concepts, or declarative knowledge in order to solve a new problem. This type of knowledge contains an element of domain-specific (or subject-specific) knowledge and gets at the idea of a learner demonstrating expertise in a particular field.

*Library example*—Problem-solving knowledge is applied in library or information literacy contexts when learners are able to troubleshoot a search or when they are able to start a search in a database with basic keywords and then search iteratively based on new knowledge gained from successive searching and reading. Learners also display problem-solving knowledge when they use a variety of search tools and sources to explore an idea and when they are able to follow through and locate the actual sources from a list of results.

*Learning strategies*—Problem-solving knowledge is easier to learn when the problems or scenarios start simply and then move to a higher level of complexity. The use of simulations or problem-based learning helps to provide a sense of real-world applicability to problem-solving knowledge.

*Appropriate for tutorials?*—The appropriateness is low—it can be difficult to come up with genuine scenarios at the appropriate level of domain-specific expertise. Situational performance is difficult to model within a tutorial without being overly simplistic. Problem-solving questions by their nature are ill-defined problems (problems with multiple solutions), so it is not easy to genuinely assess this knowledge type through multiple choice or other automatically graded solutions.

*Tutorial activities*—If you need to use a tutorial to teach problem-solving knowledge, there are still some available learning activities. One exercise could involve providing search results pages and search strings and then asking the learners to analyze them for errors or suggested improvements. Another option could involve the use of heat maps to track clicks in a "hands-on" exercise to see what decisions learners use to solve a problem. More in-depth multiple-choice questions could be crafted in order to measure higher-order learning skills such as problem solving. If you are able to provide more direct assessment and feedback that is not automatically graded, you could include open-ended questions. Finally, depending on the scope of the tutorial you are creating, you could incorporate a discussion board for learners to respond to questions and work with other learners to solve a problem.

## Cognitive Strategies

*What is it?*—Cognitive strategies describe the process of learning how to learn using techniques like metacognition and self-reflection. Cognitive strategies are not domain or subject specific and can be broadly applied to many learning situations.

*Library example*—Teaching note taking, concept mapping, or brainstorming skills as part of the research process are all part of gaining cognitive strategies for learning.

*Learning strategies*—Direct explanation of particular strategies alongside concrete examples is a helpful way to teach cognitive strategies. Guiding learners through self-questioning prompts and assigning significant writing projects that require synthesis and self-reflection help learners practice cognitive strategies in a meaningful way.

*Appropriate for tutorials?*—The appropriateness is low—while it may be possible to explain cognitive strategies with a tutorial, it is difficult to create meaningful activities in the tutorial environment that allow learners to demonstrate their use of these strategies.

*Tutorial activities*—Tutorials can be used to demonstrate cognitive strategies. This could be done with a video of the instructor—or perhaps even better, with a student—thinking aloud while using a particular strategy such as brainstorming at the beginning of the research process. In terms of incorporating activities that allow learners to practice cognitive strategies within the tutorial, multiple-choice questions asking about a variety of cognitive strategies could be used to help learners think through how they might apply cognitive strategies to their own research process. However, the best activities would involve longer, self-reflective exercises necessitating individualized feedback.

## Attitude Learning

*What is it?*—The predisposition to approach a task in a certain way is attitude learning.

*Library example*—There are several examples within library settings where attitude learning has an impact. One example is when learners experience library anxiety and approach the process of using the library, especially the library's physical space, in a fearful or anxious manner. A more positive example is when learners are able to think of themselves like a researcher and have the research self-efficacy needed to visualize themselves as a full participant in the research and learning process. Another example of attitude learning is when learners find sources first and then form conclusions based on those sources.

*Learning strategies*—Attitudes can be learned via demonstration by an instructor model. If an instructor displays a particular attitude, learners will start to emulate that attitude. Role-playing can help learners practice and adopt new attitudes. Use of case studies and simulations are another way to practice new attitudes. Additionally, attitude learning can take place through the use of discussion boards where learners can observe other participants' attitudes and adjust their attitudes by answering question prompts.

*Appropriate for tutorials?*—The appropriateness is low—because of the highly interpersonal nature of attitude learning, tutorials are not the most effective way to learn this type of knowledge. It would be difficult to give the kind of feedback needed to make changes in attitudes. In addition, some of the exercises for practicing attitude learning, such as role-playing and case studies, do not translate particularly well to the tutorial environment because the opportunity for more deeply engaging with the scenario is not as realistic. It is not impossible to make attitude-learning gains with tutorials, but it is certainly more challenging.

*Tutorial activities*—Attitude learning could be demonstrated through a video recording of a student discussing their evolving attitude toward the library and how they used specific help features in the library. Assessment components could include reading through a scenario or case study and then answering in-depth multiple-choice questions about what their behaviors might be in response to the scenario.

## Psychomotor Skills

*What is it?*—Psychomotor skills require the learner to practice skills that contain a physical element and to learn how to "perform coordinated muscular movements" (Smith and Ragan 2005, 82).

*Library example*—Remedial computer instruction, such as how to use a mouse or keyboarding skills, is an example of learning psychomotor skills.

*Learning strategies*—Demonstration with repeated, hands-on practice is the most effective way to learn psychomotor skills.

*Appropriate for tutorials?*—The appropriateness is low—the need to demonstrate with the degree of hands-on assistance required by most learners developing these types of remedial psychomotor skills makes tutorials less than ideal. However, once a certain degree of psychomotor comfort is gained, learners might be able to practice their psychomotor skills using an online tutorial.

*Tutorial activities*—A tutorial to help learners gain psychomotor skills could contain a video demonstration of how to use a particular tool, such as a mouse. After watching the video, learners could be directed through games or exercises that help them to practice mousing over and clicking on specific items.

## Summary of Knowledge Types and Tutorial Use

Thinking about what type of knowledge you are trying to teach and then examining whether or not tutorials will be an effective tool to meet your instructional goals is an important step in the process of creating a tutorial. Teaching content that includes declarative knowledge, conceptual knowledge, and procedural knowledge is an excellent use of the tutorial platform and can be effective both in terms of content delivery and providing interactivity and feedback to learners. It will be more difficult to provide engaging experiences and meaningful feedback in a tutorial setting for content that is focused on problem-solving knowledge, cognitive strategies, attitude learning, or psychomotor skills. Depending on the scope of your tutorial or whether you plan to include in-person interactivity in a hybrid or flipped course, some aspects of a tutorial platform may still be effective for teaching the latter group of knowledge types. Once you have determined whether a tutorial is an effective tool for your instructional goals, you can use the tutorial activities suggested throughout this section as a starting point to generate relevant ideas for your own topics.

# Using ADDIE to Help Guide Your Tutorial Design

Once you've determined whether and how a tutorial will help meet the identified instructional need, you can begin to think about starting the design process. A design process can act as a framework to help you think purposefully and sequentially about the learners and the learning steps involved in developing a tutorial. This book will use the iterative ADDIE model (Clark 2014) to help you create that framework (see figure 1.1). There are now many instructional design models available, but the ADDIE model is one of the most well known and provides a great deal of flexibility. This section provides an overview of the five steps of the ADDIE model to help you understand the scaffolding of the remainder of the book. As a review or an introduction (depending on your previous knowledge), the ADDIE model consists of the following steps:

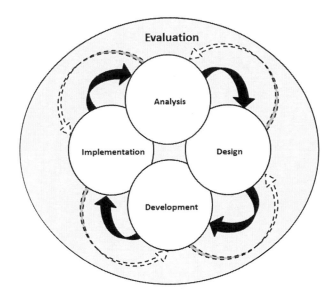

**Figure 1.1.** The ADDIE model for instructional design, which reflects both an iterative workflow and the overarching importance of evaluation. *Adapted from Clark, 2010*

A—Analysis

D—Design

D—Development

I—Implementation

E—Evaluation

These steps, which will be described in more detail in the following chapters, as well as connected to equivalent steps in the tutorial design and construction process, are meant to be dynamic and overlapping. However, in their earliest descriptions, they were viewed as more sequential than interactive. And though initially designed to be used for military training, the ADDIE model has been adapted as a process for all types of training and learning due to its flexibility and ability to interact with additional components, such as prototyping, as needed.

One caveat—while analysis is the first step in the ADDIE model, it's important to define your instructional need before beginning this process. A needs analysis can help describe the instructional need more clearly, but defining the problem is an essential starting point. For example: Do you need a more comprehensive, engaging, or concise orientation tutorial for incoming first-year students? Are your graduate students struggling with information management? Did you purchase a new sociology database that needs to be quickly explained and promoted to the right population? Once you have a handle on the problem you need to solve, the next steps of the process can be tackled more effectively.

The ADDIE model will be used in the following section to organize a series of initial questions to help you gather key information needed to begin the process of designing your tutorial. What follows will be a sketch of the steps, with greater detail filled in on the specific steps as you progress through the book.

## Analysis

*Needs analysis*—What is the problem you are trying to solve? Is a tutorial or other type of learning object the best solution for this problem, or is there another cause that should be addressed, such as better promotion of an existing resource?

*User analysis*—Who needs help with this problem? Do you have a primary and a secondary audience? What are the capabilities and potential limitations of the users you want to reach?

*Learning-environment analysis*—What is the environment in which the learners are learning (e.g., K–12, graduate education, job training)? What are the contexts in which (a) you discover this problem (e.g., class assignments, consistent reference questions, faculty requests or observations) and (b) they will use the skills they gain?

*Resource analysis*—How much time, money, equipment, and human support do you have to solve this problem?

*Review existing resources*—Has someone already solved this problem using a tutorial or other resource? Can you modify or promote an existing resource to solve this problem?

*Review what you've learned*—Is a tutorial the best solution for your problem? Do you have the data you need to move forward with this project?

## Design

*Learning objectives*—What do you want users to be able to do after interacting with this tutorial? Write two to three learning objectives that describe the goal of the tutorial.

*Assessment*—What type of learning exercises (quizzes, tasks, simulations, etc.) will be used to reinforce or evaluate learning? Does the tutorial need to interact with a learning management system (LMS)?

*Content development*—What content is essential to fulfill the stated learning objectives and equip learners to respond to assessment activities?

*Instructional strategies*—What type of knowledge are you trying to convey? What instructional strategies are recommended for that type of knowledge?

*Instructional or supplemental materials*—What content is essential to reinforce with supplemental learning materials or links to additional resources?

*Sequence instructional elements*—What is the logical way to structure the instruction? Does background information need to be briefly reviewed or instructional content scaffolded for optimal learning?

*Review what you've learned*—Do you have the design parameters in place that you need in order to move into the development phase? If you do not, then address those issues before progressing.

## Development

*Timeline*—How much time do you have to construct this tutorial? How will you specify meaningful steps that will provide measurable, achievable deadlines?

*Planning text and narrative*—How will you specify the key points you intend to cover? Time invested in an outline that grows into a script is time well invested!

*Planning graphics and navigation*—Is your tutorial heavy on images or does it have a narrative arc that images should conform to? Are you planning a multi-tutorial project? Does your interactivity plan allow users to move around the tutorial in a nonlinear fashion? A storyboard will be immensely helpful.

*Media or technology selection*—What are the best tools to use to build your tutorial? What tools are available to you or acquirable? Consider this rule of thumb—use the most stable, low-tech format that is applicable (Farmer 2011).

*Timing*—How long will your tutorial be? Short is good! Mestre (2012) recommends that screencasts be no more than one to two minutes long for skill-based tasks. Time the tutorial to allow for an average reading speed or give learners the ability to move at their own pace.

*Graphics, images, sound, and narration*—What concepts can best be communicated using visual images or narration? When are audio components, such as narration, helpful for learners, and when would a series of images or screenshots work equally well?

*Accessibility*—What accessibility features should you include? Assume that your audience may include differently abled individuals and provide transcripts to include appropriate cues for those learners.

*Review what you've learned*—Do you have what you need in order to construct a prototype or model for your tutorial and move into the implementation phase? If you do not, then address those issues before moving forward.

## Implementation

*Prototype*—Do you need to construct a prototype of the entire project or a portion thereof?

*Usability testing*—How will you recruit representative learners for brief usability testing? You may also consider testing your storyboard with representative learners for early feedback and correction.

*Promotion and marketing*—Who are your projected primary and secondary users of this tutorial? How will you let them know that this resource is available to them?

*Review what you've learned*—What changes need to be made based on the prototype and usability testing?

## Evaluation

*Summative evaluation*—How will you assess the user learning gains after interacting with the tutorial? Will that information be collected and shared with instructors (for example) or used for future revisions?

*Effectiveness of tutorial*—How does your tutorial align with your learning objectives? How are your learners performing on assessment activities (if you are capturing this)?

*Response to tutorial*—Are your intended users responding to and using the tutorial? You can collect this information via web analytics, questionnaires, surveys, interviews, observations, or testing.

*Plan for future revisions and updating*—What has changed since you published your tutorial, for example, website or curricular redesign?

# Learning from the Educational Community

Before getting into the technical elements of creating tutorials, take a look at what types of tutorials other librarians have already created and see what you can learn from these projects. You can find some projects by visiting library websites, tutorial repositories, or through reading about them in library literature. While it can be helpful to learn from others' past experiences, try not to get bogged down in the literature—the existing literature and resources about tutorial best practices, examples, and assessments is large! Instead, focus on what you can borrow or emulate. Much tutorial content is available for sharing through Creative Commons licenses. As a result, if you don't have a lot of time, it may help to begin by focusing on several well-established tutorial repositories. Here is an overview of two of the most popular tutorial repositories.

## MERLOT II—Multimedia Educational Resource for Learning and Online Teaching

The MERLOT II learning materials repository (www.merlot.org/) contains digital educational resources that can be freely used by educators from a wide variety of fields, not just libraries. However, MERLOT II does have an information literacy section. Topics covered range from basic research skills to evaluation of popular versus scholarly sources to more specific types of literacies, such as data literacy. You may also find it is a helpful source of discipline-specific instruction in areas with which you are not familiar. MERLOT II defines digital content broadly, so not all of the content is in tutorial form. Learning materials in the MERLOT II repository include lesson plans, open textbooks, quizzes, simulations, online tutorials, and more. All the materials are set up to be downloaded directly from the MERLOT II website. Materials can be peer reviewed (but not everything is) or reviewed by users with a ranking system. There is also a section of award-winning materials that showcases best practices in online learning.

## PRIMO—Peer-Reviewed Instructional Materials Online

The PRIMO database (primodb.org) is a project of the American Library Association's (ALA) Association of College and Research Libraries (ACRL) Instruction Section (IS). (Whew—now you know you're reading a book for librarians because you've gotten your dose of acronyms for the day.) As the "peer reviewed" name implies, the tutorials in this repository are carefully selected by instruction librarians to represent the highest quality tutorials on a range of library topics. There are hundreds of tutorials in this database on topics ranging from basic search skills to search skills for specific disciplines, such as business, to specific elements of the search process, such as using a database. The PRIMO tutorials are intended more for use as examples rather than for direct downloading. Links in the database take you directly to the reviewed tutorial rather than to a sharable version of the tutorial. While some of these tutorials could be easily incorporated into another library's website, most would need substantial tweaking to make them fit in with your library's website theme.

Perhaps just as helpful as the examples of these high quality tutorials themselves are surveys and interviews with the tutorial creators indicating how long it took them to create the tutorial, how many people were involved in creating the tutorial, how the tutorial was funded, and what technology they used in the tutorial-creation process. Much can be learned from the PRIMO database of surveys and PRIMO Site of the Month interviews about the nuts-and-bolts reality behind a great tutorial.

# ⑥ Initial Preparation

Now that you have considered why you might create a tutorial, instructional design ideas you might want to consider, and where to look for inspiration (or plain and simple borrowing!), it is time to begin thinking about how much planning and preparation you are going to need to do for your tutorial. Planning will be discussed much more extensively in chapter 2, but for now, it will be helpful to think about planning in terms of the scope of your project, who your audience will be, how you can break your work into smaller pieces, and what tools you will need to create your tutorial.

## Consider Your Scope

So far tutorials have been discussed as if they all fall into the same basket. But tutorials come in all shapes and sizes. There are tutorials that are short demonstrations of a relatively simple task, such as how to request an article through interlibrary loan. There are tutorials that cover a suite of linked tasks, such as generating keywords and searching in a database. Some tutorials cover a specific tool in an in-depth manner, such as a tutorial on how to use EndNote. And there are deeper concept-based tutorials that cover topics such as understanding Wikipedia and the creation of knowledge or the process involved in researching and writing a literature review. The amount of time invested in this wide range of tutorial types is highly variable, and obviously, the shorter, simple demonstration tutorials should take less time to create than the more in-depth, concept-based tutorials. As you read this book, make sure you keep your particular tutorial type in mind. Consult the PRIMO database for estimates of how long other librarians spent creating a tutorial that is similar to your concept. This book will cover a range of scenarios as examples, but make sure you are focusing on the suggestions that make sense for your context.

## Consider Your Audience

Considering the scope in terms of your topic is one element to keep in mind as you begin your project. Another element to consider is your audience. Chapter 3 will discuss both needs analysis and user analysis as a way to help you more fully understand what your learner audience needs. But before you even get to the analysis stage, it is helpful to briefly stop and think about who your audience is for this tutorial. Just as one-size-fits-all in-person instruction rarely actually does fit all, your tutorial content will probably resonate best with a particular group of learners. Thinking through who this audience is before administering a user analysis will help make sure you find the best fit for your tutorial from the beginning.

Considering your audience will also help you think about what other instructional elements you may (or may not) need to provide for your learners. For example, first-year college students will be much less familiar with a library's physical spaces. If you refer to finding a source in a physical location, you may need to provide supplemental materials with that information. In contrast, if the content is aimed at upper-division college students, you should not need to include as much background information, as too much tangential material can cause your learners to lose interest before they get to the content you really hoped they would learn.

## Build Up Your Skills

You are a learner in this process too. Just as you help novice learners in your classroom start with basic concepts and then build up to more complex ideas, start with a smaller project that lets you try a few new techniques. Even if you are working on a large project, find a smaller component of your larger project to start with. Build in some time for practice, and create early benchmarks for yourself to show that you are making progress. Finally, set limits for yourself—externally imposed deadlines may be helpful. Don't let the creation of a short demonstration video take over your life. Librarians suffer enough from perfectionist stereotypes—try not to fall into that trap!

## Tools to Assemble

Each of the chapters that follow will point you to some suggested tools that can help you with the process of creating a tutorial. Some of these tools will help you to stay organized, but most of the tools will help you with the technical aspects of creating a tutorial. Because it may take some time to get funding to purchase the technology you need or to simply order the technology and get it installed (if you don't already have some options available), it is a good idea to start thinking about what tools you might need early on. Again, the tools you choose will likely coincide with the scope of the project you are working on. However, a lot can be done with a fairly simple (and possibly inexpensive) suite of tools. For now consider assembling the following:

- Software that lets you create screenshots or screencasts—this can be as simple as Jing or as advanced as Camtasia.
- A survey tool that you can use to embed quizzes for interactivity and assessment—this can be as simple as SurveyMonkey or as advanced as Qualtrics. Note—many of the more advanced screencasting software include interactive components.
- A repository for your tutorials—this can be as simple as a LibGuide or could be server space set aside just for your tutorials.

To learn about your technology choices in more depth, read chapters 5 and 6.

## ⊚ Key Points

You have started on the journey toward creating a tutorial and have discovered there are a wide range of issues to think through when initiating a tutorial project. You now have a framework for deciding whether a tutorial will meet your instructional needs, both from the standpoint of learners and librarians. Here are some key points to take away:

- Tutorials can contribute to a learner-centered instruction program.
- Tutorials are more appropriate for delivering some types of knowledge than others, and learning strategies can be used to enhance the learning experience for each knowledge type.
- The ADDIE model provides a helpful framework for understanding the major steps of your tutorial-creation process.
- Several online repositories provide exemplary tutorials to use when looking for ideas for your own project.
- Planning ahead and breaking your tutorial project into smaller components will help make creating your tutorial simpler.

The next chapter will guide you through the steps of planning your tutorial process, whether it is simple or complex. It will focus on assembling resources, including personnel, and discuss planning strategies such as timelines and storyboards.

## ⊚ References

Arnold-Garza, Sara. 2014. "The Flipped Classroom Assessing an Innovative Teaching Model for Effective and Engaging Library Instruction." *College & Research Libraries News* 75, no. 1: 10–13.

Beile, Penny M., and David N. Boote. 2005. "Does the Medium Matter? A Comparison of a Web-Based Tutorial with Face-to-Face Library Instruction on Education Students' Self-Efficacy Levels and Learning Outcomes." *Research Strategies* 20, no. 1–2: 57–68.

Benjes-Small, Candice, and Katelyn Tucker. 2013. "Keeping Up With . . . Flipped Classrooms." ACRL Publications—Keeping Up With . . . http://www.ala.org/acrl/publications/keep ing_up_with/flipped_classrooms.

Burkhardt, Joanna M., Jim Kinnie, and Carina M. Cournoyer. 2008. "Information Literacy Successes Compared: Online vs. Face to Face." *Journal of Library Administration* 48, no. 3/4: 379–89.

Clark, Don. 2010. "A Framework for Designing Learning Environments." *Big Dog and Little Dog's Performance Juxtaposition.* http://www.nwlink.com/~donclark/hrd/learning_environ ment_framework.html.

———. 2014. "ADDIE Model." *Big Dog and Little Dog's Performance Juxtaposition.* http://www. nwlink.com/~donclark/history_isd/addie.html.

Conrad, Rita-Marie, and J. Ana Donaldson. 2011. *Engaging the Online Learner: Updated Activities and Resources for Creative Instruction.* Updated ed. Jossey-Bass Guides to Online Teaching and Learning. San Francisco, CA: Jossey-Bass.

Covey, Stephen. 2013. "Books—7 Habits of Highly Effective People—Habit 2: Begin with the End in Mind." Stephen R. Covey website. Accessed December 19. https://www.stephencovey. com/7habits/7habits-habit2.php.

Deitering, Anne-Marie, and Hannah Gascho Rempel. 2012. "Share and Share Alike: Barriers and Solutions to Tutorial Creation and Management." *Communications in Information Literacy* 5, no. 2: 102–16.

Educause. 2012. "7 Things You Should Know about Flipped Classrooms." EDUCAUSE Learning Initiative. http://www.educause.edu/library/resources/7-things-you-should-know-about-flipped-classrooms.

Farkas, Meredith. 2013. "Why I Teach Freshman." *Information Wants to Be Free* (blog). http://meredith.wolfwater.com/wordpress/2013/12/30/why-i-teach-freshman/.

Farmer, Lesley S. J. 2011. *Instructional Design for Librarians and Information Professionals*. New York: Neal-Schuman Publishers.

Mestre, Lori. 2012. *Designing Effective Library Tutorials: A Guide for Accommodating Multiple Learning Styles*. Oxford: Chandos Publishing.

Onwuegbuzie, Anthony J., and Qun G. Jiao. 2004. "Information Search Performance and Research Achievement: An Empirical Test of the Anxiety Expectation Mediation Model of Library Anxiety." *Journal of the American Society for Information Science and Technology* 55, no. 1: 41–45.

Raftery, Damien. 2010. "Developing Educational Screencasts: A Practitioner's Perspective." In *Critical Design and Effective Tools for E-Learning in Higher Education: Theory into Practice*, edited by Roisin Donnelly, Jen Harvey, and K. C. O'Rourke, 213–26. Hershey, PA: Information Science Reference.

Skagen, Therese, Maria Carme Torras, Solveig M. L. Kavli, Susanne Mikki, Sissel Hafstad, and Irene Hunskår. 2009. "Pedagogical Considerations in Developing an Online Tutorial in Information Literacy." *Communications in Information Literacy* 2, no. 2: 84–98.

Smith, Patricia L., and Tillman J. Ragan. 2005. *Instructional Design*. 3rd ed. Hoboken, NJ: J. Wiley & Sons.

Thorpe, Mary. 2008. "Effective Online Interaction: Mapping Course Design to Bridge from Research to Practice." *Australasian Journal of Educational Technology* 24, no. 1: 57–72.

Westerveldt, Eric. 2013. "The Online Education Revolution Drifts Off Course." NPR.org. http://www.npr.org/2013/12/31/258420151/the-online-education-revolution-drifts-off-course.

# CHAPTER 2

# Planning
## *Begin with the End in Mind*

---

**IN THIS CHAPTER**

---

▷ Determining what resources (both people and equipment) are required for your project and how you can gather them

▷ Reviewing what skills you already have and determining what skills you need to complete your tutorial by conducting a skills inventory

▷ Understanding the purpose of making a project timeline and learning about several tools for creating a timeline

▷ Choosing tasks to include on your timeline

▷ Estimating how much time the various components of your tutorial project might take

▷ Exploring storyboarding and some storyboarding tools

---

THIS IS THE POINT IN THE PROCESS when even though you may be ready to dive in and start scripting your tutorial, instead you should take a deep breath and back away from the keyboard. Even if you do not consider yourself to be a planner and prefer going with the flow, reining in that flow and thinking through the content and equipment you need to assemble, and the steps that make sense to follow, will almost certainly end up saving you (and your colleagues) a tremendous amount of time and frustration. You may avoid costly mistakes by being forced to consider and discard approaches that are not optimal. The more complex your project is and the greater the number of people involved, the more the preparation of a clear road map for all participants will improve the process and the final product.

Of course, planning is not necessarily a linear process, but the important elements will be described in such a way as to help you adapt them to fit your circumstances. When planning your tutorial project, the basic steps of gathering information, finding resources, and staying within your deadline will apply in varying degrees depending on the level of complexity of your project.

As you go through these planning steps, you may uncover the need for more data to inform your project, and you might have to stop and collect that data before advancing. You may also uncover the need for particular collaborators or skill sets that must be recruited or developed before continuing. Be patient with these detours—having a solid framework of data, people, and skills will help you in later phases of the project. Conversely, you may discover preexisting tutorials or other resources that will either meet your identified needs, perhaps with some revision or customization, or provide an excellent model you can use to leapfrog ahead in the process and save both time and resources. You will surely have a more clear idea of what the tutorial will look like when you have finished the planning process.

Because people are the most important resource you will draw on in all aspects of your tutorial project, the planning discussion starts by walking through some decisions involved in making sure you have the right people and skills in place to be successful.

## Solo or Team Effort: Gathering the Personnel and Skills

One of the first questions you will need to answer as you plan your tutorial project is, "Who will be involved in this project—will this be a solo effort or will there be a team?" There is no right or wrong answer to this question, but determining the answer will have major impacts on the way you plan how to structure and produce your tutorial.

If you are working as part of a team, the initial phase of your planning process should start with a meeting to inventory the skills needed to complete your tutorial. Discuss what skill sets you or your teammates bring to the table (assuming you're not already familiar with everyone's skill set). Consult the list of skills in the sidebar to help guide this skill-set inventory discussion. Divide up the tutorial project tasks based on the identified skills.

### SKILL-SET INVENTORY

- Project management, including organizational skills or proposal writing experience
- Content knowledge of the tutorial topic
- Writing skills, particularly writing for instructional purposes
- Experience with a screen-capture or screencasting tool
- Software programming expertise
- Graphic design experience
- Still or video photography experience
- Production skills, such as video or image editing, storyboarding, or narrating experience
- Usability testing experience
- Willingness to try new things

Identify gaps that need to be filled—do you need to find someone already possessing a needed skill, or should someone on the team learn that skill? Finally, make sure to check back in regularly to see how team members are feeling about their roles and how they are progressing.

If you are working on the project alone, make sure to self-assess whether or not there are any skill gaps that are potential barriers to successfully completing your project. It may be more difficult to objectively assess your own skills than those of others, but it is essential to be honest both about your skills and the time you may need to acquire additional skills. Particularly if you are on a short timeline, you may need to make design and development decisions based on your current skills rather than on those you hope to acquire.

Because few librarians have all of these tutorial-creation skills (except perhaps a willingness to try new things), it is very common for tutorials to be created by teams that bring together a variety of skill sets. Barbara Blummer and Olga Kritskaya (2009) list common players on a library tutorial development team, including

- subject librarians,
- instruction librarians,
- instructional technology specialists,
- programmers,
- graphic designers,
- multimedia specialists,
- network administrators,
- assessment professionals, and
- project managers.

Some projects may also benefit from support or consultations with other academic departments to form a more complete picture of the content to be included.

The advantages to working on a tutorial project as a team include the ability to solicit multiple perspectives, which can lead to a more carefully considered and higher-quality product. Individual project members can play to their strengths by focusing on their specific tasks. Working as a team can also provide the opportunity to observe people who have skills you would like to acquire. Finally, working with a team gives you a higher level of accountability for finishing the tutorial project and means the entire burden for success (or failure) is not on you alone.

However, there are some drawbacks to the team-based approach. A tutorial produced as a team can often take longer, as you need to negotiate or juggle multiple schedules and other competing demands. The more people involved in a project, the more necessary it will be to have someone acting as a project manager in order to keep all the participants on track and prevent tasks from overlapping. For smaller projects or for projects that need to be completed quickly, a solo effort may be the simplest and best choice.

In addition, many institutions do not have specific people who fill each of the roles listed above. In this case, you will need to determine whether you have the time and desire to acquire training in skill areas you don't currently possess or whether it is worth the cost to hire freelancers, graduate student assistants, or student workers who can augment your skills. Some commonly used "outside" skill sets are graphic design and programming.

Advantages of the solo approach to tutorial design include simplicity; because you only have to deal with one calendar, the timeline is thus only dependent on your schedule. The overall process may be speedier as a result. It is much easier to keep track of the major tutorial elements and separate themes when you have your hands on all of them. However, even a relatively simple tutorial is a lot of work that must be juggled with other responsibilities, and going it alone means there is no one to step in if there is a crisis. Finally, a single viewpoint without additional eyes on the project may make it easier to miss important omissions or errors.

To sum up—choosing whether or not you will be working in a group or by yourself will largely depend on your particular situation: the personnel available at your institution and the scale of your project. Both solo and group efforts require an honest assessment of what skills are required to complete your tutorial project and whether or not you (or your teammates) have those skills. Determine early in your planning process whether you will need to get additional training or hire people with specific expertise. Either a solo or group-produced project can turn out well as long as you match the tutorial content to your learners' needs, design with your learning outcomes in mind, and find appropriate outlets for promoting and distributing your tutorial. You'll learn how to do these things in later chapters.

## Assembling the Equipment

Because acquiring equipment can take a significant amount of time (and money), it is helpful to start planning for your equipment needs early in the tutorial planning process. Assuming you have access to basic computer equipment that you are familiar with, this section will walk through your technology-equipment needs by answering these questions:

- What hardware and software will you need to accomplish your task?
- Will you need screen-capture software or e-learning authoring software for your project?
- Do you have an appropriate skill level with those software applications that will enable you to do what you intend to do?
- Do you plan to use images that will need to be captured and edited extensively?
- Do you plan to use stock photos or will you need to collect your own images?
- Will you need video footage that goes beyond screen captures?
- Will your tutorial benefit from narration?
- If so, how will you record and edit that narration?

Several of these skills, such as audio recording or editing, video or still photography, and editing or screen-capture software, require specialized software that will be covered in chapter 5. However, plan now to purchase or borrow and learn how to use that equipment—don't wait until you are in the middle of your project! By the same token, if you will need specialized skills that can only be provided by an expert, investigate your options in this regard early in the process. This next section will discuss some creative solutions to consider if you need a resource that is not readily available.

## Filling the Gaps

When a resource need is identified for your tutorial, how can you fill a gap that your own department cannot fill? Is there someone on your staff or in your institution who is, for example, an experienced video photographer who could help you capture a lecture or class exercise for your tutorial? A talented amateur who would volunteer time to help? If you are in need of equipment your department does not possess, can a case be made for purchasing it to enable additional projects? Can it be borrowed from another department or colleague in your institution? Sometimes specialized hardware, such as audio- or video-capture equipment, can be borrowed from the information technology (IT) department or a campus entity like instructional design or a center for instructional support or excellence. There may be specialized software such as graphics-capture or editing applications may be available through an academic department. If you need actors for your video, can you find volunteers or pay theater students? It pays to be curious and to ask for help, because you never know when it might be available through an unexpected avenue. You may also be building relationships that will help solve future problems or provide expertise on other projects.

If you have access to equipment but don't have the necessary skills to use it, you may be able to fill in some gaps through classes offered by IT or even outside your institution. Remember that YouTube offers hundreds of short training videos that may enhance your skills, although the quality may vary widely. Alternatively, the basic monthly fee to use Lynda.com tutorials, which cover design, video, audio, photography, and web skills, may be worth the investment for a short period of time. Also remember that if you need to use an application or learn more about software, the software publisher often offers excellent training to its customers on its website or through online classes. Again, asking for help may garner incredible benefits—many people are pleased to be able to contribute to a worthwhile cause!

If you are in need of images, use a search engine to look for copyright-free images on the Internet. If you have a marketing department, they are likely to have institutional photos that are freely available and may save you time spent on capturing the images you need. Marketing personnel may also have expertise to share in obtaining and editing images and may have graphic design capabilities too.

Finally, if you are set on a certain technology or piece of equipment to use in your tutorial design or production and are not able to beg, borrow, or steal what you want, reality may force you to make decisions based on that lack. Don't invest an unhealthy amount of time trying to find the resources you want; concentrate on skillfully using the resources you have. Remember that a constraint often helps make a clear decision about how to proceed—accept it and exercise your creativity to find the perfect solution for you!

## ⊚ Constructing a Project Timeline

Once you have formed the initial idea of what type of tutorial you will be creating (see chapter 1), have thought through whether you will be working on your tutorial alone or in a group, and have looked at your equipment needs, it can be helpful to put together a project timeline. Project timelines can help you

- visualize the overall trajectory of your tutorial project,
- itemize the individual tasks involved with creating your tutorial, and
- set realistic deadlines for completing your project as a whole, as well as the many steps involved along the way.

Project timelines can be useful for both solo and group projects; however, it is particularly helpful to create a timeline when you are working on a group project. The timeline can be used to help you divide up tasks, to establish a sense of accountability among group members, and to make the end date clear for everyone involved. Plus, using a timeline gives you a great sense of satisfaction when you complete each individual step!

That said, don't let the project timeline creation process turn into an end product unto itself. Many people have procrastination foibles—don't let creating the perfectly color-coded timeline turn into yours. Depending on the size of the project, timelines can be effectively created with pencil and paper, an Excel spreadsheet, or software specifically made for project management. Don't be afraid to try something new, but at the same time don't feel like you have to use commercial project management software if it doesn't work for you or is overkill for your particular project.

Before discussing the tools you can use and the various components to include in a project timeline, a quick note about some assumptions of what components are already in place. First, it is assumed that the players involved with creating the tutorial have already been identified and assembled. Second, it is assumed that you have identified and begun to assemble the resources you expect to use to construct the tutorial.

## Project Timeline Tools

There are many timeline tools available, but they all achieve the same end outcome—creating timelines! If you are working on a solo project, a pencil-and-paper sketch or a Word document with tasks and dates may be just right for you. Alternatively, setting appointment notes in your calendaring system might work well. However, if you are working on a group project, it is advisable to create a sharable timeline using one of the following free options.

### Office Templates

Microsoft Office has a variety of free templates available for download. PowerPoint slides (see figure 2.1) are one option and are available at http://office.microsoft.com/en-us/templates/time-line-project-planning-examples-TC101875472.aspx.

*Pros:* If your project is relatively simple, your team is not too large, and therefore your timeline is not overly detailed, the PowerPoint templates may be right for you. A Power-Point template can easily be used in a presentation or project proposal, providing a clear overall sense of the steps involved in creating the tutorial.

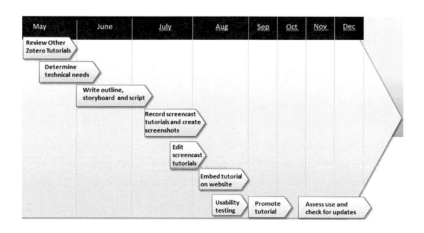

**Figure 2.1.** Sample timeline for a one-person project created with a PowerPoint template

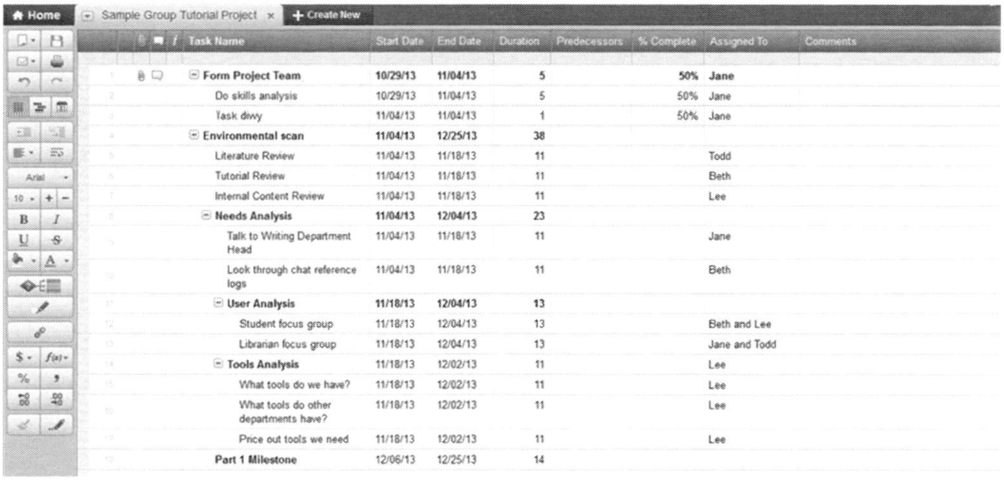



| Task Name | Start Date | End Date | Duration | Predecessors | % Complete | Assigned To |
|---|---|---|---|---|---|---|
| Form Project Team | 10/29/13 | 11/04/13 | 5 | | 50% | Jane |
| Do skills analysis | 10/29/13 | 11/04/13 | 5 | | 50% | Jane |
| Task divy | 11/04/13 | 11/04/13 | 1 | | 50% | Jane |
| Environmental scan | 11/04/13 | 12/25/13 | 38 | | | |
| Literature Review | 11/04/13 | 11/18/13 | 11 | | | Todd |
| Tutorial Review | 11/04/13 | 11/18/13 | 11 | | | Beth |
| Internal Content Review | 11/04/13 | 11/18/13 | 11 | | | Lee |
| Needs Analysis | 11/04/13 | 12/04/13 | 23 | | | |
| Talk to Writing Department Head | 11/04/13 | 11/18/13 | 11 | | | Jane |
| Look through chat reference logs | 11/04/13 | 11/18/13 | 11 | | | Beth |
| User Analysis | 11/18/13 | 12/04/13 | 13 | | | |
| Student focus group | 11/18/13 | 12/04/13 | 13 | | | Beth and Lee |
| Librarian focus group | 11/18/13 | 12/04/13 | 13 | | | Jane and Todd |
| Tools Analysis | 11/18/13 | 12/02/13 | 11 | | | Lee |
| What tools do we have? | 11/18/13 | 12/02/13 | 11 | | | Lee |
| What tools do other departments have? | 11/18/13 | 12/02/13 | 11 | | | Lee |
| Price out tools we need | 11/18/13 | 12/02/13 | 11 | | | Lee |
| Part 1 Milestone | 12/06/13 | 12/25/13 | 14 | | | |

**Figure 2.2.** Sample timeline for a group project created with an Excel SmartSheet template

*Cons:* If you have more than two to three project members, want to keep track of actual versus expected task-completion dates, or are prone to adjusting the color palette in PowerPoint for hours on end, these templates may not be robust enough for your purposes.

Microsoft Excel also offers project timeline templates in spreadsheet form; several are available at http://www.vertex42.com/ExcelTemplates/timeline.html. These spreadsheet templates (see figure 2.2), particularly the Gantt chart, which is widely used in business, are more robust than the PowerPoint templates.

*Pros:* If you plan a moderately complex project and want to be able to track more tasks, assign more project members to tasks, and track the status of a task, the Excel templates may be right for you. Excel spreadsheet templates allow for both a table and calendar view of the timeline and so can also be used to easily display progress and the overall scope of a project in a report.

*Cons:* If you are an Excel novice, the added learning curve of mastering some Excel basics might not be a wise time investment at this point.

## Project Management Software

If you find the Office templates don't meet your needs because of the size of your group, the scope of your project, or because you use a platform other than Windows, you may want to consider more specialized project management software. There are many free project management software options available. Because the software landscape changes so frequently, your best bet will be to Google "free project management software" to see what tools are currently available. At this time, Zoho Projects is one of the most useful and user-friendly tools available.

*Pros:* Zoho Projects is cloud based, which allows team members to use it from anywhere they have web access. It has alerting features that keep you up to date on when tasks are due as well as when other team members finish tasks, and it allows for much more sophisticated end reporting than either of the Office templates. Features like these should be available for most project management software options. If you need to track your time investment in a project, a more full-featured application like Zoho Projects may be essential. If alerts will help you stay on track and keep your project team connected, then trying out a tool like Zoho may be well worth your time.

*Cons:* It will take time to set up a more robust project management system, so factor this into your overall planning process in order to determine whether this component will be worth it to you and your team.

## Content to Include in a Project Timeline

Now that you have thought through the need for a project timeline and hopefully have taken a break from reading to explore a few timeline tools, it's time to consider what tasks to include on your project timeline. To help provide some structure to those tasks, return to the ADDIE model. Each step in the ADDIE model has potential tasks that can help you create a tutorial that is best suited for your audience (see table 2.1). Following an established structure like the ADDIE model can also help you visualize what is needed for your project to proceed smoothly. The following section suggests a range of tasks to consider. Of course, not all tasks will apply to every tutorial project. Use these suggestions as a guide to think through the elements that will require more of your time in order to complete your particular tutorial project.

**Table 2.1.** Potential Tasks for a Project Timeline Based on the ADDIE Model

| | EXAMPLE TASKS |
|---|---|
| Analysis | • Define what instructional goal(s) the tutorial will accomplish.<br>• Learn who might use your tutorial through discussions with stakeholders or surveys.<br>• Look for ideas, approaches, or even content you can borrow or modify.<br>• Apply for funding if needed.<br>• Solicit team members if needed.<br>• Choose the software that will work best for your needs. |
| Design | • Convene your project team and divide up tasks.<br>• Take the time to do training if needed.<br>• Beg, borrow, steal, or purchase needed equipment.<br>• Create learning objectives for the tutorial.<br>• Think about assessment activities for the tutorial.<br>• Choose the specific content you will want to include in the tutorial. |
| Development | • Create an outline, storyboard, and/or script.<br>• Find or create graphics.<br>• Consider the components you need to include to make your tutorial accessible.<br>• Practice recording your screencast (if screencasting).<br>• Record the screencast (if screencasting).<br>• Edit and make revisions (regardless of whether you are screencasting or compiling text and graphics).<br>• Publish your tutorial to the web. |
| Implementation | • Try several usability approaches, including rapid prototyping and beta testing.<br>• Revise based on what you learn in usability testing.<br>• Create a calendar of promotions activities.<br>• Hold professional development events to encourage other colleagues to use your tutorial. |
| Evaluation | • Review any interactive components (quizzes, comment fields, surveys, etc.) for feedback.<br>• Review web analytics for trends.<br>• Schedule regular updates and maintenance. |

The goal of the analysis stage in the ADDIE model is to help you determine the purpose of the tutorial and what resources you need to gather in order to create a tutorial. The main tasks in the analysis stage center around performing a needs analysis, a user analysis, an environmental scan, and a resource analysis. Examples of specific tasks to assign to your timeline could include holding informational discussions with stakeholders, researching your users' needs, conducting a literature or web search to find similar tutorials, applying for grant money, and researching and choosing the e-learning authoring tool (e.g., Jing, Captivate, or Storyline) that you will want to use.

The intention of the design stage of the ADDIE model is to help you choose an instructional framework for your tutorial. The main tasks in the design stage focus on gathering personnel and resources and creating an instructional plan. Examples of specific tasks to assign to your timeline could include convening your project team and dividing up tasks, taking the time to do training if needed, buying the necessary software or tools, creating learning objectives, selecting the content you plan to include, and planning the assessment activities.

The development stage of the ADDIE model helps you to determine the look, feel, and logical schema that will guide your tutorial. The main tasks in the development stage focus on prewriting or recording and time spent working in the actual e-learning authoring tool. Examples of specific tasks to include on your timeline are creating an outline or storyboard, writing a script, creating graphics, recording a screencast, editing and revising the tutorial components, and publishing your tutorial to the web in the appropriate format.

The implementation stage of the ADDIE model focuses on getting a usable tutorial to your users. The main tasks in the implementation stage center on usability, promotions, and professional development. Examples of specific tasks to include on your timeline are conducting rapid prototyping, conducting usability tests or beta tests, making revisions based on usability testing, creating a calendar of promotions activities, and holding a variety of professional-development events to encourage other colleagues to use your tutorial.

The evaluation stage of the ADDIE model encourages you to assess how your tutorial is actually being used and to find out what changes are needed. The main tasks in the evaluation stage focus on summative assessment, evaluating web analytics data, and regular maintenance of your tutorial. Examples of specific tasks to include on your timeline are reviewing learning assessments from the tutorial such as quizzes, reviewing web analytics data, and scheduling regular updates and maintenance.

## Time Considerations

These suggested tasks can help populate your timeline. While some of these tasks may not fit your particular situation, most of them will. Of course, your project may involve unique aspects that need to be considered and included. In addition, while different people may take longer at various stages of the process, many people frequently underestimate the time involved in editing and revising draft tutorials. Make sure to add in sufficient time to give yourself a cushion to be sure that you can make revisions as needed! That said, much of the work that goes into creating tutorials takes place in the first three steps: analysis, design, and development. Susan Smith (2010) stated that the preproduction tasks—elements included in analysis, design, and development—can take two-thirds of the total time of a project. Some examples from several librarians who have tracked how much time they spent during the tutorial-creation process provide a more concrete idea of how long some of these tasks will take.

1. A three-person project team from Florida Atlantic University Library (Ergood, Padron, and Rebar 2012) reported that they spent approximately four months creating three tutorials. Roughly three and one-half months were spent in the analysis, design, and early development stages reviewing the literature, getting training, writing a proposal, and creating a storyboard. Approximately one month was spent in the late development stages recording, editing, and publishing the tutorials.

2. A team of four Syracuse University librarians (Moekel 2010) created a tutorial as a substitute for face-to-face library instruction in their English composition classes. This team spent a total of ten months on their project. Approximately three months were spent in the analysis phase reviewing the literature and evaluating other, similar tutorials; soliciting the project team; and performing a needs and user assessment. Roughly two months were spent in the development stage creating their first module. Finally, the implementation step took four to five months to do revisions, usability testing, and final publishing.

3. At Oregon State University Libraries, an introduction to Zotero tutorial took one week to complete. This may have been due to the fact that most of the tutorial designer's colleagues happened to be on vacation that week, and there were few other distractions. Because the content was based on a previously existing outline from an in-person version of the introduction to Zotero tutorial, most of the time was spent in the development and implementation stages.

4. On a more granular level, a team from the University of Illinois at Urbana-Champaign (Bowles-Terry, Hensley, and Hinchliffe 2010) found a two-minute video took four to six hours of preparation and work to complete. However, this was just for the work that happened in the late development phase and did not include the work that went into setting the stage so that the team could do the work or any follow-up with usability testing or evaluation.

Not surprisingly, none of these examples include time estimates for the evaluation stage. This is likely because this is the ongoing work of maintenance and interacting with users and is harder to nail down in terms of specific timing. However, that does not mean that the evaluation step should be allowed to fall off of your project timeline. Instead, it may be necessary to appoint one team member to spearhead that part of the project plan so that it doesn't fall through the cracks.

## ◎ Planning Tutorial Design: Storyboarding

Up to this point, and especially in the timeline discussion, planning has been treated primarily as an element of the project management process. However, planning is also important at the tutorial-design level. One of the most popular and effective ways to plan out a tutorial design is through the use of storyboarding, a technique that will help you visualize the elements of individual tutorials, as well as the overall trajectory of a more complex project or series of tutorials.

What is storyboarding? Wikipedia (2014) defines storyboards as "graphic organizers in the form of illustrations or images displayed in sequence for the purpose of pre-visualizing a motion picture, animation, motion graphic or interactive media sequence." Storyboards are used heavily in animation and film development—and, given their common elements with instructional media, such as using text and graphics to communicate information or a message, they can be useful in planning tutorials and other instructional objects. In the case of interactive media, the storyboard is the layout and sequence in which the user or viewer sees the content or information. Most technical details involved in crafting a film or interactive-media project can be efficiently described through storyboards either as images or using additional text.

Why would you choose to include the step of storyboarding your tutorial or series of tutorials? According to an animator who has worked with the Coen brothers on films such as *Fargo*, "Storyboarding serves many purposes in addition to being an illustrated representation of a film. They [storyboards] can help you 'see' the film before you even turn on the camera, find storytelling issues, sell your idea, and get everybody working on the project on the same page" (Renée 2013). Similarly, storyboarding your tutorial can help you see your project in a more holistic way than in an outline or script, enabling you and your team to identify key concepts, detect gaps, and work out the visual plan early in the process. Even if you can't draw, images that you want to find or develop can be described in enough detail to expedite the development process. In a multi-tutorial project, storyboards provide a place to determine a common look and feel for your tutorials and a way to develop consistent graphical elements, such as images, screenshots, or fonts, that will unify the separate elements of the project. They can also help you track the concepts you want to include, ensuring that you cover what is essential as well as avoiding unintentional repetition between tutorials.

Storyboarding is an easy and forgiving method for playing with the chronology or organization of tutorial elements until you get it right and can feel less restrictive than a script or text-based outline. The visual approach of storyboarding facilitates group brainstorming so that ideas can be generated and consensus reached. It is easier to graphically specify elements that happen concurrently, and relationships between elements can be visualized and navigation planned more efficiently. A storyboard is a useful road map for prototyping a tutorial or series of tutorials before committing time and effort to that almost-final step. Finally, a storyboard can be a template for verifying the accuracy and completeness of the final product.

So how will you go about making a storyboard of your tutorial? Like timelines, the process itself can range from very simple to excruciatingly complex. A simple tutorial may be adequately served by a pen-and-paper sketch (see figure 2.3) while more elaborate and multipart creations might be appropriate for the (often very expensive) software used by animators, film studios, and software designers. In between those options, a pad of three-by-six-inch sticky notes are an inexpensive and flexible resource for sketching individual images and rearranging them easily on a wall or whiteboard. A photo of the final arrangement taken with your smartphone or camera can be shared widely and doesn't depend on adhesive integrity for its longevity! Microsoft PowerPoint slides are also useful for roughing out graphics and narration and can easily be manipulated and printed or shared.

Instructional designers and teachers use free or inexpensive software applications such as Storyboard That or Storyboard Pro, both specifically developed for educators. Storyboarding templates are easily found using your favorite search engine if you prefer to discover something uniquely adapted or adaptable to your purpose.

If you are not at all artistic and prefer to work solely in text, you might consider Celtx, another free to inexpensive application available in desktop, mobile, or online workspaces

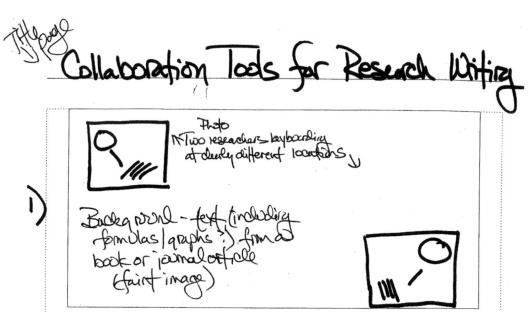

Research groups often work on group writing projects remotely from multiple locations. It is essential to use collaborative tools to store and share individual work in order for a project to be efficient and effective. This tutorial will briefly describe and compare several types of tools that are useful in any kind of collaborative writing. The focus will be tools for storing and sharing text and citation management tools for collecting and sharing citations to the relevant literature.

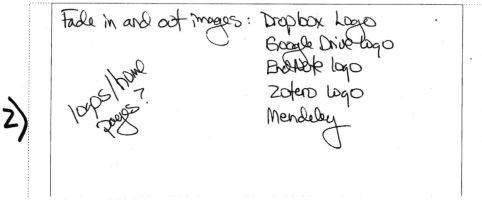

Many tools are available for storing and sharing text, images and other files. Popular tools include Google Drive and Dropbox. When any writing project involves a search of the research literature, a citation management tool such as EndNote, Zotero or Mendeley will help retrieve, organize and cite the documents effectively.
First we'll discuss Google Drive and Dropbox.

**Figure 2.3.** Example of a pen-and-paper storyboard sketch

that can be used as a stand-alone tool or collaboratively. Celtx was developed for scripting screenplays and enables parallel description of images, narration, and action.

These are a few of the many storyboarding applications available as of this writing, and when you are reading this, you may find many more. Avoid the temptation of spending too much time in the tool-discovery phase of this operation—make a selection, learn how it can benefit you, and stick with it.

The website UsabilityNet (2006) suggests the following method for assembling a storyboard once you have established the general parameters of your project through needs, user, and resource analysis and after examining similar projects for ideas and approaches.

- *Brainstorm broadly.* Include all ideas and doodlings; don't try to edit as you go, just collect initial ideas.
- *Narrow to the best ideas.* Consider your limitations, including the project requirements, time, and resource constraints, as well as the target audience. Get feedback from others to help select the best ideas.
- *Create a visual representation of your ideas.* Sketch the individual screens you will use to portray your instruction, describing the accompanying images, animations, audio, video, or text.

## Key Points

Because thoughtful planning is such an important element for determining the success of your tutorial project, this chapter has focused on a variety of strategies and tools you can use to help you both manage your tutorial project and begin planning how your tutorial will be designed. Here are some key points to take away:

- A variety of skill sets are required to create a tutorial. Decide early on whether or not you will work on the project by yourself or in a group based on the skills available to you.
- Some specialized technology and equipment are usually needed to create a tutorial. Start an inventory of the tools you will need for your project and figure out what gaps you may need to fill.
- Project management tools, such as timelines, are useful for managing all of the moving parts in your tutorial project. Begin filling in the various tasks involved in your project based on the suggestions provided in this chapter and by using the ADDIE model as a guide in order to create realistic deadlines.
- Storyboarding can be used as a technique for managing and planning the design process.

Now that you have a plan in place, the next chapter will use the ADDIE framework to discuss analysis in more depth. Creating a useful and relevant tutorial relies heavily on the work you will do during the analysis stage.

## References

Blummer, Barbara A., and Olga Kritskaya. 2009. "Best Practices for Creating an Online Tutorial: A Literature Review." *Journal of Web Librarianship* 3, no. 3: 199–216.

Bowles-Terry, Melissa, Merinda Kaye Hensley, and Lisa Janicke Hinchliffe. 2010. "Best Practices for Online Video Tutorials in Academic Libraries." *Communications in Information Literacy* 4, no. 1: 17–28.

Ergood, Alyse, Kristy Padron, and Lauri Rebar. 2012. "Making Library Screencast Tutorials: Factors and Processes." *Internet Reference Services Quarterly* 17, no. 2: 95–107.

Moekel, Lisa. 2010. "December 2010 Site of the Month." Association of College and Research Libraries. http://www.ala.org/acrl/aboutacrl/directoryofleadership/sections/is/iswebsite/proj pubs/primo/site/2010december.

Renée, V. 2013. "Video: An Inside Look at Storyboarding with the Coen Brothers' Story-board Artist." No Film School, August 26. http://nofilmschool.com/2013/08/storyboard ing-with-coen-brothers-storyboard-artist/.

Smith, Susan Sharpless. 2010. *Web-Based Instruction: A Guide for Libraries*. 7th ed. Chicago: ALA Editions.

UsabilityNet. 2006. "UsabilityNet: Storyboarding." UsabilityNet: Tools and Methods. http://www. usabilitynet.org/tools/storyboarding.htm.

Wikipedia. 2014. "Storyboard." *Wikipedia, the Free Encyclopedia*. Accessed October 30. http:// en.wikipedia.org/w/index.php?title=Storyboard&oldid=618592351.

## ⑥ More Resources

Celtx. https://www.celtx.com/.

Microsoft Excel Timeline Templates. http://www.vertex42.com/ExcelTemplates/timeline.html.

Microsoft PowerPoint Timeline Templates. http://office.microsoft.com/en-us/templates/time line-project-planning-examples-TC101875472.aspx.

Storyboard Pro. http://storyboard-pro.en.softonic.com/.

Storyboard That. http://www.storyboardthat.com/.

# CHAPTER 3

# Analysis
## *Use the Power of Information to Shape Your Tutorial*

---

**IN THIS CHAPTER**

▷ Approaching different types of analysis

▷ Conducting a learning-task analysis

▷ Conducting a learner analysis

▷ Conducting a learning-environment analysis

▷ Understanding the value of conducting a resource analysis

▷ Considering the implications of the information you gather for tutorial design

---

THE NEXT STEP IN YOUR TUTORIAL PROJECT (assuming that you have decided to use a tutorial or tutorials to address your learning problem!) is to examine your learners, their learning environment, and the type of learning task that needs to be addressed. Analysis will provide important clues and cues about how to approach your tutorial design and pedagogy. For example, the choices you make will be very different if your audience is school-aged learners as opposed to adult learners, or novices as opposed to experts on a topic. In an online environment, there may be only a brief time to engage learners before many of them will consider opting out. Using the instructional design principles behind analysis—or gathering information to help guide your decision-making process—provides the basis for strategies that capture your learners' interest and attention quickly!

You may be considering a new or unfamiliar learning topic or a population you have not previously encountered. Alternatively, you may be designing your tutorial for a stable, homogeneous population with familiar needs. You may assume that after working with a certain group for years, you can just base your tutorial on the information you have been gathering all along. That may not be the best approach, and here are some reasons why.

Consider the possibility that a constantly renewing population, such as incoming first-year students, might be less uniform than you believe, as changes within any population can be gradual and barely noticeable. Use the principle of "evidence-based" practice from the health care field, and base your decisions and choices on the best available evidence rather than on anecdotal information and unsystematic observation. Try to set aside your assumptions, even if it is only briefly, and take a fresh look at the learners, the learning environment, and their instructional needs. You may uncover subtle or perhaps significant changes that will inform your tutorial project and even your teaching practice.

Conversely, the benefit from a more exhaustive analysis of an unfamiliar population or situation is obvious, but it is important not to get caught up in analysis to the detriment of your available time and effort. Aim for "just enough" information, remembering that you will always have to generalize to some degree, otherwise each learner would need an individualized tutorial! Realistically, the urgency of your project may sometimes require you to wade in without being able to follow all recommended best practices; don't despair if you need to compress the process in order to deal with reality.

What is useful to analyze? Start with three elements well known to instructional designers: the learning task, the targeted learners, and the learning environment. The analysis of these three elements is based on the instructional design process described by Patricia Smith and Tillman Ragan (2005) and has been modified for tutorials. This chapter will also include a fourth component—available resources—in order to help you assess what resources you and your institution can devote to this task. The resource analysis section is based on your previous experience and guides you through the importance of gathering information about the resources you have and the resources you will need in order to successfully create your tutorial. You don't have to do these analyses in the exact order described here, but it is helpful to address the instructional need first. Once that need has been clarified, the information from your user and learning-environment analyses will be easier to apply and will make more sense in relation to the instructional design process. This process conforms to the principle of backward design, or beginning with the end in mind, rather than attempting to begin moving toward a desired goal without first stating what that goal is.

In order to give you clear illustrations of these analysis principles, a scenario will be used as an example throughout this chapter (see the sidebar "Scenario Context"). The

## JUST ENOUGH ANALYSIS

If time is at an absolute premium, what steps of analysis are essential? Try to collect basic information about

a. the learning goal, condensed into an outcome statement or two;
b. targeted learner information, such as age, reading level, and technological skill; and
c. what learners are already likely to know about the learning outcome.

With that level of information, you can develop a basic tutorial.

scenario will provide an opportunity to apply the various types of analysis so that you can visualize how these strategies work in a real-life situation.

# Learning-Task Analysis

The purpose of the learning-task analysis is to clearly define what learners should know or be able to do after they have completed the instructional module. The results of the analysis help determine the instructional goals and can be used to craft specific instructional objectives. These goals and objectives are used to design instruction and assessment. The following steps will help you work through the process of determining what the learner audience needs to know and how to write the resulting instructional goals and objectives.

1. Determine condition (problem/innovation/discrepancy)
2. Determine how to address that condition (instruction or another response)
3. Write initial instructional goal
4. Determine knowledge type involved
5. Divide instructional goal into logical steps or concepts, including prerequisite knowledge and prior knowledge
6. Write instructional objectives based on goal concepts
7. Verify instructional goals and objectives with teammates or content experts

The graduate nursing scenario will be used as an example throughout this section. Answers to the analysis questions are supplied in sidebars at selected intervals throughout the discussion using a "Tutorial Analysis" form. A blank version of these forms for each type of analysis is available in the appendix should you wish to use or modify it when analyzing the learning task, the learners, the learning environment, and the available resources.

## Step 1. Determine Why Instruction Is Needed

Typically instruction, in this case in the form of tutorials, is considered necessary because at least one of three conditions is occurring:

- Something isn't working. (Problem)
  *Example*—Reference staff members are reporting consistent confusion about a library website element.

- There is something new that learners need to know. (Innovation)
  *Example*—You have added a new database and want a rapid way to share how to use it.
- Institutional goals need to align with reality. (Discrepancy)
  *Example*—Students are not consistently demonstrating a concept they are expected to master as an element of core curriculum or accreditation requirements.

Determining the conditions that produce the learning task also provides clues about what strategies to use to address the instructional goal and how to describe the learning environment.

## Step 2. Determine Whether Instruction Is the Best Solution

After the initial clarification of the learning task, take time to determine whether instruction via a tutorial is the best way to address the identified problem or situation. A key step in writing instructional goals is determining that instruction actually is the best answer to the question being asked. It is possible that another solution should be pursued. In the case of consistent problems with the library website, are students truly in need of a tutorial about how to use that part of the website, or is it possible that the point of confusion needs to be identified and the website redesigned? Perhaps online instruction has already been provided to help with the problem, but the tutorial is difficult to find or use or has not been sufficiently marketed to students and reference staff. In both of these cases, designing more tutorials is not likely to provide the desired solution.

## Step 3. Write the Initial Instructional Goal

If instruction in the form of tutorials is indeed needed, what will learners need to know or be able to do after they have completed the instruction? The desired outcome is the learning goal and is focused on the curricular level rather than directly on the learners.

Working backward from the learning goal will help you to determine choices about designing learning activities and assessment. Avoid adding deadwood—unnecessary information or detail that does not help attain the learning goal. Remember that shorter is better in tutorials, and focus on the essentials only. This can be particularly difficult for content experts, according to Smith and Ragan (2005). For the scenario involving graduate nursing students, the problem is that students do not know how to do a literature search that is sufficiently rigorous for a systematic review article. So the learning goal might be to introduce key concepts in advanced literature searching for writing systematic review articles. This is a broad statement that will next be unpacked in order to create more specific learning objectives. For now, try to capture your initial thoughts as clear goals so that you can build on them as you work through the analysis and design processes.

## Step 4. Determine the Type of Knowledge Addressed by the Instructional Goal

Describing the broad instructional goal also helps determine what type of knowledge is being specified and what instructional objectives and pedagogical approach will be developed to help attain that knowledge. The types of knowledge that are best addressed by tutorials are typically declarative, conceptual, and procedural knowledge. Declarative knowledge deals with the mastery of key material about a topic, such as terminology or principles; conceptual knowledge deals with the ability to categorize and apply knowledge to new situations; and procedural knowledge defines the steps for a process, which can then be applied to different situations. Types of knowledge that are less suitable for tutorials include problem-solving, cognitive, attitude, and psychomotor knowledge. See chapter 1 for more descriptions and examples of these knowledge types.

Where does your instructional goal fit in these knowledge categories? A tutorial may certainly address more than one type of knowledge, and each knowledge type covered may require a slightly different pedagogical approach. For example, the literature search scenario topic could conceivably include declarative, conceptual, and procedural knowledge, depending on what instruction is determined to be most needed for the situation. Refer to the sidebar "Learning-Task Analysis I" to see how the first four steps of the learning analysis can be applied to the graduate nursing scenario.

## Step 5. Divide the Instructional Goal into Steps or Concepts

Once you have determined the knowledge types, divide the instructional goal into smaller steps or parts. These can be used as the basis for writing specific instructional objectives and can also help determine whether there is enough information to warrant breaking your tutorial into smaller "chunks." As you visualize the process or content on which the tutorial will be based, determine the elements that are essential to share. This can be accomplished most easily when addressing procedural-knowledge situations such as how to use interlibrary loan, which can be easily separated into individual steps. When dividing the instructional goal, also consider the following questions:

- What does the learner need to know before interacting with your tutorial in order to understand it (prerequisite knowledge)?
- Should prerequisite knowledge be scaffolded throughout this tutorial or addressed in another instructional module?
- What is the learner likely to know prior to viewing the instruction (prior knowledge)?

Collecting the essential elements of your instructional goal, the prerequisite knowledge and prior knowledge will help later when it is time to design assessment methods.

## Step 6. Draft Specific Learning Objectives

The essential elements of the instructional goal are the basis of instructional objectives. Instructional objectives "specify the desired change in the learner's knowledge" (Mayer 2011) and are intended to guide the preparation of lessons or lesson segments that will help the learner achieve the desired learning outcomes. Instructional objectives should be clear and measurable. When the objectives address either the cognitive or declarative knowledge types, they should potentially include both lower-order thinking skills (e.g., remember, understand, and apply) and higher-order thinking skills (e.g., analyze, evaluate, and create) from Benjamin Bloom's cognitive taxonomy (Anderson and Krathwohl 2001).

## LEARNING-TASK ANALYSIS I: DETERMINING THE PEDAGOGICAL APPROACH

*Graduate Nursing Student Scenario*
(See blank form in appendix)

| Describe the initial condition that requires instruction | Is it a:<br>☒ Problem<br>☐ Innovation<br>☐ Discrepancy | Short description of condition:<br>*Graduate nursing students do not know how to do a comprehensive literature search for a systematic review.* |
|---|---|---|

**Is instruction the best method to address this condition, or are there other factors causing the problem/innovation/discrepancy?**
*Instruction about comprehensive literature searching is not available to distance students. They do not have consistent opportunity for face-to-face instruction or consultation.*

**Write the elements of the instructional goal below:**
**Content** (what will be learned):
*How to perform a comprehensive literature search in multiple databases*

**Context** (how knowledge will be used):
*Systematic collection of relevant literature for systematic review articles*

**Assessment** (how attainment of knowledge/skill will be measured):
*Compare to process specified for performing a systematic review*

**Combine the goal elements into an instructional goal statement:**
*To introduce key concepts of advanced literature searching for writing systematic review articles.*

**What type of knowledge will learners be expected to gain after interacting with this tutorial? Check all that apply.**

☒ Declarative (*systematic review background*)          ☐ Problem solving
☒ Conceptual (*apply searching techniques to systematic*          ☐ Cognitive
   *review*)          ☐ Attitude
☒ Procedural (*process of systematic review*)          ☐ Psychomotor

Verify the goal, goal steps, and learning objectives with members of your tutorial team or a content expert.

The learning objectives for your tutorial should contain the following elements:

- What will be learned (content)
- How that knowledge will be used (context)
- How successful attainment of knowledge will be determined (assessment)

These elements can be combined using a three-part format that is often seen in library instruction—verb phrase plus "in order to" plus why (Gilchrist and Zald in Cox and Lindsay 2008). Using this format, the learning objective might sound something like this:

> After completing this tutorial, the learner will be able to [verb phrase] perform a comprehensive search in multiple databases using the prescribed steps in order to [why] collect relevant literature for a systematic review.

This statement is focused on the learner and contains the elements of a learning objective as follows:

- Content—how to perform a literature search in multiple databases
- Context—systematic collection of relevant literature
- Assessment—follow the prescribed steps for performing a systematic review

Draft the instructional goals and objectives for your tutorial and then take some time to ponder them and solicit feedback from content or teaching experts to help you refine them. In some ways, the learning goal is fairly self-evident, but the steps to reach that goal are trickier, so clarifying the steps (i.e., learning objectives) is worth considering carefully. Writing learning objectives will be covered in greater detail in chapter 4 when tutorial design is discussed. At this point, try to write a clear draft of the objectives based on the instructional goal that you can then refine in the design step.

## Step 7. Request Feedback on Goals and Objectives

Finally, once the learning goal and initial learning objectives have been written, ask several people, particularly those who are teaching the same class or discipline, for their feedback on the goal and objectives before you launch into the next step. If you are working with a team, this step may already be built into your learning-task analysis, but if you are working solo, include this checkpoint to help ensure that an essential piece of information is not forgotten and that you have clearly described the learning objectives arising from the instructional goal.

Instructional goals and learning objectives are the critical foundation on which instruction will be built—take time to thoughtfully consider exactly what learners will gain from the tutorial and how you will present the information you want learners to retain. Take a look at the final set of learning objectives for the nursing literature search scenario in the sidebar "Learning-Task Analysis II." Is this amount of information reasonable to address in a short instructional tutorial? If you think it may be too much, you are probably right! Breaking learning objectives into shorter chunks or modules will be discussed in chapter 4.

## Learner Analysis

Now that you have a clearer picture of the instructional goal, it's time to gather information about the target learner population. Who are these people, and why might this tutorial be important to them? Your tutorial design should take the target population into account. You may identify more than one population you wish to target, but it's best to limit yourself to describing the primary and perhaps the secondary population. If your

# LEARNING-TASK ANALYSIS II: DETERMINING PRIOR KNOWLEDGE AND LEARNING OBJECTIVES

*Graduate Nursing Student Scenario*
(See blank form in appendix)

**Use the concepts or steps of the instructional goal together with likely prior knowledge and prerequisite knowledge to write instructional objectives.**

**Learning Goal:**
*To introduce key concepts of advanced literature searching for writing systematic review articles.*

**Steps/concepts of the instructional goal:**
*Describe a systematic review*
*Define the process of performing a systematic review*
*Discuss selecting databases appropriate to the topic*
*Demonstrate using database functionality to search efficiently and effectively*

**Prerequisite knowledge needed (and if it will be covered in coursework or in other instruction):**

*What is a systematic review?(not previously addressed)*

*What is a comprehensive literature search?(not previously addressed)*

**Prior knowledge likely (and if it will be covered in coursework or in other instruction):**

*What is peer-reviewed literature? (coursework)*

*Where is the library homepage? (coursework)*

*How are library databases accessed and selected for your topic? (database searching tutorial)*

**Learning Objectives:**
*In order to collect literature for a systematic review, the learner will:*

*Distinguish between the level of rigor for a typical literature review and a literature review for a systematic review article.*

*Describe the steps taken to perform a systematic review, including the collection of literature.*

*Select topically appropriate databases to search.*

*Consistently and correctly execute the steps for collecting literature for a systematic review article.*

tutorial will be open to anyone who wishes to use it, you cannot hope to describe all of the potential learners in your analysis, so concentrate on the group that you intend to target. However, Smith and Ragan (2005) recommend gathering as much information about potential learners as possible because critical aspects or characteristics may not become apparent until later in the design or development process.

If you're already familiar with your population, you may have a good handle on their characteristics. Remember to stay inquisitive and observant and avoid sweeping assumptions so that subtle changes don't evade your notice! The questions below are meant to serve as a starting point for gathering information. You may uncover more questions to answer as you work through the process. Below are the details that you should consider gathering about your primary or target population.

- *Age.* What is the age of the group that you expect to use this tutorial? Differing levels of complexity will be appropriate for different age levels and scholarly attainment. An obvious example is that instruction appropriate for middle school students is not appropriate for graduate students.
- *Developmental stage or reading level.* Is your population at a consistent developmental stage or reading level? This will influence the level of vocabulary in your tutorial and the complexity of the information you share.
- *Motivation for learning.* Why is this information important for the targeted learners? Will they interact with your tutorial in order to earn a grade or for personal enrichment? Can the connection to something that is relevant to the learner be made explicit in order to increase motivation? Some educators consider motivation to be the most important aspect of successful instruction (Dick, Carey, and Carey 2001). Evaluating your learners' motivation level is important, as is considering how it might be enhanced.
- *Cultural background.* Do your potential learners come from a homogeneous background that may influence their approach to your instruction? A positive answer may need to be taken into account during tutorial design, while a negative answer, indicating a more heterogeneous population, may suggest that a more generic approach is required.
- *Learning/cognitive style or preference.* Homogeneity in this characteristic is difficult to determine without either testing or interviewing your population or without interacting with them directly in an instructional situation. It's difficult to design online or in-person instruction that addresses every learning style, so concentrate on providing multidimensional instruction in order to reach as many learners as possible.
- *Technological expertise.* How comfortable are your learners with the technology needed to view and interact with your tutorial? If their comfort level is low, the technology may need to be explained or taught as a preamble to or an element of the tutorial. If your institution requires the use of a particular platform or technology for e-learning, that specific technology should be chosen rather than another in order to minimize confusion.
- *Language.* What is the primary language of your intended learners? If there are many learners whose primary language is not English, it is even more critical to consider carefully your word choices and always strive for simplicity and clarity. Consider testing the readability level of your text and adjusting it to the reading level of your anticipated audience or in some cases, providing multiple versions of tutorials in different languages.

- *Prior knowledge of topic.* What are your learners likely to know already about this topic? Are there any common misconceptions that can and should be corrected? While some instructional designers specify motivation as an important predictor of instructional success, others say prior knowledge is the most critical characteristic influencing learners. Learning is constructed by adding new knowledge to what is already known, so knowing learners' current level of understanding is crucial. Tutorials can include a pretest that directs learners through different learning paths depending on their prior knowledge. In formal learning, courses that precede the intended instruction, as well as future classes it prepares students for, should be considered in order to build on established skills in addition to developing the capabilities that are expected for the next steps in the curriculum. If the tutorial is part of a series of tutorials, the series should be carefully designed to avoid needless repetition and to scaffold the essential principles. If a tutorial will supplement face-to-face instruction, learn as much as you can about the objectives of that instruction and review them with the instructor or coordinator regularly in order to synchronize them as much as is practical. Additional learner characteristics are described for the graduate nursing scenario in the sidebar "Learner Analysis."

How is information about potential learners gathered? Direct experience and observation in the classroom or at the reference desk will provide opportunities to gather basic learner information. There may be a need to interview or survey a target population for which little opportunity to interact or observe currently exists. Instructional colleagues are a rich source of information about learner groups with which they are familiar. When a tutorial has been requested for a specific course or discipline by an instructor, that instructor will be an important source of information about his or her students. Instructors are often very aware of areas in which their students are not skilled or comfortable, enabling tutorial design to focus on those potential areas of identified need. It may be advisable to administer a pretest to a target population to uncover more data about their starting point for learning. Information about demographics, grades, majors, current educational status, reading levels, and other aggregated data may be available through published institutional records or via a query to your institution's enrollment management department. Examination of prerequisite class syllabi and departmental curricula may also provide a better grasp of students' existing knowledge.

# Learning-Environment Analysis

Learning-environment analysis helps determine the context for the desired instruction at the institutional as well as the individual level. What is the physical and technological environment in which learning will take place? How should the learning environment be taken into account when designing instruction? Analysis may be formal and extensive for an unfamiliar environment and potentially less extensive for a familiar or less complex environment. Even a relatively brief reflection, review, and investigation of the educational environment will help avoid ineffective investment of time and effort on a misdirected approach or a strategy that will not be well received by instructors or students for institutional reasons. The sidebar lists learning-environment characteristics that you will need to analyze.

# LEARNER ANALYSIS: WHAT ARE THE CHARACTERISTICS OF YOUR TARGET POPULATION?

*Graduate Nursing Student Scenario*
(See blank form in appendix)

**Target population:** *Graduate nursing students*

**Age:**
*Adult*

**Developmental stage/reading level/academic attainment:**
*College graduates, some have been in clinical practice and out of school for many years and others are recent graduates. Most are nursing students, but some students are nutrition science or health and kinesiology graduate students.*

**Motivation for learning:**
*Students recognize that competent performance of literature searches is a key skill for their capstone research project. Most are realistic about their current skill level and eager to improve as needed.*

**Cultural background:**
*Ethnically diverse*

**Learning/cognitive style or preference:**
*Unable to determine*

**Technological expertise/comfort:**
*Students have differing levels of technological expertise but all are comfortable with basic word processing, e-mail, searching the Internet and viewing online video. They have some understanding of key health science databases, but many have not recently performed literature searches. Many are new to distance learning but are becoming familiar with the requisite technology quickly.*

**Language:**
*Fluent in written and spoken English; most are native English speakers.*

**Prior knowledge of topic:**
*The learners can distinguish systematic review articles from primary research articles.*

What additional information about target learners should be gathered before proceeding?

- The mission and philosophy of the larger organization
- The curriculum into which instruction must fit
- Available technology and learning facilities
- Instructors who will use the proposed tutorial

## The Larger Organization

What are the mission, philosophy, and taboos of the larger organization? The framework within which instruction will be delivered should be considered for clues about how to design the instruction. A clear understanding of the mission, philosophy, strategic plan, or core curriculum of the parent institution will help uncover the characteristics most likely to influence the learning environment. For example, if an institution has a strong commitment to help students develop information literacy skills, then instruction that fulfills that commitment might reasonably be expected to be widely assigned and accessed, although individual instructors may have different attitudes. Conversely, if there is a strong institutional belief that students should have already graduated from secondary education with all the information literacy skills they need for life, the attitude toward information literacy instruction may be much less positive.

## Curriculum

What is the curriculum into which the instruction must fit? In order to integrate instruction into a broader curriculum, the curriculum itself must be understood. The curriculum for a particular program or major is often clearly described in the information for prospective students considering that path. Familiarity with prescribed courses of study will provide details that enhance and focus the instructional content of a tutorial. For example, a curricular strategy that stresses hands-on learning may suggest the inclusion of learning activities involving psychomotor knowledge and opportunity for abundant practice. In another example, you may already know that a particular science curriculum encourages beginning students to think of themselves as scientists, then to consider how scientists read and understand the scientific literature, and finally provides opportunities for them to investigate and explore scientific literature on their own. Familiarity with this approach may suggest how to structure a tutorial for that group of students.

## Technology and Learning Facilities

What type of technology is typically used by learners? Where will learning take place? If students are using uniform technology, as in the case of campuses where laptops are provided for each student, tutorial design should be tailored to that technology. Will students typically access instruction using mobile devices? If so, the tutorial should be designed to work on major mobile platforms as well as larger-screen computers. If learning labs are available and are expected to be a major access point for this instruction, their capabilities should also be considered during design, as should the conventions of the institutional e-learning platform or course management system. In many cases, there is not one single platform used by potential learners, so learning technology will need to be available on multiple platforms. Conversely, if students have little or inconsistent access to technology, low bandwidth options may need to be considered carefully as part of the tutorial design.

## Instructors

What characterizes the instructors who will be using or assigning this tutorial for instruction? They may have clear preferences about how instruction is delivered to their students. For example, instructors in a particular department may have a positive attitude toward online instruction, while those of another department question its utility and express a preference for face-to-face instruction. Inconsistent acceptance of e-learning may necessitate careful marketing of an online tutorial, employing strategies such as sharing research about the effectiveness of online instruction in order to help encourage instructor buy-in. The need to address skepticism may erode the effectiveness of online instruction and suggest that a different instructional avenue could be more effective to pursue. In some cases, a required course with a large enrollment may be taught by many individual instructors, and thus acceptance of e-learning may vary widely from class to class, although learning goals and objectives are uniform. See chapter 7 for more strategies about how to encourage instructors to use your tutorial.

Consult the sidebar "Learning-Environment Analysis" for the learning-environment characteristics for this chapter's graduate nursing scenario.

## ⊚ Resource Analysis

This portion of the analysis is intended to help determine what resources you and your institution can devote to the design and implementation of this tutorial project. No one has everything they need at hand, so it is important to investigate your options before you start determining the design and development parameters of your project. Resource analysis will enable you to determine what resources are readily available; what resources need to be acquired; or, if they cannot be acquired, what strategies can be used to fill the perceived gap. Remember that the lack of a desired resource can be used to decide the elements of your design, so even if it is initially disappointing, a lack can become a useful limit and even a spur to creativity.

In general, any instructional design project, including a tutorial, is likely to require some resources from the categories in the sidebar "Resource Analysis Elements," each of which will be discussed in more detail. If you spend some time analyzing the resources you need and learning the skills you do not currently have early on, your project will not be stalled by the need to acquire a new skill or resource on the fly!

## Personnel/Skills

As a team is being assembled to design and produce the proposed tutorial, useful skills to include on the team or to consider seeking out include

- content knowledge of the tutorial topic (liaison librarian or instructor);
- experience with the selected tutorial-creation technology;

- software programming expertise;
- graphic design experience;
- writing, particularly instructional writing such as learning goals and objectives;
- still or video photography;
- acting or narration;
- production skills (video/audio/image editing, storyboarding, or narration);

- usability testing experience;
- project management; and
- a sense of adventure and a willingness to try new approaches and learn new skills!

An initial list of personnel that may be able to provide these skills includes subject librarians or disciplinary faculty, instruction librarians, instructional technologists or designers, programmers, graphic designers, multimedia specialists, network administrators, assessment professionals, and project managers. Now is the time to conduct the skills inventory that was suggested in chapter 2!

Scan the team or inventory your own skills (if working solo) to determine where there may be gaps in your desired skills list. Is there a formal or informal leader on the team who can help determine what skills need to be sought, or will the team approach that task together? If a skill deemed essential is not possessed by the team or the solo practitioner, possible approaches to remedy this are to find someone with that skill who can join or consult with the team or to designate a team member to learn the skill. Finding someone with the necessary skills may be the speediest solution, but it adds personnel and complexity to the team and will potentially increase the cost of the project. Learning the skill yourself may be the best solution for the long term, but that solution adds time to the process and may not be realistic.

If a particular skill is not currently available or possible to learn in the time available, can the tutorial be designed without it? Is there someone outside of your library who could be asked to provide the skill? It might be possible to consider recruiting volunteers if resources and budgets are not optimal.

## Equipment

If you are fortunate, all of the equipment you need will be readily available, but if not, consider some creative ways to beg or borrow access to what you need. Here is a list of commonly used tools for assembling an online tutorial:

- Hardware and software, including screen-capture or e-learning software
- Video or still cameras
- Audio equipment (digital recorder and microphone)
- Specialized areas for audio and video recording
- Audio, image, and video editing
- Collaboration tools

Depending on your organization, specialized equipment may be easy or difficult to access or borrow. The campus information technology division or instructional design department are good possibilities to investigate for specialized equipment that your library may not have. Screen-capture or e-learning software may include image-, audio-, and video-editing capabilities. Many librarians have some level of audio, video, or still image capture available on their desktop or mobile devices, so consider that option if more specialized equipment is not available.

You may also want to consider using collaboration tools such as Google Drive or Dropbox in order to have a central point for collecting all of the project elements as they are developed. It can be much easier to coordinate the project if you can view what others are doing and tailor your own work accordingly. Even if you are working solo, a central gathering point that is stored in the cloud may offer advantages for working efficiently both at home and in the office. A large multipart project, such as a coordinated suite of tutorials, may also benefit from project management software so that completed elements can be efficiently tracked and the project kept moving on its timeline. Review the ideas for timeline and project management software included in chapter 2 early in your process to determine whether they might be useful for your project.

## Network Resources

Where will tutorials be hosted? Is video and image storage space available on a server or on the web? Tutorials involving screencasting or other video content produce very large files—the typical size is difficult to quantify, but theoretically the sky is the limit. Free video storage may be available on the web through a service such as YouTube, but that often includes limitations such as mandatory advertising, storage-space limits, and reduced video quality. Local hosting is typically the most flexible option as hosted tutorials can be freely shared or reside behind a firewall. They can even be password protected if that is desired (Notess and LITA 2012). The location for tutorial files may be determined centrally; consult your information technology team for more information if finding this information is not obvious at your institution.

## Time

Time is almost always a critical resource and is typically in short supply. Most librarians are constantly busy, and adding an additional project to an already heavy workload can be daunting. If specialized personnel are theoretically available to you but are completely booked for the next six months, they certainly won't be able to help with a tutorial that must be completed by the end of the summer. Additional time constraints may include rush requests from instructors who have no idea how much effort goes into creating an instructional tutorial and therefore don't allow sufficient time for planning and preparation.

There usually isn't a way to clear someone else's calendar, and it may not be advisable to refuse a request to create a tutorial if there are strategic reasons for making a tutorial for that requestor. Try to provide a realistic overview of how much time is involved for a typical tutorial project and negotiate a compromise that works for all of the parties. It is helpful to have some experience with tutorial design and production so that you can make an informed estimate of the time required for a requested project (see chapter 2 for time estimates from other projects). The best long-term solution may be to explain what

# RESOURCE ANALYSIS: ASSESSING THE TOOLS
# AND SKILLS NEEDED FOR YOUR PROJECT

*Graduate Nursing Student Scenario*
(See blank form in appendix)

## Personnel/skills

| Need | Have | | Need | Have | |
|------|------|---|------|------|---|
| ☐ | ☒ | Content knowledge | ☐ | ☒ | Writing |
| ☐ | ☒ | Tutorial-creation technology | ☐ | ☐ | Acting |
| ☐ | ☐ | Programming | ☒ | ☐ | Narration |
| ☐ | ☐ | Graphic design | ☐ | ☐ | Video/audio production |
| ☐ | ☒ | Still photography | ☒ | ☐ | Usability testing |
| ☐ | ☐ | Video photography | ☐ | ☒ | Project management |
| ☐ | ☒ | Collaboration tools | ☐ | ☐ | Other _____ |

**What personnel or skills are needed and not currently available? How will you meet that need?**
*Haven't decided on narration yes/no but have found it helpful in the past. May be able to recruit a student for this.*

*Notes: Digital audio recorder in undergraduate library. Planning to use Dropbox to share script and image files with team; support available for Camtasia. Nursing liaison will provide content expertise*

## Equipment

| Need | Have | | Need | Have | |
|------|------|---|------|------|---|
| ☐ | ☒ | Screen-capture software | ☐ | ☒ | Still camera |
| ☐ | ☒ | E-learning/tutorial software | ☐ | ☐ | Video camera |
| ☐ | ☒ | Audio recorder | ☒ | ☐ | Soundproof area—audio capture |
| ☐ | ☒ | Microphone | ☒ | ☐ | Video-recording studio |
| ☒ | ☐ | Stock photography | ☐ | ☐ | Audio/video editing |
| ☐ | ☐ | Other _____ | ☐ | ☐ | Other _____ |

**What equipment or software is needed and is not currently available? How will you meet that need?**
*Soundproof area; construction in usual area makes recording difficult.*

*Notes: Camtasia available across campus; multiple resources for assistance.*

## Network Resources

**Will tutorial video and image files be locally hosted or stored on the Internet/in the cloud?**
*Locally.*

**Are there limits to this storage space?** *Some, but files not anticipated to be large.*
**Are the files easily accessed for revision and updating?** *Password protected; contact IT for this.*
**If there are access options, how can they best be resolved?** *None.*
**Are there storage costs involved for local or remote file storage?** *No.*
**Who is the key resource person for local/remote storage issues?** *Gerry A. in IT.*

## Time

**When is this tutorial needed? How much time do you have before the deadline?**
*Needed for fall semester, four weeks to complete.*

**Are key personnel available to work on this project in order to meet the deadline?**
*So far, so good. Amy P. will be on vacation from 7/14 to 8/4 so will need to schedule usability testing around that absence.*

**If key personnel are not available, how will that affect the design/production/implementation portions of the process?**
*See above.*

is optimal versus what is possible in order to move forward with an instructional or liaison relationship. In some circumstances, what might be possible is to find an existing tutorial with the right content that can be shared quickly and then propose developing a more customized tutorial for the future. Sitting down with the requestor to evaluate a few tutorials and asking for feedback on the final choice can also provide pertinent information to guide the development of future instruction. See the sidebar "Resource Analysis" for a breakdown of the resources available for the graduate nursing scenario.

## Key Points

Now that you've worked through the steps of examining the learning task, learner, learning environment, and resources, you should have a much clearer vision of what content your tutorial might cover, what resources are available for your project, and how to take the characteristics of the learners and the learning environment into account as you approach the design phase of the process. Here are some key points to take away:

- It's crucial to have a good grasp of the available resources when determining how to approach a tutorial project. Time spent determining the instructional task and analyzing the learners and the learning environment will help you construct a realistic framework for your project.
- If you have very little time to design a tutorial, consider an abbreviated analysis of the learners, the learning task, and the prior knowledge your learners are likely to have. Alternatively, find a tutorial that includes the desired content and use it as a bridge to developing a more customized tutorial.
- Resource analysis will provide the information necessary in order to assemble the required resources well before they are called upon—no last-minute scrambling to find something or learn how to use it!
- If a resource cannot be found, borrowed, or learned, your tutorial design will have to be adapted to that reality. Limits can help focus your choices, so view them in a positive light!

Chapter 4 will guide you through the design process of refining learning objectives, choosing instructional strategies, planning assessment, and selecting and organizing the content of your tutorial. This is where you will start to see your preparation work pay off!

## References

Anderson, Lorin W., and David R. Krathwohl, eds. 2001. *A Taxonomy for Learning, Teaching, and Assessing: A Revision of Bloom's Taxonomy of Educational Objectives*. Abridged ed. White Plains, NY: Longman.

Dick, Walter, Lou Carey, and James O. Carey. 2001. *The Systematic Design of Instruction*. 5th ed. New York: Longman.

Gilchrist, Debra, and Anne Zald. 2008. "Instruction & Program Design through Assessment." In *Information Literacy Instruction Handbook*, edited by Christopher N. Cox and Elizabeth Blakesley Lindsay, 164–92. Chicago: Association of College and Research Libraries.

Mayer, Richard E. 2011. *Applying the Science of Learning*. Boston: Pearson/Allyn & Bacon.

Notess, Greg R., and LITA (Library and Information Technology Association) (U.S.). 2012. *Screencasting for Libraries*. The Tech Set, no. 17. Chicago: ALA TechSource.

Smith, Patricia L., and Tillman J. Ragan. 2005. *Instructional Design*. 3rd ed. Hoboken, NJ: J. Wiley & Sons.

# Designing Your Tutorial
## *Choosing and Organizing Your Content Intentionally*

---

| IN THIS CHAPTER |
| --- |

▷ Crafting learning objectives for your tutorial to help focus your tutorial content

▷ Planning your summative assessment strategy

▷ Determining what unique instructional strategies to use when designing a tutorial

▷ Designing a tutorial using a variety of content elements

▷ Understanding the value of organizing a tutorial in a logical and flexible way

---

INSTRUCTIONAL DESIGN PRINCIPLES have been used at every step along the way in this book. As a result, you may feel like you have been designing since chapter 1. This is not a coincidence as instructional design models like ADDIE are not meant to be used linearly but should be revisited throughout each step of your tutorial-building process. However, in this chapter, the components that go into design will be more intentionally discussed.

The design process starts with several big-picture elements—crafting learning objectives and forming an assessment strategy. Beginning with the big-picture view will give you a foundation to return to if you have a tendency to get too mired in the details as you are designing more specific elements of your tutorial. Again, depending on the size and scale of your tutorial, the complexity of your big picture may vary, but the principles of using learning objectives and corresponding assessment strategies remain constant regardless of the scale of your project. After that basic foundation is established, the importance of choosing instructional strategies tailored to the tutorial context, choosing a variety of ways to deliver your content, and choosing a plan for organizing your tutorial will be discussed.

## ⟳ Learning Objectives

Chapter 3 described how to create instructional goals and began the discussion of how to create learning objectives to help guide the learning-task analysis. Crafting targeted learning objectives during the design phase helps you to think concretely about what you want your learners to be able to do after they have completed your tutorial. A typical and helpful first step in creating learning objectives is to consult Benjamin Bloom's Taxonomy of Educational Objectives (Anderson and Krathwohl 2001). Bloom's taxonomy (or Bloom's revised taxonomy) is frequently consulted in the process of creating learning objectives because the suggested learning verbs (e.g., *recognizes, interprets, applies, analyzes*) provide a clear way to assess how well and to what extent your learners have mastered the content. Educators have expanded the original learning verbs that Bloom developed into extensive lists that are helpful to consult when writing learning objectives.

Instructional designers recommend a straightforward formula for piecing together a learning objective. Start with a learning verb (like those found in Bloom's taxonomy) that describes what the learner will do with the content covered in the learning experience, then explain why the learners are learning that content. The result should be a clearly assessable objective (Dick, Carey, and Carey 2004). Or you can combine this method of creating learning objectives with the three-step process described in chapter 3: begin by crafting a learning goal that includes a description of what will be learned (content), followed by an explanation of how that knowledge will be used (context) and a plan for how successful attainment of that knowledge will be determined (assessment; see figure 4.1).

With practice, creating clear learning objectives should become a relatively straightforward exercise that keeps you focused on your end learning goal. When designing a tutorial, it is important to keep learning objectives simple so that the resulting learning activities don't try to do too much all at once. For example, the first two learning objectives in the sidebar were separated into two components: one focuses on primary- and secondary-source comparison and the other on catalog and database recognition. The learner does not need to demonstrate simultaneous knowledge of primary sources (example 1) and database use (example 2). However, these two objectives could connect as part of a logically organized instructional sequence. Separating objectives into smaller

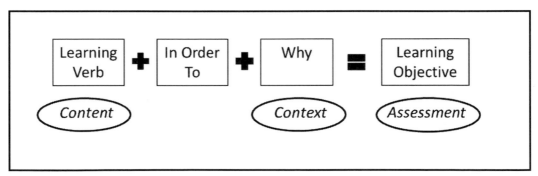

**Figure 4.1.** Designing learning objectives with content, context, and assessment in mind. *Adapted from Gilchrist and Zald, 2008*

Example 1: Students will be able to **compare** [learning verb] *different characteristics of primary and secondary sources* [content] in order to find appropriate sources for their research paper [context].

Example 2: Students will **recognize** [learning verb] *the difference between the catalog and the database links* [content] in order to find books and articles for their research paper [context].

Example 3: Users will **recall** [learning verb] *the steps of downloading an e-book using the vendor software* [content] in order to add e-books to their own personal e-reader device [context].

chunks enables you to design learning activities for each learning component. This makes the learning task easier for the learner and helps make the instructional strategy simpler to plan and the objective easier to assess.

When designing your tutorial, learning objectives are a helpful way to guide you, the instructor. However, it is not necessary to overtly share your learning goals with your learners. Researchers have found that learners ignore introductory text (Mestre 2012), and extraneous text in general has been shown to take away from the learning experience (Clark and Mayer 2011). So rather than beginning a tutorial with a detailed and laborious description, like the learning objective in example 3 stating that users will be able to recall the steps of downloading an e-book using the vendor software in order to add e-books to their own personal e-reader device, choose navigational labels with short descriptions such as "How to download e-books" or "Add e-books to your e-reader." Design your tutorial to demonstrate the purpose of the content and context to your learners without needlessly bogging them down in instructional jargon.

## ◎ Planning Your Big-Picture Assessment

Because tutorials are usually shorter learning experiences that often take place outside of a classroom environment, there are several big-picture, practical, technology-based considerations to keep in mind as you plan how you will assess learning in your tutorial. The learning objectives you create can and should foreshadow what you will assess. Therefore, one consideration is which of your learning objectives are actually assessable within the tutorial environment? For example, think about the three learning-objective examples used above. Based on these three examples, within the online tutorial environment you can assess:

Example 1: Students' ability to compare different characteristics of primary and secondary sources

Example 2: Students' ability to recognize the difference between the catalog and the database links

Example 3: Users' ability to recall the steps of downloading an e-book using the vendor software

These content elements can all be assessed using a variety of automated quizzing options such as multiple-choice, true/false, or sequence drag-and-drop questions.

However, it is more difficult to assess more long-term or applied learning with online tutorials. Unless you are meeting with your learners in person, for example, if you are using a tutorial in a hybrid or flipped course or have a specific plan to see examples of finished products of student work online, you may never see direct application of learning. As a result, looking back at the earlier learning-objective examples, within the tutorial environment you would not be able to assess:

Example 1: Whether your students found appropriate primary and secondary sources for their research paper

Example 2: Whether your students found books and articles for their research paper using the library catalog and databases

Example 3: Whether your users were able to add e-books to their own personal e-reader device

Assessing those end products of learning would require more direct contact with learners and demonstration of the use of their acquired knowledge than is usually feasible in the tutorial environment. Design your learning objectives and your assessment to align with the realities of data collection within the online-tutorial environment.

When considering your big-picture assessment as part of the design process, another factor is the capabilities of the learning measurement tools available to you. For example, if you are using a simple survey tool like SurveyMonkey to collect your assessment responses, you have the option to create multiple-choice, true/false, rating, matrix, and fill-in-the-blank questions. However, if you are using newer versions of Adobe Captivate or Articulate Storyline to build your tutorial, the graded question types include multiple choice, fill-in-the-blank, true/false, word bank, matching drag and drop, matching drop-down, sequence drag and drop, sequence drop-down, and hot spots. As a result of the greater range of question types available in Captivate or Storyline, you can plan for different types of assessment than you could if you were using SurveyMonkey. So while it may be possible to assess a user's ability to recall the steps of downloading an e-book using a tool that only allows multiple-choice responses, more realistic learning might be assessed using a tool that allows users to arrange the steps using a sequence drag-and-drop question. Design your learning objectives and your assessment to align with and maximize the tools available to you.

Another assessment consideration as you begin designing your tutorials is to determine how your assessment results need to be reported. If you are at a college or university that uses a learning management system (LMS), you may need to integrate your tutorial quizzes with your campus LMS so that student responses can be recorded for specific classes. Many e-learning authoring tools, such as Adobe Captivate, Articulate Storyline, and Techsmith's Camtasia, allow quiz scores to be integrated into an LMS using an Internet protocol called SCORM (sharable content object reference model). However, compatibility between e-learning authoring tools and an LMS are highly dependent on your version of both the e-learning authoring tool and the LMS. Check to make sure that the two tools play nicely together before making assumptions about what will happen with learners' quiz results. E-learning authoring tools will be discussed in more depth in chapter 5.

Not every instructor needs the automatic integration of quiz results to assess learning objectives. Some workable assessment alternatives include the ability for learners to print out a certificate of completion at the end of a tutorial to show to an instructor, the option to e-mail quiz results directly to an instructor, or the collection of anonymous responses to polling-style questions. Any of these solutions can provide you with some level of assessment of your learning objectives. Knowing what is technologically possible to assess before you design your content will help you make more realistic choices about the level of learning that can be assessed.

## Instructional Strategies

This is the point where designing instruction for an online tutorial begins to diverge significantly from in-person or course-based (either in-person or online) instructional strategies. While in-person and course-based instruction may relay similar subject knowledge, make use of graphics, and incorporate assessment activities, the way these elements are designed and integrated into a tutorial cannot be directly translated from an in-person or course-based instructional experience. Some educators claim that designing online activities is very similar to designing in-person learning experiences (Conrad and Donaldson 2011). However, the types of online learning experiences these educators describe are full-term online classes where there is direct interaction with both instructors and fellow students. Online tutorials rarely fit that mold.

Some of the differences between tutorials and other types of classroom experiences, both in-person and online classes, are the asynchronous nature of tutorials, the way learners can choose their own pacing and navigational path through a tutorial, the manner in which interaction is possible in tutorials, the distractions presented simply by placing students within an online environment, and learners' expectations of time investments (see table 4.1). Teaching in an asynchronous, unmediated learning environment means that you, the instructor, won't be available to direct learners' attention simply with your presence, your entertaining jokes, your engaging demeanor, or by using the traditional instructor/student power differential. You will need to use other techniques to engage your learners in a tutorial.

Similarly, in-person classroom activities such as paired discussions, walking around and observing students' computer monitors, or asking for a show of hands in response to a question don't translate directly to the tutorial environment. And embedding your content in the online environment means that learners may be easily tempted to surf over to another tab while watching your tutorial or may skip practice exercises and jump to the very end of the tutorial. In addition, because learners typically engage with tutorials on "their time" outside of class time, they are usually unwilling to watch long tutorials, so you will need to keep your tutorials short! Current recommendations suggest that "short" means one to two minutes (Mestre 2012; Oehrli et al. 2011). However, having your tutorial embedded within the online context where learners already do most of their work also brings with it advantages that you can incorporate to maximize learning.

**Table 4.1.** Differences between Tutorials and In-Person and Virtual Classroom Instructional Strategies

| DIFFERENCE | CLASSROOM STRATEGY | TUTORIAL STRATEGY |
| --- | --- | --- |
| Asynchronous, unmediated delivery of content | Engaging delivery; social pressure; instructor/student power differential | Demonstrating relevance; tight fit to learning objectives; use of visual examples |
| Instructor-driven pacing and sequencing | Ordering learning activities in a sequential manner; making content available at specified intervals | Allowing learners to move at their own pace; providing a variety of ways to navigate through the tutorial |
| Fewer interaction opportunities | Active learning exercises; instructor observation of student work; polling for immediate feedback | Formative assessment activities; rich explanatory feedback to formative assessments; scaffolded learning choices for more advanced learners; conversational tone |
| More online distractions | Ask students to put away phones; classroom control software | Short tutorial chunks; demonstrating relevance; reduced cognitive load |
| Different time expectations | Students are committed to the scheduled course time | Short tutorial chunks; learner control of navigation |

The use of instructional strategies and pedagogical techniques will help you to design instruction best suited for the tutorial environment. The following instructional strategies are covered in this section:

- Designing based on learning objectives and the knowledge type(s)
- Using cognitive load theory to maximize learning retention
- Creating a conversational tone

## Back to Basics: Learning Objectives and Knowledge Types

One of the key instructional strategies for designing and deciding what information to include in your tutorial is to refer back to your learning objectives and assessment goals. Make sure the content that you plan to cover is finely attuned to your learning objectives so that you are not tempted to go off track or provide additional information "just in case" (remember your goal is to keep tutorials under two minutes in length). This is also the time to check and see whether the learning objectives need to be divided into smaller chunks or whether any of your learning objectives are so similar that only one of the objectives needs to be covered. Learners in the online environment are wary of spending too much time on any one topic and are often looking for practical information, so avoid unnecessary repetition in your learning objectives; they should be clearly related but distinct.

Narrowing the focus of your tutorial to a few clearly defined skills will lower the chances of confusing your learners and will help them stay on track. For a smaller project, limit yourself to no more than the two to three ideas or steps you really wish to address. For a larger tutorial project, focused chunks can be created through the use of interconnected modules in order to maintain the principle of including no more than two to three ideas or steps per module.

Learners prefer to have the control to navigate between many short segments or modules of a tutorial rather than feeling trapped inside a long tutorial. Learners often

**Table 4.2.** Choosing Visual Examples by Types of Knowledge[1]

| KNOWLEDGE TYPE | WHAT IS IT? | USEFUL VISUAL EXAMPLES | EXAMPLES |
|---|---|---|---|
| Declarative Knowledge | Learning baseline facts; memorizing terminology | Infographics | A table with library terms and their definitions; a screenshot of a citation with the parts labeled |
| Conceptual Knowledge | The ability to apply knowledge to new situations; the ability to categorize information | Infographics, animations, worked examples | A series of screenshots of source types combined with audio illustrating evaluation skills |
| Procedural Knowledge | Knowing how to do things in a particular order and then applying these procedures to a new situation | Infographics, animations, worked examples | A decision-tree diagram walking through how to use the library catalog; a series of screenshots illustrating how to request a book via interlibrary loan |
| Problem-Solving Knowledge | Combining previously learned procedures, concepts, or declarative knowledge in order to solve a new problem. This type of knowledge contains an element of domain-specific knowledge. | Real-world scenarios | A scenario asking students to walk through an information problem as if they were a professional in their field |

[1]Adapted from Smith and Ragan 2005 and Clark and Mayer 2011.

do not use the Pause button in videos and do not break the content into segments on their own (Clark and Mayer 2011). As a result, if you plan to use screencasts or videos, remember to keep them no longer than two minutes, or build in a "Continue" button after chunks of content so that users don't have to choose when to stop and start the videos.

Another strategy is to design instruction based on the type or types of knowledge your tutorial addresses (see table 4.2). The type(s) of knowledge you are addressing will help determine the best way to deliver your content. The following section on designing tutorial content and managing cognitive load will suggest design examples that match up with the knowledge types most suitable for the tutorial environment.

## Managing Cognitive Load

Focusing on core learning objectives and matching the type of knowledge you wish to address to appropriate delivery methods helps you to address learners' cognitive load needs. Cognitive load theory is the idea that working memory can only handle a limited amount of information at any one time (Miller 1956). The amount of information a learner can process depends on

- how much the learner already knows about the topic;
- how complex the learning objectives are; and
- how much pacing control a learner has over the delivery of the instructional materials.

When designing an instructional strategy for a tutorial using cognitive load principles, refer back to your learner analysis to determine how advanced your learners are (see chapter 3). If you are primarily targeting novice learners, make sure the learning objectives are at an appropriate complexity level and your instructional materials aren't too long so that learners only need to process a limited amount of information at one time. If you are primarily targeting advanced learners, make sure the learning objectives aren't too simple and that you include options for learners to choose their own pacing or navigation through the tutorial so that they can more quickly go to the parts of the tutorial that are newer or more relevant for them. If you will be serving learners with a variety of expertise backgrounds, try to make sure instructional materials are brief and that your tutorial has as much navigational choice as possible.

Another way to incorporate cognitive load principles into your instructional strategies for designing a tutorial is to separate background and supporting information about how to do a task from the procedural steps involved in completing the task (Nguyen and Clark 2005). For example, look at the differences between these two lesson plans for a tutorial addressing "the learning objective" from example 2 used earlier:

Students will recognize the difference between the catalog and the database links in order to find books and articles for their research paper.

### LESSON PLAN 1: SUPPORTING INFORMATION INCLUDED WITH PROCESS STEPS

*Step 1.* Open the library's homepage. Click on the catalog link. Using the catalog is a way to find books, videos, maps, government documents, and journals at our library.

*Step 2.* Enter your keyword search. Try to limit your search to two to three main ideas for more successful results.

*Step 3.* In another tab, open the library's homepage and click on the database link. The library subscribes to many databases, including some that cover specific subject areas; some that contain specific types of sources, such as newspapers; and some that cover a broad range of subject areas. Use library databases to find newspaper articles, scholarly articles, conference proceedings, government documents, and more.

*Step 4.* Choose a subject database using the subject-selector drop-down menu. Librarians create guides that help point you to databases connected to specific subject areas. Choose the subject area that most closely matches your research question.

*Step 5.* Enter your keyword search. Try to limit your search to two to three main ideas for more successful results.

*Step 6.* Compare the results list you receive from both the catalog and the database searches.

Lesson plan 1 includes supporting information with the procedural steps of the task, while lesson plan 2 separates the supporting information from the procedural tasks (see the sidebars). Separating supporting information from procedural steps helps to reduce the learners' cognitive load and allows them to focus on the learning task.

## Be a Real Person

One final instructional strategy to keep in mind as you design your tutorial is how to create a feeling of interaction or connection even in this unmediated context. Some ways to create connections with your learners are to

- use a conversational tone in your text and audio components;
- use first-person pronouns (I, we) when referring to yourself as the instructor;
- use second-person pronouns (you) when referring to the learners; and
- be polite when providing feedback.

Including the feeling of a "visible author" (Clark and Mayer 2011, 199) allows the learners to visualize a real instructor with thoughts and advice and can help learners feel more engaged with the material.

# ⊚ Designing Tutorial Content

Now that you know how to craft learning objectives, have some assessment strategies, and understand appropriate instructional strategies for the tutorial environment, it is time to begin thinking about the content you will include in your tutorial. Design decisions for three types of content will be covered:

- Subject knowledge
- Graphics, audio, and text
- Assessment activities

This section will discuss how planning for and using each of these three content types together, rather than treating them as isolated design elements, will result in a richer learning experience.

## Designing Subject-Knowledge Content

You are likely to be a subject expert on the topic of the tutorial you are designing (or hopefully you at least know more than your students!). As a result, it can feel natural to think of transferring your knowledge to your learners by simply recording your spoken description of how to perform a certain task or technique, such as using subject headings to find more sources for a research assignment. Or you may be tempted to write out a description of a process you want to explain, such as evaluating the credibility of a particular source. However, cognitive scientists have found that because of the highly visual nature of the online learning environment, what learners see is often more important than what you say (Clark and Mayer 2011). As a result, these experts recommend beginning the design process by designing your content around the use of visual examples rather than around a narrative or transcript.

Visual examples that help to explain subject-knowledge content can come in several forms. Worked examples, real-world scenarios, animations, and infographics are all types of visual examples that can guide the design of a tutorial. It is difficult to fully separate out the principles of designing these visual examples for portraying subject knowledge from design decisions about what the visuals should look like, and the two ideas may overlap at times. This first section will focus on how to design visuals in order to relay subject knowledge, while the following section will address how to design visuals, as well as audio and textual information, for the best perceptual and cognitive experience.

### Infographics

If your tutorial will be addressing declarative, conceptual, or procedural knowledge, the visualizations that work well for describing this type of content are infographics or animations (see table 4.2). Infographics are simply visual images used to represent information or data. They include visual examples such as screenshots, diagrams, and decision-making trees. If you have ever included a Venn diagram in an explanation of Boolean operators, you have used an infographic. They can contain a combination of text and images to help walk the learner through the information you are trying to convey. Infographics work particularly well as a basis for explaining declarative, conceptual, and

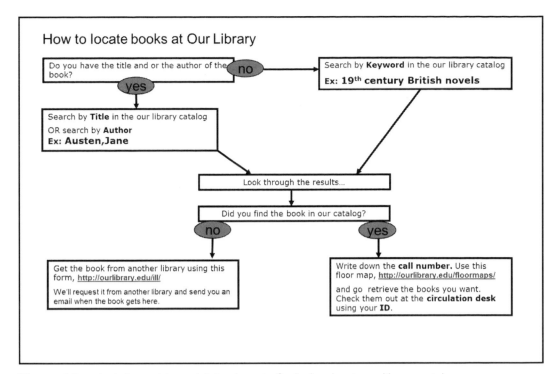

**Figure 4.2.** An infographic explaining how to find a book using a library catalog

procedural knowledge to novice learners, because they can help learners form a mental model of the information that they are trying to learn.

An example of using an infographic to explain procedural knowledge is a simple decision tree to walk through finding a book using a library catalog (see figure 4.2). This decision tree walks new users through the scenario of finding a book with basic prompts such as "Do you know the title or author of the book?" and "Did you find the book in the catalog?" Because these questions result in simple yes or no responses, learners should then be able to practice finding books on their own using this model to guide their actions. If you believe terminology like *catalog* or *call number* might be new for your users, consider explaining this declarative knowledge in a separate part of the tutorial, such as a glossary, or with callouts or pop-up boxes above these terms on the infographic itself.

## Animations

Animations are images that contain motion and can help show changes over time, or they can demonstrate a complicated manual skill such as knitting and can help facilitate conceptual- and procedural-knowledge learning (see table 4.2). However, cognitive scientists have found that a series of static images illustrating the same content is actually as or more effective than animations (Clark and Mayer 2011). This is because a series of static images allows learners to think through the images at their own pace, processing the information faster or slower depending on their learning needs, which allows for more active learning. This finding mirrors that of librarian Lori Mestre (2012), who found that students were better able to re-create a library search after watching still screenshots than after viewing a video screencast. This finding may be a relief for you if you don't have a programmer available to create slick animations or if you do not have time to learn advanced screencasting software.

If your tutorial includes content that demonstrates information changing over time, think of ways that you could communicate that information step by step using static images. Building on the example of illustrating how to find books in your catalog, you could take screenshots of the steps involved in the process. This might be a multistep process to illustrate where the catalog link is; where the keyword, author, and title fields are; how to locate a result in the search results list; and how to find the call number. This information probably could be conveyed in three or four still screenshots. Explaining how to request a book from another library may require an additional module, depending on the complexity of your interlibrary loan or consortial library system. Breaking those two elements of the book-finding process into separate components, regardless of whether you use still screenshots or a video screencast, can help the user focus on one learning objective at a time.

## Worked Examples

Worked examples are useful for teaching procedural and conceptual knowledge (see table 4.2). They help to either teach specific tools (procedural knowledge), such as how to use the citation management software Zotero or a specific subject database, or to teach specific concepts (conceptual knowledge), such as how to determine when to use a particular type of database or how to evaluate when to use scholarly articles or trade publications. Ruth Clark and Richard Mayer define worked examples as "a step-by-step demonstration of how to perform a task or solve a problem" (2011, 224). Many library tutorials contain worked examples in the form of simulations or video screencasts. However, few tutorials provide the learner with the opportunity to complete some of the intermediate steps. Clark and Mayer (2011) recommend introducing a new concept with a fully worked example. Next, demonstrate some of the example, but allow learners to complete some steps on their own. Follow that experience with an example learners need to fully complete on their own. With a little tweaking and the addition of some intermediate learning opportunities, many library tutorial topics can fit the worked-example model.

Here is one example of how to transition to using a worked example to explain subject knowledge. In a tutorial on how to use Zotero, the module on how to troubleshoot problems using Zotero's online documentation and forums previously just provided links to the documentation and forums. To change this module to a worked example, the author provided a practical demonstration about how to use Zotero's help in context. This context can be provided by first using a fully worked example showing how to access the Zotero help tools, using a demonstration search, and illustrating how to use the information that results from a search (see figure 4.3).

The next step could be a partially worked example including a demonstration of a search in Zotero's forums, followed by a quiz asking learners to choose the result from a search results list that looks most relevant to the assigned help search topic. This exercise could be done using either a screenshot of a results screen with hot spots enabled or learners could choose from a list of prepopulated multiple-choice questions with realistic search-result options.

The last step in this worked example would direct learners to independently access Zotero's help documentation, perform their own topical search in the Zotero forums, and choose the search result that was most relevant for their question. Their success with this step could be assessed with a yes or no question asking whether or not they were able to answer their help question successfully.

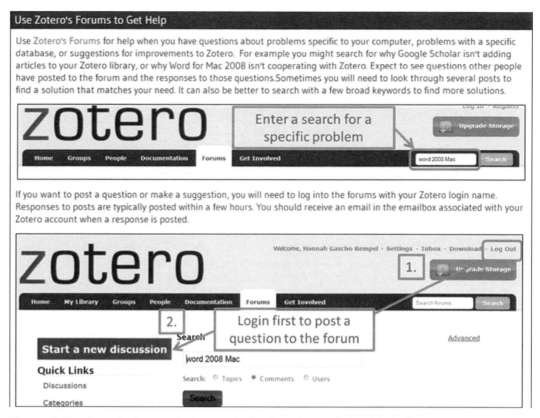

**Use Zotero's Forums to Get Help**

Use Zotero's Forums for help when you have questions about problems specific to your computer, problems with a specific database, or suggestions for improvements to Zotero. For example you might search for why Google Scholar isn't adding articles to your Zotero library, or why Word for Mac 2008 isn't cooperating with Zotero. Expect to see questions other people have posted to the forum and the responses to those questions.Sometimes you will need to look through several posts to find a solution that matches your need. It can also be better to search with a few broad keywords to find more solutions.

If you want to post a question or make a suggestion, you will need to log into the forums with your Zotero login name. Responses to posts are typically posted within a few hours. You should receive an email in the emailbox associated with your Zotero account when a response is posted.

**Figure 4.3.** A worked example demonstrating how to use Zotero's help features

Worked examples pair well with follow-up practice questions or exercises using new scenarios or slightly different tools, such as Zotero's FAQs page. However, because worked examples are often used to help learners gain procedural knowledge, it is also important to include practice questions or prompts that require learners to think about the concepts involved in the process or task that they are learning. Including self-reflective questions along the way helps learners avoid the trap of simply memorizing a set of steps that are either quickly forgotten or that they can't transfer to a new situation. Self-reflection opportunities also help address the fine line librarians often need to walk between teaching learners how to use specific tools and teaching learners concepts that they can transfer to new situations.

Using the Zotero help documentation scenario described earlier, some useful self-reflective prompts could begin by asking learners to start thinking about how and when they use the help resources. For example, "What kinds of questions match best with what you can expect to find in Zotero's documentation pages?" and "What kinds of questions match best with what you can expect to find in Zotero's forums?" Those specific tool-based questions could be followed by broader troubleshooting questions, prompting learners to reflect on how they prefer to search or how they think through a problem. For example, "What works better for you—searching or browsing? Why?" and "Where do you start when you run into roadblocks?" While the responses to these prompts may not be captured in an assessment question, including questions that ask the learner to pause and think metacognitively is a proven way to help encourage deeper learning (Clark and Mayer 2011).

## Real-World Scenarios

Real-world scenarios help build problem-solving knowledge through the use of relevant and authentic problems or questions (see table 4.2). Types of scenarios can include case studies, problem-based learning, and simulations. Scenarios are particularly helpful for advanced learners who can connect the concepts illustrated to real-life examples and scenarios of their own. In addition, some e-learning experts suggest that scenarios, such as problem-based learning, can be particularly helpful for online learners who may need an additional sense of relevance and connection (Conrad and Donaldson 2011).

However, as was noted earlier in this chapter, designing online tutorials is different than designing an online class. Students may be less invested in spending a lot of time delving into a particular case study or problem that doesn't seem to get them immediately to relevant information. When students were asked to choose a character and corresponding scenario in a tutorial, Mestre (2012) found that the students in her study preferred to skip over the information about the characters and just wanted to get to the more explicitly applicable content. Just as with the other example types, scenarios are most effective if they are focused on a few clearly defined learning objectives. In addition, learners value the relevance provided by scenarios more than "fun learning" offered through a game. Games often focus on lower-level skills that are difficult for the learner to transfer to an actual learning situation (Clark and Mayer 2011). Resist the temptation to design an overly involved scenario with extraneous information or to spend a lot of time thinking up fun activities that end up simply falling into the extraneous information category.

An example where a scenario could be effective is with an advanced audience like the graduate nursing students described in chapter 3. A problem-based learning scenario could be developed for that learner group to show a professional in the nursing field trying to choose topically appropriate databases to search. A patient with a specific medical condition could be described to give context for why the professional needs to do the search. Details about the patient's age and gender could be included to help the graduate nursing students decide on the most appropriate search tools. In addition, a description of what search tools are available to the professional could help provide a greater sense of authenticity. After students have worked through the problem facing the nursing professional, provide them with correct examples of how to approach the search so that they can alter their search process if necessary. It can also be helpful to ask them to consider additional examples, such as different medical conditions or patient histories, in order to allow the students to continue to build on what they have learned in the scenario.

To summarize this section on designing the delivery of topical content in a tutorial, start with infographics, animations, worked examples, and real-world scenarios as the focal point for delivering your topical content. This approach aligns with the visual nature of the tutorial environment and can help provide students with models to foster continued learning. Using this strategy doesn't mean that text or audio shouldn't be used to explain and deliver topical content. Rather it means that the visual medium of an online tutorial requires a special design approach. The next section will discuss how the elements of visual examples (or graphics) and audio and text work can be designed to complement each other in order to help maximize learning within the tutorial environment.

## Designing Graphics, Textual Content, and Audio Content

### Graphics

Before discussing how to design graphics, textual content, and audio content together, it is helpful to keep in mind a few principles about how to design graphics themselves. Keep your graphics uncluttered and clear. Visual learning tools should remain focused on your learning objectives, just as when you were designing subject-knowledge content. As a result, don't include extraneous visual information "just in case." Choose visual information that serves a direct learning need. Avoid the temptation to include what Ruth Clark calls "decorative visuals" or visuals that may look interesting—for example, a picture of a happy undergraduate student—but that don't explain any concepts or relationships related to the learning experience (2009, 36). Such decorative visuals actually have been found to inhibit learning because they distract or sometimes confuse the learner.

Most of the time, graphical information such as images, diagrams, screenshots, or screencasts will be used in concert with text or audio. However, there are some cases when it can be beneficial to include a graphic by itself. Graphics that demonstrate relationships, changes over time, or that help learners interpret complex information can stand on their own (Clark and Mayer 2011). Some graphics that help to facilitate these kinds of learning are matrices, models, diagrams, time series, or tables. Allowing learners to interpret these graphics on their own rather than providing the text or audio with "your" version of how to think through the idea can also help to enhance learning because they allow learners to create their own mental maps or ways of thinking about a concept.

### Text and Graphics Together

While a few standalone graphics may be useful, it is much more common to build a tutorial that includes some combination of text, audio, and graphics. Learners have been found to understand visual examples more easily if text explanations are included on or very close to the image. The further the text is from the image, such as in captions, the harder it is for learners to make the connection between the information in the text and the visual (Clark and Mayer 2011). Whenever possible, try to place key explanatory text directly on the graphic itself.

For example, in figure 4.4, the image from a Zotero tutorial on how to add websites to a Zotero library contains images and text that are separate from each other. In contrast, figure 4.5 shows a revised version of this graphic with key text embedded in the screenshot itself. The second figure still has additional explanatory text near the visual for those learners who may want or need more context, but the key information for learning this procedural task can be gained just by looking at the graphic itself.

One final note about using graphics and text together: novices to a topic learn best when graphics and text are used together; however, learners with a more advanced understanding of a topic learn better if they can create their own mental model rather than adapting what they know to someone else's conceptualization of an idea. Advanced learners have been found to learn equally well either from text and graphics together or from text alone (Clark and Mayer 2011).

### Audio and Graphics Together

Because of the way the brain processes information, cognitive scientists have found that "presenting words in audio rather than as on-screen text can result in significant learning

1. If you want to add a website that doesn't display a Zotero icon in the URL bar, there are **two ways** to add the website to your Zotero library. If using the Zotero library in the bottom portion of your Firefox browser, click on the **"create new item from current page"** icon on the Zotero toolbar while viewing the website you want to add.

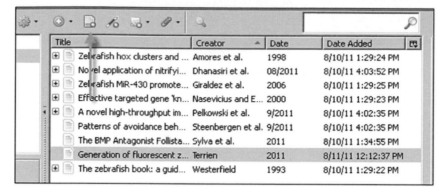

| Title | Creator | Date | Date Added | |
|---|---|---|---|---|
| Zebrafish hox clusters and ... | Amores et al. | 1998 | 8/10/11 1:29:24 PM | |
| Novel application of nitrifyi... | Dhanasiri et al. | 08/2011 | 8/10/11 4:03:52 PM | |
| Zebrafish MiR-430 promote... | Giraldez et al. | 2006 | 8/10/11 1:29:25 PM | |
| Effective targeted gene 'kn... | Nasevicius and E... | 2000 | 8/10/11 1:29:23 PM | |
| A novel high-throughput im... | Pelkowski et al. | 9/2011 | 8/10/11 4:02:35 PM | |
| Patterns of avoidance beh... | Steenbergen et al. | 9/2011 | 8/10/11 4:02:35 PM | |
| The BMP Antagonist Follista... | Sylva et al. | 2011 | 8/10/11 1:34:55 PM | |
| Generation of fluorescent z... | Terrien | 2011 | 8/11/11 12:12:37 PM | |
| The zebrafish book: a guid... | Westerfield | 1993 | 8/10/11 1:29:22 PM | |

2. Alternatively, if you are using the Zotero library either in a Firefox tab or if you are using Zotero Standalone, **right-click** anywhere on the website you want to add and choose Zotero>Create Web Page Item from Current Page from the menu.

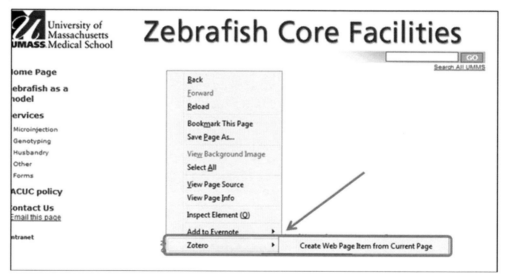

**Figure 4.4.** Graphic with text separated from the image

gains" (Clark and Mayer 2011, 115). While it may seem like providing visuals, text, and audio together would help many learners, this has not been found to be the case. Instead, the combination of all three elements overloads learners, and they are unsure of what elements to focus on. This occurs because reception of the audio information and the visual information is divided across two separate cognitive channels; the brain processes information more effectively if it only needs to use one channel.

The exceptions to this rule are if the learners cannot process spoken words well, for example, if the learners are English-language learners or have learning disabilities. In these cases, provide closed captioning that can be turned on or off or provide a separate text file so that not all learners need to watch the text and listen to the audio together. Audio recordings in combination with clear visuals can be a powerful instructional tool, but the design principles discussed earlier still need to be followed. The audio recording should be short and directly tied to the learning objectives.

1. To add a website that doesn't display a Zotero icon in the URL bar, there are **two ways** to add the website to your Zotero library.  First, go to the website you want to add to your library. Next, if you are using **Zotero for Firefox**, use the "create new item from current page" toolbar icon to add the page.

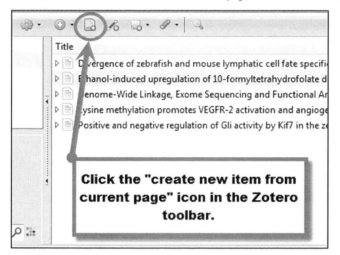

2. Alternatively, if you are using the Zotero library either in a **Firefox tab** or with **Zotero Standalone**, right-click anywhere on the website you want to add and use the Zotero menu option.

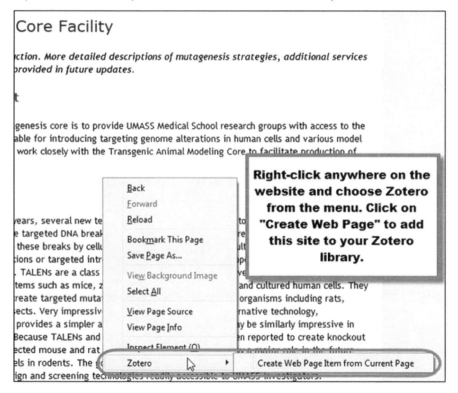

**Figure 4.5.**    Graphic with text embedded in the image

## Designing Assessment Content

Earlier in this chapter, big-picture assessment considerations were discussed. Most big-picture assessments are summative assessments, meant to more formally demonstrate whether learners have met the learning objectives at the end of the learning experience. Formative assessment, or feedback throughout the learning experience that helps learners gauge if they are on the right track, will now be discussed as a type of content that can be designed and integrated throughout tutorials in order to help encourage reflective learning. This type of assessment need not be graded and can usually be administered as self-tests.

While it can be simplest to design quizzes based on facts covered earlier in the tutorial, this type of assessment promotes low engagement and shallow processing of the content. This kind of assessment is sometimes referred to as "regurgitative." While you may need to collect some of this information at the end of your tutorial for reporting or grading purposes, this should not be the only way to encourage and evaluate learning within the tutorial. Chapter 8 will discuss ways to create meaningful objective questions, such as multiple-choice questions, that can be used either for formative assessment or to assess learning at the end of your tutorial. A more engaging type of assessment involves "deliberative practice." Deliberative practice assessment requires reflection by the learner and should build toward larger learning goals. Here are some deliberative or self-reflective formative assessment examples for a tutorial on database searching:

- How broad or narrow were the keywords you used to search for your question?
- When you started your research project, was searching or browsing in the database more helpful?

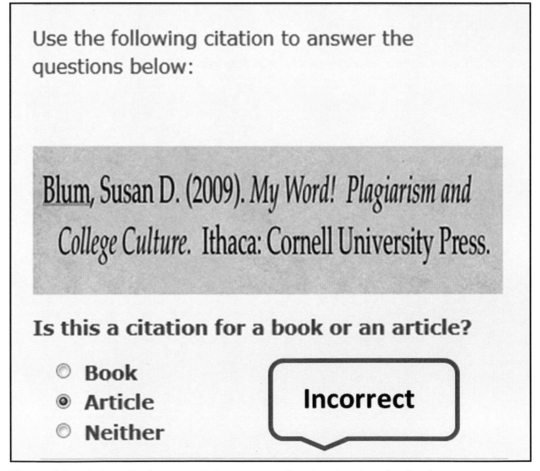

**Figure 4.6.** Automatically generated response without explanatory feedback

While purely fact-based multiple-choice questions on their own don't always encourage deep learning, including a variety of question types can help learners stay engaged. Use multiple-choice questions attached to specific examples in order to make the questions feel more relevant. Another helpful formative assessment technique is to use several different contexts while maintaining the focus on the same main principle to let learners see how principles work under different conditions. This type of assessment helps learners transfer what they have learned to new contexts. For example, in a tutorial on how to use facets as a way to narrow search results, learners could first try a search exercise using facets in an online shopping website, followed by a search in a web-scale discovery system, followed by a search in a subject database. Using realistic examples helps learners see the relevance of the assessment exercises.

Because this assessment is meant to be formative, the feedback you provide can be as valuable as the exercises themselves. When using multiple-choice or other automated options, use the options built into most e-learning authoring tools to give explanatory feedback for both correct and incorrect responses. The explanatory feedback should go beyond a simple "correct" or "incorrect" and should illustrate the rationale behind the correct answer (see figures 4.6 and 4.7 for examples of feedback without and with explanatory feedback). In addition, researchers have found that sticking to feedback focused on the learning task is more helpful than feedback focused just on the learner, such as "well done." Feedback aimed at the learner makes them focus on their ego rather than on the learning task (Clark and Mayer 2011).

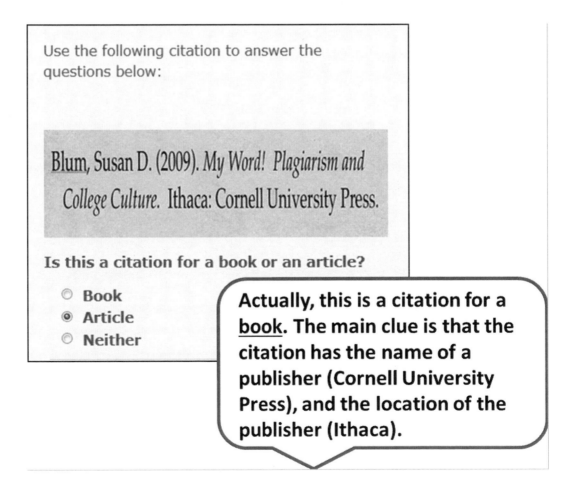

**Figure 4.7.** Automatically generated response with explanatory feedback

Finally, practice is more helpful early on in the tutorial, but you don't want learners to burn out with too many formative assessment exercises. Again, keeping a tutorial short is important for retaining learners' attention. Practice balancing the four content types of subject-knowledge content; graphical, textual, and audio content; and assessment content as you design your tutorial so that learners are engaged and meet the learning objectives without feeling either overwhelmed or bored.

# Sequencing Tutorial Content

Once you have chosen and designed your tutorial content, the next step is to determine the most logical way to sequence the tutorial content. For many people, it is difficult to truly separate out content design from organizational design. This section will more explicitly address how you can use an organizational framework and provide clear navigational strategies to design your tutorial to make the content most approachable for your learners. This section will wrap up with an overview of storyboarding as a tool to help you view and evaluate your content and organizational strategy.

Before determining organizational strategies, revisit your learner analysis in order to determine whether background information needs to be presented or whether instructional content needs to be scaffolded in a particular way based on what your learners already know. This is also a good time to remember that tutorial content should be broken into brief chunks or modules that address two to three ideas at the most. Depending on the size of your tutorial, you will have more or less organizing fun ahead of you!

## Organizational Framework

A tried and true way of organizing instructional content is based on instructional design principles (Smith and Ragan 2005). Course instructors are often encouraged to organize their content into the following four segments (see table 4.3):

- Introduction
- Body
- Conclusion
- Assessment

Organizing instructional content into these discrete organizational elements may be more practical with a term-long class or with a longer tutorial. Depending on the size of your tutorial and the resulting number of modules, you may either choose to explicitly use this organizational framework or you may combine multiple elements of this framework into a single module or introductory slide. Regardless of the size of your tutorial project, paying attention to the instructional events that go into the standard organizational framework can help you make sure that you are providing your learners with a logical way to navigate through the instructional material.

## Introduction

There are four instructional events possible in the introduction to a tutorial: gaining attention, establishing purpose, arousing interest or providing relevance, and giving

**Table 4.3.** Organizational Framework and Suggested Instructional Events[1]

| ORGANIZATIONAL ELEMENT | INSTRUCTIONAL EVENTS | TIPS FOR TUTORIALS |
|---|---|---|
| Introduction | 1. Gain attention or focus<br>2. Establish purpose<br>3. Arouse interest and promote motivation or relevance<br>4. Give overview of lesson | • Keep the introductory elements short.<br>• Focus on relevance. |
| Body | 1. Recall relevant prior knowledge<br>2. Explain and demonstrate content or knowledge, including examples<br>3. Include learning strategies, such as self-reflective prompts<br>4. Learner practice with supervision, e.g., self-tests or scenarios<br>5. Feedback to practice exercises | • Include visually relevant examples to communicate content knowledge.<br>• Provide explanatory feedback beyond "correct" and "incorrect" for self-test exercises. |
| Conclusion | 1. Summarize<br>2. Transfer learning, learner practice within different contexts<br>3. Remotivation and closure, providing context for learning, signaling that the tutorial is complete | • Keep the conclusion elements short.<br>• Focus on learning transfer.<br>• Create a clear ending, either in the form of a final screen or a clear textual or audio sign-off. |
| Assessment | 1. Summative assessment<br>2. Provide feedback, usually in the form of a score or a grade, along with a way to receive more help | • Provide clear resources to online and in-person help resources. |

[1]Adapted from Smith and Ragan 2005.

an overview of the lesson. Because learners' willingness to spend time on extraneous information is limited within the tutorial context, try to streamline your introductory elements as much as possible. Gaining attention can be as simple as introducing the title or main topic of the tutorial so that learners know the tutorial has begun. Establishing the purpose of the tutorial can be combined with elements of the instructional events of providing relevance and giving an overview of the lesson. Don't belabor the purpose of the tutorial, especially if learners are being directed to your tutorial for a specific class or task. In those cases, learners should be able to understand the purpose based on guidance from their instructors.

Focus your introductory efforts on providing relevance for your tutorial in order to help motivate learners to complete the instruction. Make the connection to tangible outcomes obvious and then provide an overview of the lesson. In some cases, it may be appropriate to provide an overview of the learning objectives (in jargon-free language); other times it may be more helpful to briefly summarize the main outcome that learners will come away with and allow the navigational elements, such as the table of contents or module headings, to indicate the topics to be covered.

## Body

The body of the tutorial is the main focus for knowledge delivery and contains five instructional events: recalling relevant prior knowledge, explaining and demonstrating content or knowledge, incorporating learning strategies, providing opportunities for learner practice, and giving explanatory feedback for practice exercises. There are a variety of options in a tutorial for helping learners recall prior knowledge or for explaining what you expect learners should already know. This may be an opportunity to use branching to allow learners to go to an alternative part of the tutorial depending on how much they already know about the topic. Alternatively, this could be a place to link to supporting materials if learners' knowledge is not at the expected level.

Most of the body of your tutorial should focus on explaining and demonstrating content, hopefully with the use of visually engaging examples, and on providing opportunities for learner practice in the form of self-tests, worked examples, or scenarios. Remember to include opportunities for learners to process what they have learned and create their own mental model through the use of self-reflective prompts. The explanatory feedback you provide for the formative assessment learning opportunities in the body will serve as another opportunity for demonstrating the content and reinforcing knowledge.

## Conclusion

The conclusion contains three possible learning events: a summary of content covered, promotion of learning transfer, and the opportunity to remotivate learners and provide closure. A brief summary of what was covered serves to remind learners of the main learning objectives along with an illustration of the relevance of the content. However, just as with the introductory learning events, in the tutorial context it is important to keep this summary and explanation of relevance short so that learners do not view the information as extraneous. Instead, focus on providing opportunities for transferring learning to new contexts either by providing additional learning exercises situated in different settings or by giving learners self-reflective prompts that allow them to provide the new learning context.

Providing closure to a tutorial is helpful in order to let the learners know that the tutorial is finished. Don't make learners wonder whether the website crashed or the video closed on its own. Provide a clear ending slide, screen, or module along with text or audio indicating that learners have reached the end of the tutorial.

## Assessment

The assessment part of the organizational framework contains two instructional events: summative assessment and feedback and an explanation of how to get more assistance. Not all tutorials will require the collection of summative assessment information, so if you do not need to administer a score, certificate, or grade, you do not need to include this step. However, all tutorials should provide some way for learners to get more help, either in the form of a contact person or department or in the form of additional instructional materials.

## Navigational Strategies

After having carefully sequenced the overall content for your tutorial, you will now need to give up some control! In contrast to a classroom setting, in tutorials learners should be able to choose their own path through the instructional content. Regardless of how linearly or logically you set up your tutorial content, some learners will still want to be able to jump ahead to the content that most closely matches their information need. Designing your tutorial with navigational strategies that allow learners to do this while still providing a clear outline of the learning arc will help learners achieve that need for control.

One way to give learners navigational control is by designing content in modules. Modular design helps your learners to be more flexible and choose their own path through your content. Next, make sure to include some type of site map to allow users to visually understand the overall plan or connection between the modules. One of the most easy-to-use site maps is a table of contents sidebar (see figure 4.8). Tables of contents can be particularly helpful as a navigational guide if a tutorial is somewhat long or complex or if learners are new to the content. The headings used in the table of contents should be clear and free of jargon.

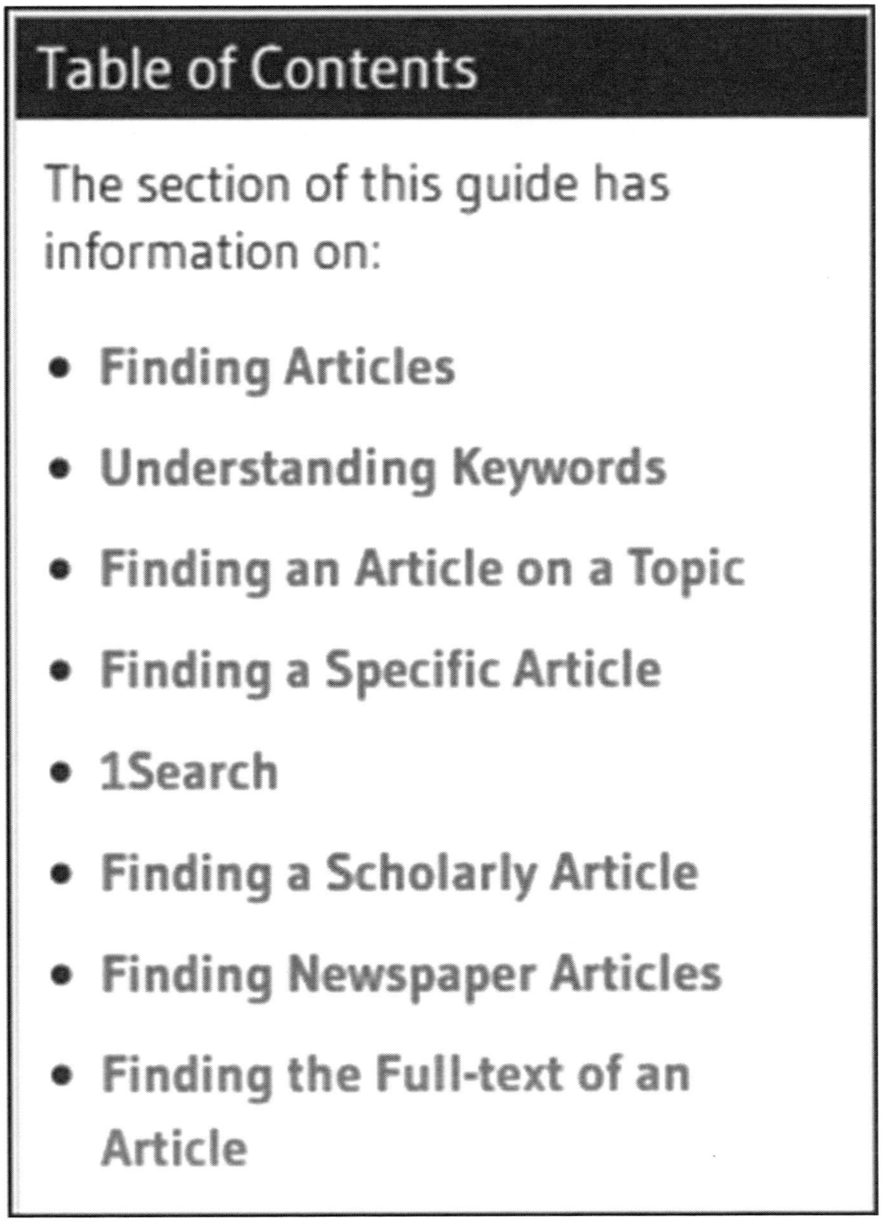

**Figure 4.8.** Example of a click-able table of contents site map

## Table of Contents

The section of this guide has information on:

- **Finding Articles**

- **Understanding Keywords**

- **Finding an Article on a Topic**

- **Finding a Specific Article**

- **1Search**

- **Finding a Scholarly Article**

- **Finding Newspaper Articles**

- **Finding the Full-text of an Article**

- Modules
- Table of contents
- Forward and backward arrows

Another important navigational element is the use of forward and backward arrows on the top and bottom of the page to help navigate between modules. Having the arrows in both places will make it more likely that learners will see these navigational elements. The arrows also give learners control over the pacing of the tutorial as learners need to actively click on the arrows in order to advance to new content.

There are some additional navigational elements that you might consider using but that aren't as crucial or clearly beneficial as modules, table of contents site maps, and arrows. If your tutorial-creation software has the option to include a progress bar, this can be a helpful signal to indicate how much content remains in the tutorial. Some tutorials include tabs or drop-down menus. However, research has not yet found that these navigational elements are particularly helpful (Clark and Mayer 2011). In fact, researchers looking at LibGuides design found that learners didn't see the tabs at all (Pittsley and Memmott 2012). As a result, relying on tabs as the only or primary navigational strategy is not advisable.

While it is important to provide learners with some navigational control, not all learners are equally able to choose the best path for themselves. Novice learners have been found to make relatively poor navigational choices simply because they don't know enough about the subject area and the language associated with the subject to make appropriate choices. In contrast, more advanced learners who already know something about the subject area or learners who have some metacognitive learning strategies in place will make better navigational decisions and will benefit from the option to skip ahead to newer or more advanced content (Clark and Mayer 2011). However, for all types of learners, providing a logical structure and navigational plan helps learners to see the connection between ideas and helps many learners feel confident that they have mastered the learning objectives. If a tutorial is too unstructured or if learners are allowed to aimlessly explore through the tutorial contents with no clear learning goal, they will be less likely to learn what you intend for them to learn.

## Storyboarding: Design Tools for Organization and Visualization

As discussed in chapter 2, storyboarding is an excellent way to visualize both individual elements of a tutorial as well as the overall trajectory and organization of your tutorial project. Storyboards can range from a simple pen-and-paper sketch to more professionally generated online graphics. With either approach, the main goals of storyboarding are to

- give a snapshot of the content elements;
- indicate how the content will be illustrated (visual elements, assessment exercises, narration, etc.);

**Table 4.4.** Examples of Storyboarding Tools and Their Benefits

| STORYBOARDING TOOL | BENEFITS |
|---|---|
| Pen-and-paper sketch | Cheap, design anywhere |
| Sticky notes | Cheap, flexible, easy to rearrange on a wall, take a picture to capture various iterations |
| Microsoft PowerPoint slides | Cheap if you have Microsoft Office already; easy to manipulate, share, or print |
| Storyboard That | Has a free version, online tool, has an educators' version |
| Celtx | Has a free version; available in desktop, mobile, or online versions; helpful for more text-intensive design |
| Twine | Free, open source, can download to your desktop, publish to the web for sharing, can incorporate text and images |
| XMind | Has a free version, pro version is $99, can download to your desktop, publish to the web for sharing, includes template diagrams |

- see how the content elements are connected;
- choose navigational strategies;
- find gaps in your content; and
- see the tutorial more holistically.

Table 4.4 includes an overview of some free and inexpensive tools that can be used to design storyboards. The storyboarding tools with the smallest learning curve are those tools you likely already use: pen and paper, sticky notes, and Microsoft PowerPoint. See figure 4.9 for an example of a storyboard created using PowerPoint. These simple tools will work well for projects that are not too large and if all of the collaborators are geographically close together.

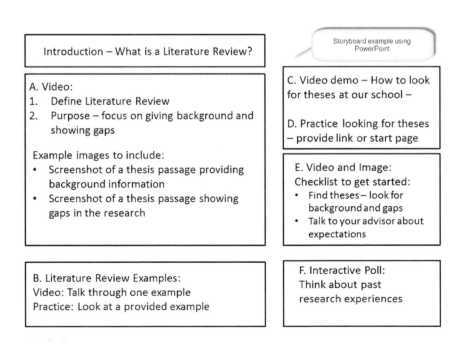

**Figure 4.9.** Example of a storyboard created using Microsoft PowerPoint

**Figure 4.10.** Example of a storyboard created using Twine

The online storyboarding tools have a somewhat higher learning curve but may be worth your time if you have a larger project that includes more navigational elements or if you and your collaborators need more sophisticated sharing options than are readily available with the off line versions. See figure 4.10 for an example of a storyboard creating using Twine, and see figure 4.11 for an example of a storyboard created using XMind.

Remember not to get distracted by creating the perfect storyboard but rather let the process of creating a storyboard help you see what content may be redundant or lacking, to see how content can be organized, and to see how you are using visual and assessment exercises throughout. Taking the time to create a storyboard will help you better communicate your ideas to other collaborators and will help you build a more robust and learner-friendly tutorial.

## ⊚ Key Points

Designing a tutorial involves strategically thinking through everything from the instructional strategies you will use to how you will incorporate the content you want to include, how you will organize the information, and how you can realistically assess learning. Here are some key points to take away:

- Beginning your design process with clear learning objectives will make it easier for you to focus on what you want your learners to know and will make it easier to determine appropriate assessment strategies.
- Designing a tutorial is different than designing classroom or course-based instruction. Capitalizing on the unique attributes of this online delivery method will help you maintain your learners' interest and increase their potential for deep learning.
- Content delivery in a tutorial relies on the interplay of visual examples, opportunities for practice, and short explanations via audio or text.

**Figure 4.11.** Example of a storyboard created using XMind

- A combination of logically interconnected modules and opportunities for learners to control their own navigational steps through a tutorial will result in higher satisfaction for learners of a variety of backgrounds.

Now that you understand the underpinnings of good design you are ready to begin developing your tutorial. Chapter 5 will address the process of selecting technology tools, and chapter 6 will guide you through developing an outline, writing a script, choosing your media, producing your tutorial, and making sure your tutorial is accessible.

# ◎ References

Anderson, Lorin W., and David R. Krathwohl, eds. 2001. *A Taxonomy for Learning, Teaching, and Assessing: A Revision of Bloom's Taxonomy of Educational Objectives*. New York: Longman.

Clark, Ruth Colvin. 2009. "Give Your Training a Visual Boost." *Training & Development*, April: 36–38. http://www.clarktraining.com/content/articles/VisualsForLearning.pdf.

Clark, Ruth Colvin, and Richard E. Mayer. 2011. *E-Learning and the Science of Instruction: Proven Guidelines for Consumers and Designers of Multimedia Learning*. 3rd ed. San Francisco, CA: Pfeiffer.

Conrad, Rita-Marie, and J. Ana Donaldson. 2011. *Engaging the Online Learner: Activities and Resources for Creative Instruction*. Updated ed. Jossey-Bass Guides to Online Teaching and Learning. San Francisco, CA: Jossey-Bass.

Dick, Walter, Lou Carey, and James O. Carey. 2004. *The Systematic Design of Instruction*. 6th ed. Boston: Allyn & Bacon.

Gilchrist, Debra, and Anne Zald. 2008. "Instruction & Program Design through Assessment." In *Information Literacy Instruction Handbook*, edited by Christopher N. Cox and Elizabeth Blakesley Lindsay, 164–92. Chicago: Association of College and Research Libraries.

Mestre, Lori. 2012. *Designing Effective Library Tutorials: A Guide for Accommodating Multiple Learning Styles*. Oxford, UK: Chandos Publishing.

Miller, George A. 1956. "The Magical Number Seven, Plus or Minus Two: Some Limits on Our Capacity for Processing Information." *Psychological Review* 63, no. 2: 81–97.

Nguyen, Frank, and Ruth Colvin Clark. 2005. "Efficiency in E-Learning: Proven Instructional Methods for Faster, Better Online Learning." *Learning Solutions E-Magazine*, November 7: 1–7. http://www.learningsolutionsmag.com/articles/245/efficiency-in-e-learning-proven-instructional-methods-for-faster-better-online-learning.

Oehrli, Jo Angela, Julie Piacentine, Amanda Peters, and Benjamin Nanamaker. 2011. "Do Screencasts Really Work? Assessing Student Learning through Instructional Screencasts." *ACRL 2011 Conference Proceedings* 30: 127–44. http://0-www.ala.org.catalog.wblib.org/ala/mgrps/divs/acrl/events/national/2011/papers/do_screencasts_work.pdf.

Pittsley, Kate A., and Sara Memmott. 2012. "Improving Independent Student Navigation of Complex Educational Web Sites: An Analysis of Two Navigation Design Changes in LibGuides." *Information Technology and Libraries* 31, no. 3: 52–64. doi:10.6017/ital.v31i3.1880.

Smith, Patricia L., and Tillman J. Ragan. 2005. *Instructional Design*. 3rd ed. Hoboken, NJ: J. Wiley & Sons.

# CHAPTER 5

# Development
## *Tools for the Task Ahead*

---
**IN THIS CHAPTER**
---

▷ Discovering the range of tools available for tutorial creation

▷ Determining how to choose technology tools for your project

▷ Learning about major examples of each type of tool

▷ Finding new tools for your project

▷ Developing techniques for learning how to use new tools

THIS CHAPTER LOOKS AT THE TYPES of tools available for tutorial creation, their characteristics, and some specific examples. In their 2011 article, Anne-Marie Deitering and Hannah Gascho Rempel reported on a survey of instruction librarians and identified the need to learn new technology as a significant hurdle to creating tutorials. So if you feel some trepidation when thinking about learning how to use new tools, take heart—you are not alone! The intent of this chapter is to provide a framework for considering specific tools that best fit your individual project as well as your institutional needs and circumstances. Technology is changing so rapidly in the e-learning world that no book can hope to be comprehensive or current by the time it is published, so in this chapter you will be pointed to resources that will help you find information about the most recent tools and reviews about them, as well as information about how to use them. In chapter 6, processes for assembling your tutorial using the tools in this chapter will be discussed, along with best practices for making tutorials more accessible.

## Getting Started with Tutorial-Creation Technologies

As you consider what tutorial-creation tools to choose, several assumptions about the resources you have in terms of support, training capacity, and time are important to address. First, if you are planning a complex, multipart, highly interactive and interrelated set of tutorials, it is assumed that you will have the support of instructional designers or information technology experts with access to specialized tutorial-building technologies. If that support is not available, it would be prudent to choose a less complex technology solution or to budget time to negotiate a steep learning curve. Second, once you have chosen a particular technology tool, it is assumed that you have the time and access to training so that you can learn enough about the tool to construct engaging and effective tutorials with a reasonable investment in outside training or self-education. Even free tools often provide some training and support, and users of commercial as well as free resources often share information and support with each other. You don't have to wait until you are an expert to make a good tutorial!

Because the most important and potentially mystifying technology to master are e-learning authoring tools (which may also be called e-learning development tools), those will be the first resources discussed in this chapter. Depending on the technology you choose, you may need additional tools like screen capture or audio editing to fulfill your design goals, so the initial choice of an e-learning authoring tool will inform other choices. When you begin to examine e-learning authoring tool resources, first investigate what your institution is currently supporting and determine how those resources might fit your instructional needs. For example, if you already have institutional access to software such as Techsmith's Camtasia or Adobe Captivate (both widely used for e-learning and library tutorials), that may make your choice much simpler. In addition to reduced upfront costs, you are likely to find technical assistance and instruction available on campus and experts to consult with when learning a tool that is already widely used by your colleagues. A campus department for instructional design or learning focused on information technology may be able to steer you to campus resources quickly.

## E-learning Authoring Tools

There are a variety of tutorial-authoring or e-learning tools to consider, correlating with the many types of tutorials that are possible to create. At one end of the spectrum, tutorials can be Word documents or PowerPoint presentations saved as PDFs, designed for learners to work through step by step. At the other end of the complexity spectrum, tutorials can include audio, video, screenshots, captions, interactivity, or quizzes in order to provide a richer and more self-directed learning experience. Choosing the right tool to help you accomplish your tutorial-design goals can be a dizzying prospect. See table 5.1 for a sample rubric that takes into account an array of tool characteristics that you will need to consider as you choose an e-learning authoring tool.

Consider the following aspects when choosing e-learning software:

- *Design needs*—If you plan to produce a small number of simple tutorials, it may not be cost effective to invest in an expensive e-learning tool that takes a long time to master. If you are designing an integrated suite of tutorials and intend to include complex graphics, narration, quizzing, and interactivity, this will be more easily accomplished with versatile and powerful tools. Try to match tool capabilities with your current needs, as well as including some consideration of future needs for expanded e-learning.

**Table 5.1.** Sample Decision-Making Rubric Based on Tool Characteristics*

| TOOL ASPECTS | MEETS NEEDS (2) | PARTIALLY MEETS NEEDS (1) | DOES NOT MEET NEEDS (0) |
|---|---|---|---|
| *Design Needs* | Tool capabilities match your design needs now and into the future. | Tool capabilities match some of your immediate design needs or future needs, but not all. | Tool capabilities do not match your design needs. |
| *Budget* | Tool cost matches your budget. | Tool cost somewhat more expensive than your budget can handle or may take more costs than anticipated to get running. | Tool cost is entirely out of the question for your current budget. |
| *Learning Curve* | You or your team members are already comfortable with using the tool. | You or your team members have used some elements of the tool before, but some training will be needed. | You will need to spend a significant amount of time training yourself in how to use the tool. |
| *Output Formats* | Tool provides a final product in the formats you need. | Tool provides most of the formats you need, but the choices are limited. | Many other tools will be needed to adjust the tutorial to a final format. |
| *Accessibility Options* | Tool provides simple methods for creating a fully accessible tutorial. | Tool provides some options for creating an accessible tutorial. | Tool does not provide an accessible final product. |
| *Platform* | Tool works on both Mac and Windows computers. | Tool works on the platform that most of your team uses. | Tool does not work on the platform that your team uses. |
| **Total Rating Score:** | | | |

*Suggested ratings are included in parentheses.

- *Budget*—The price tag for e-learning tools can range from free to thousands of dollars. If your budget is limited, there are excellent free options to investigate, but you may need to spend more time in order to understand the capabilities and limitations of those options. Many commercial options offer discounts for purchase by educational institutions, so factor that into your calculations when investigating pricing. Also consider that you may be able to negotiate a different price than that which is publicly shared, so find the person in your organization who is responsible for purchasing or negotiating licenses and ask for help acquiring the tool you want.
- *Learning curve (and time available for learning)*—Consider how much time you have to devote to learning a new tool and what tools you or your team members may already be skilled at that can be used for your project. Simple and effective tutorials can be produced with tools that are relatively easy to learn. Comprehensive tools that allow editing of more than one aspect of the tutorial, such as audio, video, navigation, and timing, will typically be more complex and difficult to master than tools with limited capabilities. The time it takes to become competent in a tool is not easily quantified, but looking at the tool itself, watching videos about how to use it, or talking with colleagues who are familiar with a specific tool are all useful

methods for estimating the effort required. Many commercial products offer a free trial that can help you determine how difficult it is to use. Once you have mastered one development tool, it will be easier to add another to your repertoire if, for example, your institution shifts support to another tool or you move to an institution with different resources available for e-learning.

- *Output formats*—For years, the majority of tutorials were shared in web browsers using the Adobe Flash format (SWF), which requires an Adobe Flash Player plug-in, a separate software component, to deliver multimedia elements such as video and audio. The ubiquity of mobile platforms and new operating systems that do not use Flash, such as Google's Android, suggest that HTML5, which was designed to deliver multimedia capability to mobile devices and browsers without using plug-ins, is a more widely accepted platform to design for in the future. Most development tools provide a range of output choices for finished tutorials; in some cases, it may be useful to save a tutorial in more than one format, such as both Adobe Flash and HTML5, depending on what you know your learner population is using. While Flash is still widely used and continues to be useful, most experts tend to agree that HTML5 will gain increasing popularity, particularly for its ability to deliver multimedia on mobile platforms (Ganci 2013).
- *Accessibility options*—The ability to add captions, narration, tab navigation, and other aids to accessibility is not limited to expensive packages but should be considered for all tutorials. Commercial software options typically include at least some accessibility options, while free resources often do not.
- *Platform*—If you are working with a large team, it's a good idea to make sure that you are all working on the same platform, whether that is Windows, Mac, or another operating system, and that your tutorial-development software is compatible with it. The platforms that your users are likely to view the tutorial on should also be taken into account when choosing output formats. Many current output formats, like HTML5, are (relatively) platform neutral.

Once you have thought through some of your basic requirements for an e-learning authoring tool, you can then transition to considering a specific tool to acquire. Table 5.2 includes a range of tool examples and their characteristics that were available at the time this book was written.

One element that influences the type of e-learning development tools you will choose is a consideration of how the content will be displayed and how your learners will interact with that content. Table 5.2 describes a range of output-type options, from text-based documents to animated images. Many of these tools are flexible enough that they can be used to develop more than one type of tutorial. Even if you plan to start out simply, versatile tools offer more options for your future online tutorial designs. For example, Camtasia can produce tutorials based on PowerPoint presentations, as well as record and edit screencasts and develop animation. A web-based tutorial may contain animation or screenshots, and a video tutorial is often based on a PowerPoint presentation. Even a simple text-based tutorial will generally be shared on the web, requiring someone involved in the process to have web-authoring skills. However, to help clarify the components that can go into developing a tutorial, the next section describes the characteristics of each of the output types.

**Table 5.2.** Major Types of E-learning Authoring Tools with Examples

| TUTORIAL OUTPUT TYPE | CHARACTERISTICS | TOOL EXAMPLES (2014) | PROS AND CONS |
|---|---|---|---|
| Text based | Document-based tutorials; static; no interactivity | • Adobe PDF<br>• Microsoft PowerPoint<br>• Microsoft Word | Pros:<br>• Easily developed and shared<br>• Useful in low-bandwidth situations<br>Cons:<br>• Linear and static |
| Web based | Webpage based; one or a series of pages that can be interactive | • Adobe Dreamweaver<br>• Adobe Flash<br>• LibGuides by Springshare | Pros:<br>• Interactive options<br>• Work on most platforms<br>Cons:<br>• Flash is declining in favor as it doesn't work with mobile devices and newer operating systems |
| Presentation based | Tutorial elements easily built from presentation slides—narration and interactivity can be added; slides can be turned into video or can be the basis for more feature-rich tutorials | • Adobe Presenter<br>• Articulate Storyline<br>• Microsoft PowerPoint<br>• SoftChalk | Pros:<br>• Easily developed and shared<br>• Presentation software is familiar and widely available<br>Cons:<br>• Linear design |
| Screenshot or screencast | Computer-screen activity recorded as separate images or video clips; captions and narration added | • Adobe Captivate<br>• Articulate Screenr<br>• Techsmith Camtasia<br>• Techsmith Jing<br>• Techsmith Snagit | Pros:<br>• Can clearly communicate with less text<br>• Useful when demonstrating a multistep skill like database searching or citation management<br>Cons:<br>• Requires more bandwidth<br>• Requires server space to save media |
| Videos | Recorded still or video; edited to optimize order, captions, narration, timing | • Apple iMovie<br>• Kaltura<br>• YouTube<br>• Windows Movie Maker | Pros:<br>• Create a personal connection<br>Cons:<br>• Editing requires a steep learning curve<br>• Requires high bandwidth |
| Animation | Separate images combined into a series that provides the illusion of movement on the screen | • Adobe Flash<br>• Adobe Captivate<br>• GoAnimate<br>• Pencil<br>• Powtoons<br>• Synfig<br>• Techsmith Camtasia | Pros:<br>• Animation can be engaging<br>Cons:<br>• Difficult to make accessible<br>• Can contain problematic cultural references |

## Text-Based Tutorials

Text-based tutorials may be advantageous in situations when a student just wants to check a piece of information or refresh his or her memory because they can be rapidly skimmed for answers instead of watched from beginning to end to glean the desired information. They are also useful where low bandwidth might be anticipated, such as in rural areas or developing countries. However, text-based tutorials are not typically recommended due to their linear structure and lack of interactivity. Another negative is that the low level of sophistication may signal to younger or media-savvy learners that the tutorial is not a high-quality production and might even make them suspect its legitimacy. The potential to be fairly wordy arises when using a text-based platform; this can make it easy to ignore best practices of conciseness, which other tutorial output types encourage.

Even a text-based tutorial is likely to be shared via the web, so some knowledge of web authoring and the ability to store files to a web server is still necessary. Text-based tutorials are produced using widely available tools such as Microsoft PowerPoint or Adobe PDF, so the learning curve for both design and production is typically quite low. This also means that they can be developed relatively quickly and inexpensively. Output formats include typical document files like PDFs, so text-based tutorials are compatible with multiple platforms and can be easily used with web-based screen readers or self-voicing browsers to provide text-to-speech narration for visually impaired learners.

## Web-Based Tutorials

Web-based tutorials can add elements of interactivity and learner control much more easily than text-based tutorials. If your institution has a web presence, there may be commercial web-authoring tools such as Adobe Dreamweaver, Adobe Flash, or LibGuides by Springshare available to use for tutorial development. Free options for web authoring like WordPress, Weebly, or Google Web Designer are also available.

The learning curve for these tools can vary—some require at least basic HTML coding or programming skills, while others, called WYSIWYG (What You See Is What You Get) editing programs, are more intuitive and easier to master. Because these tutorials are saved as webpages, their output can typically be viewed using major browsers and thus present few platform issues. Accessibility options will vary with the web-editing resource, but most are configured to provide basic accessibility options.

## Presentation-Based Tutorials

Tutorials based on a presentation format, such as Microsoft PowerPoint slides, are in a format that is already familiar and widely used, though not always highly regarded due to their linear design elements. However, working from presentation slides provides some potential design options that are quite attractive. Narration can be recorded directly into a presentation using an external microphone, and presentations made in PowerPoint can be converted into video and saved as a Windows Media Video (WMV) file. Because presentation software is so ubiquitous—PowerPoint is included in standard versions of Microsoft Office—it already exists on most office computers and therefore doesn't require an extra purchase.

Some e-learning resources, such as Adobe Presenter, can be based on PowerPoint presentations and are designed to augment the presentations in order to produce more interactive and engaging tutorials. Other resources, such as Articulate Storyline, Camtasia, and Captivate, can incorporate PowerPoint slides into video tutorials in order to easily add text, captioning, and transitions. The output can be saved in numerous media file types, as well as PDFs. Similarly, SoftChalk allows the incorporation of PowerPoint or Word files as a starting point for designing tutorials. Presentation-based tutorials can range from a relatively low learning curve (PowerPoint with narration) to a much more involved design (Articulate Storyline) when branching, quizzing, and other interactivity elements are added. Microsoft Office 2010 provides an Accessibility Checker for Word, Excel, and PowerPoint that identifies potential accessibility issues and suggests corrections.

## Screenshot- or Screencast-Based Tutorials

Tutorials employing screenshots or screencasts as a major element are particularly useful for point-of-need demonstrations of databases and other research tools or for computer-based skills such as citation management. While many vendors may offer excellent online instruction for their databases, libraries can easily provide customized screencasts incorporating nuances from the local library's website in order to prevent confusion for their users. This can be particularly useful in distance-learning situations in which it is almost impossible to be too clear. Simple screencasts are easily obtained and often need minimal editing to be both presentable and useful (Belanger and Izenstark 2011).

There are excellent free screencasting tools available, including Jing and Screenr, as well as more powerful and expensive commercial tools. The learning curve is not steep for simple screencasts with minimal editing and can in some cases be almost instantaneous! A little practice combined with informal feedback from your colleagues can help you feel more comfortable with this technology fairly quickly. Screencast and screenshot output formats vary, but most resources produce output in widely used media formats such as Flash, MP4, or HTML5 for screencast files or TIFF, JPG, or PNG for screenshot files. Free tools typically do not offer many accessibility options for tutorials, but commercial software provides a variety of features, such as tabbed navigation, captioning, and narration.

## Video-Based Tutorials

Video-based tutorials capture live action and narration as a basis for instruction. They can be particularly useful for library orientations, presenting the librarian to his or her patrons, and marketing the library or its services (Leeder 2009). Video footage can be captured using a video camera, a digital still camera with video capability, or a smartphone or tablet and can be edited to include captions or narration for accessibility. Many people have become amateur video artists and are confident capturing simple video clips, but expert video capture and video editing have a fairly steep learning curve, and the requisite equipment and software for each can be quite expensive.

Video clips can be edited in most e-learning software as well as in more specialized video editors like iMovie and Windows Movie Maker. Web-based services such as YouTube, which some institutions use to distribute their tutorials, also provide basic video-editing capability. Video-based tutorials and animation tutorials, described in the next section, both tend to output very large files, which may not be best for learners where bandwidth is low and access to the Internet is slow.

## Animation-Based Tutorials

Animation combines still images into a series that provides the illusion of movement on the computer or movie screen. It can spark interest and engagement in learners, particularly those who have grown up saturated with media. While live video is visually literal, animation provides a more conceptual view of instructional content and often can illustrate more clearly what is difficult to see in live video (Lipkowitz 2013). Animation is particularly useful for demonstrations involving "knowing how," or procedural knowledge, versus "knowing what," or declarative knowledge (see chapters 1 and 4 for knowledge types), and can be used to produce a stand-alone tutorial or as an element to enhance another type of tutorial (Lander and Lundstrom 2013).

Dedicated animation software such as GoAnimate, Powtoons, or Adobe Flash Professional (all commercial) are able to produce animated tutorials, as can e-learning authoring tools (e.g., Camtasia, Captivate) that include animation as part of their toolkit. There are also many free animation options available, including Pencil and Synfig. Adding animated sections to a tutorial to provide humor or appealing transitions doesn't have to be difficult, but developing an entire animated tutorial with characters and dialogue will demand more skill and a steeper learning curve. Animations file formats include MP4, Flash, or animated GIF files that can be viewed on multiple browsers and platforms. Animated tutorials can be difficult to modify for accessibility (which will be discussed in more depth in chapter 6), and they may also cause confusion for learners of different cultures.

## Commercial versus Free Software Choices

As you can see, there are many factors to consider when choosing tutorial-creation tools. Likely you will use a combination of the tools and strategies described above in order to create your tutorials. It is also likely that some of the limiting aspects such as budget or learning curve may be more important to you at different phases of your career. Currently, one philosophical as well as practical choice many libraries face is whether to use commercial or open-source software.

Some institutions have even taken the step of developing their own tutorial-authoring software in order to meet specific needs after considering the options that already exist. The University of Arizona, for example, developed Guide on the Side (GoTS) (http://code.library.arizona.edu/gots) when they identified the need for scalable, interactive, and pedagogically driven online database instruction but did not find a platform that met all of their specifications. GoTS is an open-source product that has been widely adopted by other institutions and recognized by the ACRL Instruction Section as a "model of the future of library instruction" (Farkas 2012). This product and other open-source, library-focused tools are well worth considering if they fit your particular needs.

A caveat to consider when assessing commercial versus free e-learning development tools: as is true with many computer applications, free sources can be incredibly well designed and useful, but they may lack the virtue of longevity and are not guaranteed to be available for the long term. If you base a series of tutorials on a resource that suddenly disappears (case in point: Xtranormal, a popular animation resource), it can throw a big monkey wrench in your plans. Free resources may also present problems such as adding malware to your computer when you download the free tool, so be sure to read reviews when available, ask your colleagues to share their experiences before you leap, and download carefully! Commercial resources are likely to be around for a while; be updated regularly; have developed robust instruction, training, and support; and possibly be more responsive to customer requests.

Use these characteristics as a guide for making tool choices regardless of what tools are currently available. For examples of some major e-learning authoring tools available at the time this book was written, with a focus on some differences between commercial and freely available tools, see table 5.3.

**Table 5.3**. Commercial versus Free or Open-Source E-learning Software Comparison*[1]

| | COMMERCIAL | | | FREE OR OPEN SOURCE | | |
|---|---|---|---|---|---|---|
| | CAMTASIA STUDIO | CAPTIVATE | STORYLINE | GUIDE ON THE SIDE | JING | SCREENR |
| Publisher | Techsmith | Adobe | Articulate | University of Arizona | Techsmith | Articulate |
| Audio record/ edit | Yes | Yes | Yes | No | Record, not edit | Record, not edit |
| File output options | HTML5, SWF, AVI, MP4 | HTML5, AVI, MOV, FLV, MP4, SWF | HTML5, FLV | Web-based, displays live webpages | SWF | SWF, MP4 |
| Viewer control | Pause, navigate, volume | Pause, navigate, volume | Pause, navigate, volume | Self-paced, navigation | Pause | Pause |
| Quizzing | Yes | Yes | Yes | Yes | No | No |
| SCORM/ LMS integration | Yes | Yes | Yes | No | No | No |
| PowerPoint import | Yes | Yes | Yes | No | No | No |
| Branching | Yes | Yes | Yes | No | No | No |
| Accessibility— Section 508 compliance | Captioning, no tabbed navigation | Tabbed navigation, captioning | Tabbed navigation, captioning | Captioning, working on adding accessible features | No tabbed navigation, captioning with Screencast.com Pro | Tabbed navigation, no captioning |
| Unique features | Screencast.com for storage, sharing; Google Drive integration; video tables of contents | Autosizing for multiple device screens | Translation and right to left language support; rich cast of animated characters | Library centric, open source; guidance is provided when user interacts with live webpages | Screencast. com, tutorials, tech support, 5-minute limit on videos | No download needed; works from Macs or PCs; easily share links to video |

*As of 2014

[1]Adapted from Slebodnik and Riehle 2009.

# ⑥ Scripting Tools

Once you have chosen an e-learning authoring tool, if you are creating a tutorial with an audio component, it is time to start on the nuts and bolts of developing your script. Perhaps you are weary of hearing that planning and, by extension, scripting are very important parts of the tutorial process. Maybe you think that you are just going to wing it because you have taught this class at least twenty times! There are plenty of reasons to write at least a simple script or outline for your tutorial narration no matter how familiar you are with the instructional content. Even if you are a talented improviser, forgetting one word or recording unnecessary words (like *umm . . .*) can lead to multiple re-recordings or more complicated audio editing. A script will help you keep your narration clear and concise and avoid fumbling for an elusive word. When it is time to update your tutorial, it will be much easier if you have a script to modify, rather than having to transcribe your narration (or someone else's narration) before deciding what changes to make. And when you write captions in order to provide greater accessibility, your script is a ready-made source for that text.

Writing a script doesn't have to be a difficult process. If you record the narrative you have already honed over multiple iterations, you will have a good draft that can then be edited into a serviceable script. A script should be written to reflect spoken conventions rather than written conventions (no one will "hear" your well-thought-out semicolons!) and in a way that makes it engaging for the target audience. A simple narrative can easily be roughed out as part of the storyboard, which can then do double duty as the script. A complex series of interacting tutorials will benefit from more detailed and formal scripts that allow you to detect and edit out redundancies, synchronize images and narration during storyboarding, and insert transitions early in the process.

At the bare minimum, the scripting or screenplay resource you choose should allow you to arrange dialogue in parallel with screen images in order to visually indicate simultaneous processes. Scripts or screenplays can be written in your familiar word-processing software, which often provides templates for screenwriting that make the process of coordinating screenshots and other graphics with narration easy. Microsoft Word, for example, has a template called "Screenplay," and additional Word options can be found on Wikipedia or Word user forums.

One well-regarded option is Celtx (see figure 5.1), desktop screenwriting software that provides templates for document types such as screenplays and AV scripts. The basic version is free, and the website includes helpful tutorials and a robust community forum. Wikipedia lists many other screenplay options that range from basic and free to highly specialized and expensive (http://en.wikipedia.org/wiki/List_of_screenwriting_software).

# ⑥ Tools and Specifications for Creating Graphics

Tutorials need not consist of only text or screenshots—carefully chosen graphics can enhance any type of instruction. Still images can be just as effective as video, and some would say that they are more effective as images decrease cognitive load for tutorial users when compared to video (Mestre 2012). Remember the discussion of tutorial design in chapter 4—make sure your images are chosen to support actual learning and are not tangential or purely ornamental. Image types include still images, video, screenshots or screencasts, and animation. The following section describes the range of formats and im-

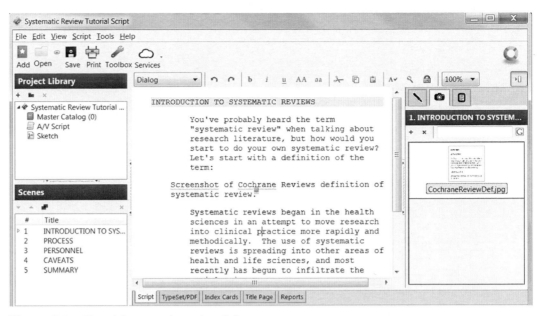

**Figure 5.1.** Tutorial screenplay using Celtx

age types that are commonly used in creating graphics. Having a deeper understanding of what kind of file type to use will make your tutorials both more visually pleasing and more technologically accessible for your learners.

## Still Images

Still images are produced in either raster (also known as bitmap) or vector formats (Smith 2010). Raster images are made up of pixels and are not easily resized or scaled up without becoming pixelated. Therefore, they should be constructed in the required image size in order to avoid resizing or in the highest resolution possible if resizing is anticipated. Raster image quality is related to the amount of data contained in the image, with larger amounts of data displaying as higher-quality images and high file sizes being the norm. Raster or bitmap files are used when photographic image quality is required, so they are often referred to as image editors. Common file formats include bitmap (BMP), graphic interchange format (GIF), tagged-image file format (TIFF or TIF), and Joint Photographic Experts Group (JPEG or JPG). Raster images can be imported, created, and edited in programs like Adobe Photoshop, which is the industry standard, and in abundant commercial and free image editors, such as Gimp.

Vector images consist not of pixels but of mathematical descriptions that are translated in order to produce images. Vector images are not restricted to rectangular shapes and can be resized or scaled without degradation of the image quality. They are typically used for illustrations and type, so you may hear them referred to as illustration software. Vector images do not increase in file size as the image size increases, so they are much smaller than raster files. Common vector file formats include scalable vector graphics (SVG), Adobe Illustrator (AI), and computer graphics metafile (CGM). Vector graphics are created and edited in graphics software such as Adobe Illustrator, Adobe Flash, and CorelDRAW. Free vector-graphics options include Inkscape, OpenOffice Draw, and FatPaint. File formats that provide support for both raster and vector graphics include Adobe portable document format (PDF) and Adobe Flash (SWF).

Screenshots, which are still images of the computer screen, can be obtained using the built-in screenshot capability of many browsers (e.g., Windows Explorer, Safari, and Google Chrome) or using specialized screen-capture software like Snagit or SnapDraw. Screen-capture software can often be manipulated in order to capture a specified portion of the computer screen, allowing unnecessary information to be filtered out of the resulting image. Some software allows scrolling beyond what is initially visible on the screen, enabling larger amounts of visual information to be captured. Screen-capture software often provides basic image-editing functions such as cropping, resizing, special effects, and even the addition of captions, arrows, and other visual cues. A series of carefully planned screenshots can provide much of the visual information obtained from a screencast (discussed in the next section) but may be less useful when showing a dynamic process, like dragging and dropping a file. Dynamic processes may be more coherently demonstrated using a screencast rather than a screenshot. Individual screenshots can be extracted from screencasts if still images are the best fit for your design plan as well as your learners' projected bandwidth capabilities. Both screenshots and screencasts provide excellent visual information and can be edited and captioned in order to enhance their instructional utility.

## Videos

Video files are increasingly delivered as streaming media, which enables them to be downloaded in a continuous stream while being viewed rather than downloaded from a server before being viewed. Streaming media is captured, saved as digital files and edited, and encoded with the appropriate video codec, a device that enables the compression and decompression of digital video. Common codecs for streaming media include MPEG4, WMV, and RealVideo. MPEG4 is designed for interactive multimedia and includes specifications for video, audio, and interactivity. The device that is used to view streaming video must also be installed with the codec used for that media's output. After being encoded, a step that occurs when the file is saved in a particular format, the file is ready to be delivered through a web platform. The technical issues involved go beyond the scope of this discussion, but saving video files in a widely used format will usually ensure that they can be viewed without difficulty. Some video is still delivered in formats such as AVI (audio video interleave) or QuickTime that require a separate downloading step, so be aware of this when choosing output formats. Waiting for the download step to complete can be a hurdle for learners in a hurry, so video clips in these formats should be kept to less than a minute in length whenever possible.

Screencasts, or moving images of computer-screen processes, are obtained using specialized software like Screenr or Captivate and provide a detailed demonstration of multistep processes such as performing a database search. Screencasting tools come in two general types: frame-based tools and full-motion-based tools. Frame-based tools capture screen activity in static images that are generated each time a new activity takes place on the computer. For example, if you are demonstrating a database search, a new frame is captured when you (1) click on the database link, (2) type in a search term, and (3) click on the Search button, producing a total of three new frames. Frame-based tools often provide an audible cue, such as a camera shutter sound, when a frame is generated so that you know exactly when an image is being captured. It is simple to replace a single frame if the image is not exactly what you wanted to record and easy to delete unwanted images from the sequence.

Full-motion-based tools produce a movie of computer-screen activities, usually capturing about thirty frames per second even when there is no screen action. Typically, the first step of the process you wish to capture is set up on the computer screen, you tell the software to begin recording, you complete the process that is being demonstrated, and finally you halt the recording. If there is an error on the screen, like a pop-up box appearing when an e-mail is received during the recording, the recording must be redone. It takes more skill to use full-motion-based tools, as jerky movements of the mouse are recorded equally jerkily and you must avoid obstructing relevant content with the cursor (which is harder than it sounds!). In addition, the files resulting from full-motion recording of a screen activity like a database search will be much larger than those of a frame-based recording of the same process because of the greater number of images captured. Screen-capture tools of either type save the recorded activity in a proprietary file format. Files are edited and then published or produced in a video format of your choice, like MPEG4 or AVI.

Animation in tutorials can add visual interest and humor to encourage learner engagement. A tutorial can be completely animated, or animation can be used selectively to illustrate complex concepts and principles, to transition between sections, and to illustrate instructional scenarios and simulations. Animated characters are easier to control than human actors, and media-savvy students may enjoy the multisensory experience that animation can provide. New animation tools do not require drawing skill; they provide preformatted characters and drag-and-drop tools to insert characters and other objects into the scenes you wish to create. For example, Articulate Storyline comes preloaded with an initial group of characters and provides the option to purchase additional groups of characters. Storyline also simplifies the construction of animated scenes and scenarios by dragging and dropping the desired elements on the screen. Animation is output in animated GIF, Flash, Shockwave, and CSS3 files.

## Finding Graphics

Engaging graphics can be purchased, produced, or borrowed. Stock images may be entirely sufficient in order to enhance the design needs of your tutorial. They are widely available, often free or inexpensive, and typically of excellent quality. You can also produce your own digital photos or video clips using a camera, smartphone, or video camera and edit the images in graphics editors like Adobe Photoshop or use any one of numerous free resources like Picasa. Most editing applications provide basic image editing such as cropping, sizing, special effects, or contrast adjustment and can save edited photos and images in multiple file formats.

Rather than creating all of your own graphics, you can sometimes find graphics that you can borrow and reuse. Free still images and video clips can be obtained by searching for them using a search engine. For example, Google's Advanced Image Search allows you to specify images that are free to share and even to modify. Another option is Creative Commons, which offers a search function called CC Search that provides access to a variety of independent resources such as Flickr, Google Images, YouTube, and SoundCloud for images, music, and other media that can be royalty free (see figure 5.2). While the search results are not all necessarily Creative Commons compliant, their status can be determined quickly. To check the copyright status of an image you are considering, perform a "reverse image search" using a free service like TinEye, which will find the original source of an image and verify its status (Morgan 2013).

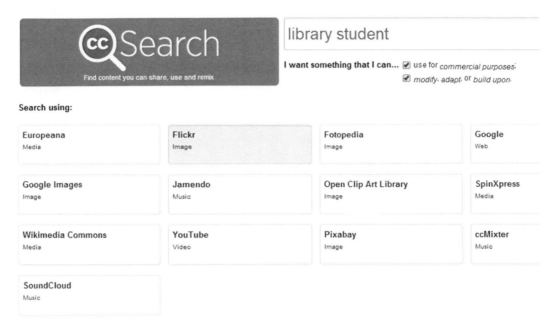

**Figure 5.2.** CC Search initial search screen

A quick search for "library student" using CC Search to access Flickr yields many interesting images that can be quickly scanned and downloaded. It is worth emphasizing that royalty-free videos and still images may not be free of charge to download, so proceed with caution! Video images can also sometimes be obtained for free, and clips can be useful for background. Simple video editing such as trimming and combining video clips and adding audio, metadata, and other enhancements can be done within YouTube's Video Editor and other video editors, as well as within the commercial e-learning software options.

For very simple image needs, you might consider using clip art, which is widely available as part of packages like Microsoft Office and can also be found free through web searches of resources like the Creative Commons CC Search page (http://search. creativecommons.org/). However, be careful not to overuse clip art images as they can quickly contribute to cognitive overload without providing any substantial learning value. When searching for these images, try to find ones that are freely downloadable for use or modification and download the highest resolution of each image that is available. If an image needs to be edited, starting with a high-resolution image will produce a higher-quality end product.

Investigate local sources like your college or university development office that have often assembled a library of institutional photos for use in webpages and development materials and have already secured permission to share them. Historical images can often be obtained for free from sources such as the Library of Congress and other digital history archives. Even if a site is described as containing "public-domain" images, movies, music, or art, individual works should be checked for copyright restrictions before being repurposed for your tutorial. Rather than segueing into a long discussion of copyright restrictions and issues at this point, please consider refreshing your copyright knowledge by reviewing one of the many excellent resources that will help you avoid missteps in this arena. As an example, Columbia University provides an exhaustive guide to public-domain resources through their Copyright Office (http://copyright.columbia.edu/copy

right/copyright-in-general/public-domain-resources/). Most institutions have resources to help their students avoid plagiarism—if you feel at all uncertain about using a particular image or video clip, carefully investigate your options and err on the side of caution!

## ⑥ Tools and Specifications for Using Audio

If you plan to add narration or music to your tutorial, choose and use it carefully. Nothing is more distracting than inaudible or confusing narration or music that is loud and unremitting. Adding audio increases the amount of effort required to design and produce your tutorial, as well as the cognitive load for your users, so make sure that the audio enhances your message. Adding musical background throughout is usually too distracting—consider a brief clip to introduce your tutorial and perhaps another to close it. Studies show that adding both audio and text to an image may distract users to the point of detrimentally affecting their learning achievements, so narration that repeats screen text may be more confusing than reinforcing (Mayer and Moreno 2003).

Audio is typically recorded in one of two types of file formats: lossless or lossy. Lossless audio files preserve much of the audio quality of the original source, while lossy files are compressed in order to save file space, and the sound quality can be slightly diminished. Common lossless file formats are WAV (waveform audio file format), AIFF (audio interchange file format), and Apple Lossless, and common lossy formats include MP3 (Moving Picture Experts Group audio layer III) and AAC (advanced audio coding). These distinctions are probably most important to audiophiles who plan to convert their audio files to other formats in the future, but they do have implications for your tutorials too. In general, lossy formats such as MP3 files are adequate for audio, including both music and narration, and are much smaller than lossless files. MP3 files are also very common and widely supported.

The commercial versions of e-learning software, including the three described in table 5.3 (Camtasia, Captivate, and Storyline), allow the insertion and editing of audio. Generally, narration can also be recorded directly into these resources using an external microphone or downloaded when recorded using a digital recorder. Audio is saved as an MP3 or WAV file and edited to remove errors and improve timing and volume, then synchronized as desired with the other elements of your tutorial. Many authoring tools use some form of timeline that allows audio and visual elements to be synced in a linear fashion and then previewed to fine-tune the results.

Audio files can be downloaded or produced. Fair use of copyrighted items, including music, is supported under U.S. copyright law, so it is possible that short audio clips can be incorporated (with credit) from commercial music. To avoid any appearance of copyright violation (especially important when making tutorials about plagiarism or copyright!), it is advisable to use royalty-free audio clips and properly credit the audio that you use with permission. Royalty-free audio can be found through a CC Search (see above) or from web services like Jamendo and SoundCloud.

Producing audio, typically narration written specifically for your tutorials, may sound intimidating but does not need to be a daunting process. Recording directly into the development tool with an external microphone or using a digital recorder to capture narration and uploading the resulting audio files into your e-learning authoring tool are both straightforward processes. Another possibility is installing and using the text-to-speech capability of many resources like Windows (Word, PowerPoint, Excel) and Apple (Text to Speech). Computer-generated voices may be more distracting than human narration in some ways and less distracting in other ways, but computer-generated voices are almost always easier to generate than recording a human voice.

Audacity (http://audacity.sourceforge.net/) is a free, widely used open-source and cross-platform audio editor and recorder. Narration is recorded by Audacity using a microphone or mixer, and audio files of many formats can be imported for editing. Recorded sound is edited in order to correct sound quality, timing, and volume; erase static and other background noises; remove vocals; mix tracks; and add special effects like echo and reverberation. Audacity can be used on Windows, Mac, and Linux machines, and its output file options include WAV, AIFF, and MP3. Audacity has a robust library of tutorials and other training materials, including one specifically for teachers and students who are just getting started with Audacity. Apple's Garage Band (http://www.apple.com/mac/garageband/) is another free software resource for recording, mixing, and sharing music tracks.

Chapter 6 will recommend best practices for narration, but at minimum, narration should be clear and audible. Most e-learning programs will allow direct recording via an external microphone into your PowerPoint presentation or tutorial and provide simple editing of embedded audio files.

## Finding New Tool Possibilities

Now that you've started to think about tool possibilities, how can you identify the best tools for your project? There are many possibilities for identifying new tools, both commercial and free. One resource that can be surprisingly valuable when you are trying to get a handle on the universe of learning technology is Wikipedia. Well-curated lists and links to current examples of screenwriting software, screencasting and screen-capture applications, digital audio editors, web design, presentation software, public-domain images, video-editing software, and collaboration tools will guide you to recent as well as archived information and often to reviews of useful tools. For a good snapshot of currently available tools, consider Wikipedia as a starting point.

Another source that can be quite useful is Softonic (http://en.softonic.com/). Softonic provides searchable and downloadable descriptions of free and commercial software and applications that work with Windows, Mac, Android, and mobile platforms. Links to full, trial, and commercial versions of software are provided through the Softonic website. A search for "screen-capture software" found 139 programs, sortable by factors such as relevance, ratings by Softonic or users, and number of downloads in the last month. Softonic reviews each entry, providing a brief overview, pros and cons, and links to free downloads and to publishers' websites in order to learn more about the software and purchase it. The company Softonic is based in Spain, and its reviews are available in multiple languages. A word of caution—many free download sites, including Softonic, are plagued with issues like malware, which can hitch a ride on your downloaded application and infect your computer workstation. Read reviews of download sites before using them; be sure that you are clicking on the link to download the software you want (whether free or commercial) and not on a link for an advertiser. Hover your cursor over the download link and check the URL before clicking! For a sample review of Snagit from Softonic, see figure 5.3.

Your colleagues can also be a rich source of ideas for tools that they have tested and deemed useful. A message asking for tool suggestions submitted to a discussion list like

# Snagit

Buy now and receive your purchase via email

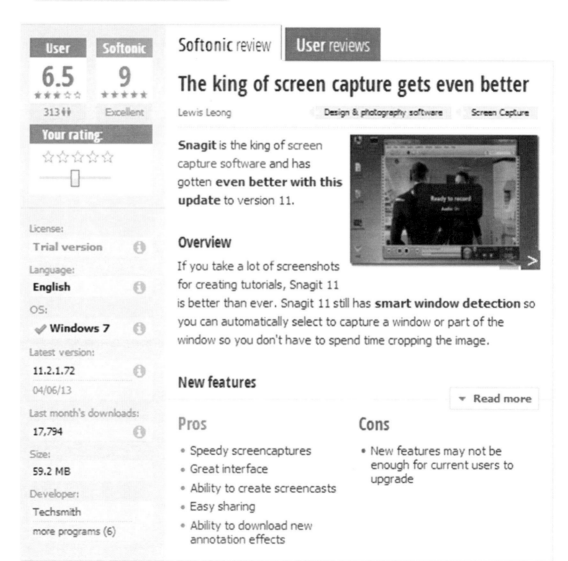

| User | Softonic |
|------|----------|
| 6.5 | 9 |
| ★★★☆☆ | ★★★★★ |
| 313 | Excellent |

**Your rating:**

☆☆☆☆☆

**License:**
Trial version

**Language:**
English

**OS:**
✔ Windows 7

**Latest version:**
11.2.1.72
04/06/13

**Last month's downloads:**
17,794

**Size:**
59.2 MB

**Developer:**
Techsmith

more programs (6)

**Softonic** review    **User** reviews

# The king of screen capture gets even better

Lewis Leong          Design & photography software      Screen Capture

**Snagit** is the king of screen capture software and has gotten **even better with this update** to version 11.

## Overview

If you take a lot of screenshots for creating tutorials, Snagit 11 is better than ever. Snagit 11 still has **smart window detection** so you can automatically select to capture a window or part of the window so you don't have to spend time cropping the image.

## New features

▼ **Read more**

## Pros

- Speedy screencaptures
- Great interface
- Ability to create screencasts
- Easy sharing
- Ability to download new annotation effects

## Cons

- New features may not be enough for current users to upgrade

**Figure 5.3.**   Softonic review of Snagit software

the Information Literacy Instruction Discussion List (ILI-L) from the ACRL Instruction Section will quickly garner recommendations from instruction librarians and may spark a lively discussion of pros and cons. ILI-L is a members-only discussion list that has over five thousand members and is hosted by the American Library Association. Your state library association or other professional group may have a similar discussion list that you can tap into—discussion lists can also help you identify experts in your chosen e-learning tool who might help you when you run into snags. Read the blogs of instruction librarians who you have found to be "early adopters" of new technology to see what they are reading about and testing out. Consider contacting an instructional designer at your home institution who might be able to steer you toward useful tools and provide occasional support. The eLearning Guild, a professional organization for instructional designers, publishes a useful trade journal, *Learning Solutions Magazine*, which publishes reviews of e-learning software, as well as practical articles about designing instruction. Basic membership in the eLearning Guild is free and provides access to *Learning Solutions*, as well as useful information, classes, workshops, and conferences.

## Learning to Use New Tools

It can be helpful to consider how to approach a new tool that you want to add to your personal toolkit. Patti Shank (2011), an instructional designer, recommends that when you are first starting to learn a new application you should first install it (always a good practice) and then take a deep breath and look for tutorials provided by the vendor. Some vendors have basic or even extensive lists of tools on their website—look for "Training," "Support," or "Resources" or call customer service if you come up short. Tutorials may be included on the installation disks if they come with your new program. For a complex program like a tutorial-authoring application, it may be helpful to attend a class, either online (e.g., through Lynda.com) or in person, in order to dive into it quickly and confidently. If the tool is used by your institution and supported by the information technology department, they may offer classes to faculty and staff. Attending a local class may be a great opportunity to find others who are either experts or new learners and who can provide expertise and support.

Other possibilities for learning new tools or skills include finding (or forming) an enthusiast or user group on the Internet, checking with professional colleagues (like those on the ILI-L discussion list) for expertise and support, purchasing the appropriate instruction manual or Dummies book, or looking for conference workshops that align with your needs. Sometimes the best way to learn a new tool is simply to use it—think of a short tutorial that you can design and produce quickly (maybe a topic you're personally interested in rather than something for work) and put the unfamiliar resource through its paces while you become familiar with it. Remember that many commercial tools offer the possibility of a free trial. Using the trial version can be time well spent in evaluating and learning a new tool while assessing its fit for your own needs.

## Key Points

Now you have had the chance to take a tour of the types of tutorial-development tools that are available to you. Take some time to consider and match the best tools to your tutorial design needs, realizing that the perfect tool may not be possible to find (or some-times to afford).

- There are numerous tools available for tutorial authoring—choose the tools that most closely match your design, budget, learning curve, platform, output, and accessibility needs.
- Free tools may necessitate more investment in time and self-education to master and may disappear unexpectedly. Commercial tools offer more support, training, and possibly longevity.
- Learning a new tool takes some time and effort, but that investment will pay off in skills that help you learn the next tool that you tackle to solve a problem.
- There are many resources for free audio, video, and graphics files for your tutorials. Be aware of copyright issues before you download!

In chapter 6, the focus will shift to using these tools—how to plan and produce the audio, video, and graphics elements that you will then edit into the final form you will share with your learners.

## References

Belanger, Jackie, and Amanda Izenstark. 2011. "Tips & Trends: Screencasting." ACRL Instruction Section Tips and Trends. http://www.ala.org/acrl/sites/ala.org.acrl/files/content/aboutacrl/directoryofleadership/sections/is/iswebsite/projpubs/tipsandtrends/2011winter.pdf.

Deitering, Anne-Marie, and Hannah Gascho Rempel. 2011. "Share and Share Alike: Barriers and Solutions to Tutorial Creation and Management." *Communications in Information Literacy* 5, no. 2: 102–16.

Farkas, Meredith. 2012. "In Practice: The Guide on the Side." *American Libraries* 43, no. 5/6: 43–43.

Ganci, Joe. 2013. "Toolkit: Tools for Delivering eLearning with HTML5 (Part 1)." *Learning Solutions Magazine*, August. http://www.learningsolutionsmag.com/articles/1236/toolkit-tools-for-delivering-elearning-with-html5-part-1.

Lander, Beth, and Kacy Lundstrom. 2013. "Animations." ACRL Instruction Section Tips and Trends. http://connect.ala.org/node/212927.

Leeder, Kim. 2009. "Learning to Teach through Video." *In the Library with the Lead Pipe*, October. http://www.inthelibrarywiththeleadpipe.org/2009/learning-to-teach-through-video/.

Lipkowitz, Gary. 2013. "Tips for Using GoAnimate in eLearning." *Learning Solutions Magazine*, February. http://www.learningsolutionsmag.com/articles/1110/tips-for-using-goanimate-in-elearning.

Mayer, Richard E., and Roxana Moreno. 2003. "Nine Ways to Reduce Cognitive Load in Multimedia Learning." *Educational Psychologist* 38, no. 1: 43–52.

Mestre, Lori S. 2012. "Student Preference for Tutorial Design: A Usability Study." *Reference Services Review* 40, no. 2: 258–76.

Morgan, Matt. 2013. "How to Find Free Images with Google's Advanced Image Search." Search Engine Watch, August. http://searchenginewatch.com/article/2289302/How-to-Find-Free-Images-With-Googles-Advanced-Image-Search.

Shank, Patti. 2011. "Beginning Instructional Authoring: Learning How to Author." *Learning Solutions Magazine*, November. http://www.learningsolutionsmag.com/articles/791/beginning-instructional-authoring-learning-how-to-author.

Slebodnik, Maribeth, and Catherine Fraser Riehle. 2009. "Creating Online Tutorials at Your Libraries: Software Choices and Practical Implications." *Reference & User Services Quarterly* 49, no. 1: 33–51.

Smith, Susan Sharpless. 2010. *Web-Based Instruction: A Guide for Libraries*. 3rd ed. Chicago: American Library Association.

## More Resources

Bozarth, Jane. 2013. *Better Than Bullet Points: Creating Engaging E-learning with PowerPoint*. 2nd ed. Hoboken, NJ: Wiley.

eLearning Guild. http://www.elearningguild.com/.

Lynda.com. http://www.lynda.com/.

# Development
## *Putting the Pieces Together for All Learners*

▷ Creating accessible tutorials for learners of all abilities

▷ Writing scripts that are clear and easy to follow

▷ Communicating effectively with graphics

▷ Determining when and how to record simple audio to reinforce learning

HAVING SELECTED, ACQUIRED, AND GAINED some insights into how to use the tools that will help you implement your tutorial, it's now time to use them to produce the pieces (the text, graphics, and audio) that will then be assembled into the final form of the tutorial. Depending on the complexity of your project, the final steps may take a few hours or many days, even weeks, to complete. However, your prep work is complete, and this stage can be very exciting as you see your ideas start to take recognizable shape! For motivation, keep in mind your final goal of an excellent instructional tutorial that benefits your learners as you proceed.

In this chapter, you will be strongly encouraged to consider how to make your tutorials more usable and accessible for learners of all abilities, a practice that provides a wide range of benefits. In addition, this chapter will discuss how to assemble the components of your tutorial. While it is not possible to discuss every form of the tools you will be using and the processes you might follow for your specific tutorial project, this chapter will provide general guidelines and best practices to help guide your production and assembly process.

Providing disabled individuals with comparable access to electronic information is a legal requirement for all federally funded agencies and institutions in the United States according to the Section 508 amendment to the Rehabilitation Act of 1998. Since that requirement went into effect, criteria for Web Content Accessibility Guidelines (WCAG 1.0) were developed and revised (WCAG 2.0) by the Web Accessibility Initiative (WAI) of the World Wide Web Consortium (W3C). These criteria are provided on the WAI website (http://www.w3.org/WAI), along with a great deal of information and supporting resources to help you fulfill the criteria. While accessibility recommendations are generally written for webpages, they are also specified for multimedia resources. Tutorials are natural targets for providing accessible content as they are tools that all learners will be using, regardless of their physical abilities or distance from your library. Accessibility is as much about removing barriers for all learners as it is about providing accommodation for disabled learners.

What are the benefits of accessible tutorials? Making the content accessible fulfills standards that are accepted worldwide, such as those recommended by W3C, as well as fulfilling legal requirements like Section 508 standards in the United States. Accessibility increases the effectiveness of the instruction you provide by offering more than one way for learners to interact with the information. Additionally, accessibility by definition allows your instruction to reach a wider audience and helps train learners with different abilities, broadening the pool of potential learners and fulfilling institutional expectations of social responsibility.

There are two levels of accessibility to consider. The first level of accessibility is accomplished by design features that provide usability, such as a logical structure, a consistent navigation scheme, clear graphics, appropriately sized fonts, and adequate contrast between graphical elements and the screen background. This level of accessibility, which is more commonly referred to as usability, benefits all learners—including disabled learners, learners using mobile devices, aging learners, and learners whose first language may not be English. The second level of accessibility, which is more specific to learners with disabilities, is typically provided by tutorial-authoring software or assistive technology and includes captions, alternative text labels, and features that optimize use by a screen reader, such as a right-to-left, up-to-down organizational scheme. Table 5.3 outlined several e-learning authoring tools that can create accessible tutorials. Choosing one of these tools is essential if you seek to create a tutorial that is accessible to learners with a variety of abilities.

While creating tutorials for learners with certain physical disabilities may require the use of specific e-learning authoring software, creating usable tutorials that work for all learners is something that can be done with many tools. Elements that build in usability for all learners can be created using universal design, a philosophy that seeks to provide flexible resources and environments that are usable by the greatest number of people possible without special adaptation. One widely quoted rule of thumb states that if your webpage (or tutorial) is not usable, the most sophisticated aids to accessibility will not make it accessible (Smith 2014). Whereas assistive technology helps individuals overcome particular barriers to learning or living, universal design strives to eliminate barriers in the initial design process in order to increase opportunities for the widest possible range of users (Rose et al. 2005).

When applied to learning, universal design gives users options such as

- the ability to customize displays;
- alternatives to auditory or visual information;
- clear syntax and structure;
- illustration of key points using multiple media;
- the option to learn more background knowledge; and
- the highlighting of critical features, patterns, ideas, and relationships.

These are all strategies that can be used in tutorial design to optimize the presentation of content and increase usability, as well as to enable learners to navigate through the tutorial in a way that suits their individual preferences and abilities.

## Usability Best Practices

Creating usable and accessible tutorials is first and foremost about presenting web-based information clearly. The first strategy for making your tutorial more usable from an accessibility standpoint is to use clear, consistent graphics and text fonts with adequate contrast between elements. All learners will most easily absorb content from tutorials with clear, uncluttered graphics and fonts and a consistent visual and color theme. Additionally, providing adequate contrast between elements helps learners with visual disabilities. WebAIM provides an online Color Contrast Checker (http://webaim.org/resources/contrastchecker/) that compares foreground and background colors in RGB hexadecimal format to verify and modify color choices. The WAVE accessibility checker (http://wave. webaim.org/) evaluates contrast within webpages as part of its accessibility analysis. The use of sans serif fonts such as Verdana or Tahoma, which were specifically developed for use in electronic media, in font size that is large enough (greater than 10 point) is also advisable for greater readability.

Another strategy for creating usable and accessible tutorials is to provide consistent navigational cues and directions. All learners benefit from clear, consistent navigational cues that help them proceed through a tutorial with less confusion. But having consistent navigational tools also helps learners who are using a screen reader learn how to use your tutorial more easily. Navigation links should remain consistent in appearance and order throughout the tutorial. A link to return to the homepage or to the beginning of the tutorial should be included throughout the resource. You may want to consider including a Help button for additional navigation cues or for clarifying navigational strategies at the beginning of your tutorial.

Just as you learned in chapter 4, providing learners with choices about how they navigate through tutorial content makes learners more satisfied. It also makes your tutorial more accessible. Consider including consistent landmarks such as a tutorial map or outline that can be accessed as learners move through the tutorial to help them choose their own order or skip elements that are not necessary. If you include video content, learners should be able to stop or replay the video if they need more time to read and use the content.

Following chapter 4's instructional design suggestion of ensuring that the reading order of the content is logical and intuitive is another helpful strategy for creating an accessible and usable tutorial. Usability is optimized when web (or tutorial) content is designed to fit into a logical heading structure or outline. Clearly labeled elements help visually challenged learners determine where they are on a page and move through the content with confidence. Screen readers move through the content on a page in a linear fashion, converting screen text and graphics labels to speech, so the reading order of a webpage or tutorial should help facilitate that flow.

Another strategy is to clearly highlight important concepts for your learners. Directing learners to important concepts helps them prioritize learning and form mental models in order to organize the desired content. Use highlights or symbols such as arrows and text boxes to draw learner attention to important concepts and content. Finally, avoid flashing objects. Rapidly flashing screen elements can potentially trigger seizures in learners with seizure disorders. They can also distract any learner from important information.

## Accessibility Best Practice

The second level of accessibility involves principles that are more directly related to access by disabled learners by following Web Content Accessibility Guidelines (WCAG). These guidelines were developed to provide web-design options to meet specific needs of people with disabilities. The acronym POUR (perceivable, operable, understandable, and robust) is used to summarize this design approach (http://webaim.org/articles/pour/). These guidelines include making content:

- *Perceivable*—Available to the senses, including sight, hearing, and/or touch. A key principle of accessibility is transformability, which means that the form of content can be transformed so that it can be perceived by learners with different abilities. For example, instead of being visually read, text can be narrated. And instead of being viewed, graphics can be described.
- *Operable*—Forms, controls, and navigation can be operated using a keyboard, as well as a mouse, without time constraints or flashing elements that can trigger seizures. Learners are provided help navigating, finding content, and knowing where they are in the tutorial.
- *Understandable*—Text content is readable and understandable, navigation is consistent, and webpages appear and operate in predictable ways. Learners are helped to both avoid and correct mistakes.
- *Robust*—Content is compatible with and can be used reliably by a variety of tools that the learner may need, including assistive technologies, such as screen readers and screen magnifiers (WebAIM 2013).

There are several POUR-based techniques for accessibility strategies that can be applied in tutorials. Start by checking whether your tutorial works with keyboard-based navigation rather than just mouse-based navigation. Learners with mobility difficulties or visual disabilities may find the mouse difficult to maneuver and the cursor difficult to see. Using the Tab button or up, down, right or left arrow keys on the keyboard to maneuver through a tutorial provides the learner with more individual control. This adaptation is typically provided by tutorial-authoring software. It is not recommended to restrict navigation only to the keyboard, as existing keyboard shortcuts may conflict with keyboard navigation.

Another important strategy for making tutorials accessible is to provide captions or transcripts. Hearing-impaired learners benefit from real-time captions that highlight and explain the information conveyed by narration. Visually impaired learners will benefit from text alternatives for nontext content such as graphics. According to Section 508 law, a printed transcript is not a substitute for real-time captioning, so both should be provided. However, your tutorial script can be used as the basis for both the captions and transcript text. Captions should be situated close to the element being described in order to help learners make the connection between them.

Similarly, provide audio description of important visual information. Visually impaired learners will benefit from thoughtful narration and audio instructions throughout online tutorials. The audio descriptions can be provided by screen readers as well as through recorded narration. Your tutorial should provide learners with the option to give the screen reader full control as screen-reader users often prefer familiar screen-reader narration over narration recorded with an unfamiliar voice or vocal pace.

Another important habit to establish is to label graphics with alternative text providing brief descriptive information. In most tutorial-authoring tools, this is referred to as "alt text." Alt text is also useful if your images break or disappear for some reason. The alt text will still display and will give learners (and you) an idea of what content was supposed to be there. Screen readers use alt text to provide visually disabled learners with audible descriptions of images, buttons, other graphical elements and navigation instructions. Alt text should be brief and descriptive. WebAIM provides a wealth of information

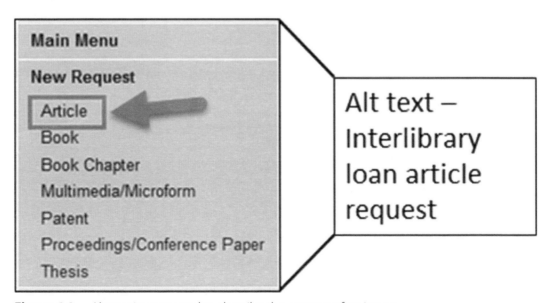

**Figure 6.1.** Alternative text used to describe the content of an image

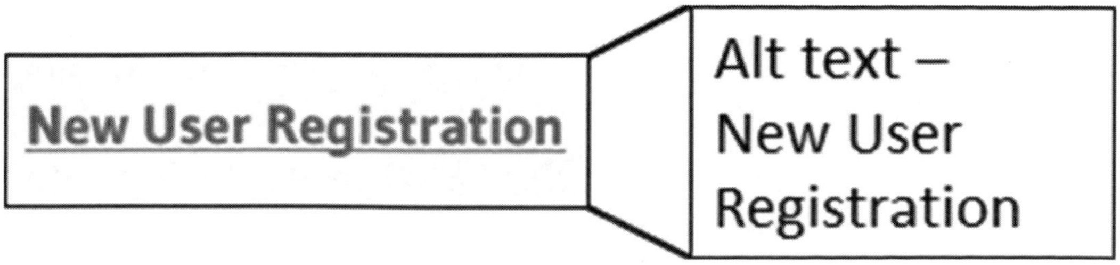

**Figure 6.2.** Alternative text used to describe the function of an image

about effective alt-text labeling techniques for links and images (http://webaim.org/tech niques/alttext/). These techniques include suggestions about how to describe the image content (such as a photo or other graphic) and the image's function (such as a button or link). The amount of information you should give in the alt text depends on how much information is provided in the text on the rest of the page. Try to be brief while describing both the content and the function of the image. Figure 6.1 shows an example of alt text for a content-based image. Figure 6.2 shows an example of alt text for a link, which is a functional image. There is no need to label an image as a screenshot, image, or link (that is usually apparent), and alt text should only be provided for images that are significant (i.e., not for "decorative" graphics that do not relate to the tutorial's learning objectives). Images may be labeled as "null" if they are decorative as a cue to skip over them.

Finally, avoid information conveyed solely using color. Learners who are color blind may not be able to distinguish instructions or callouts that are denoted solely by color or by a change in color. Graphical means of emphasis such as arrows or underlining links will provide direction that is clear to all learners. See table 6.1 for tutorial-design accommodations that are suggested for specific disabilities such as visual, hearing, mobility, and cognitive impairment.

## Best Practices for Assembling a Tutorial

Now that you've considered how to make your tutorials more usable and accessible, the next topic to address is how to produce the pieces such as a script, graphics, or audio that can be edited individually and assembled to form your finished tutorial. Because both words and graphics are powerful in their own right and even more so when combined,

---

### TIPS FOR CREATING ACCESSIBLE TUTORIALS FOR LEARNERS WITH DIFFERENT ABILITIES

- Provide keyboard navigation.
- Provide captions or transcripts.
- Give audio descriptions for important visual information.
- Label graphics with alternative text to provide brief descriptive information.
- Avoid conveying information using only color.

**Table 6.1.** Tutorial Design Suggestions for Learners with Specific Disabilities[1]

| LEVEL OF ABILITY | EXAMPLES | TYPICAL ADAPTATIONS | TUTORIAL DESIGN SUGGESTIONS |
|---|---|---|---|
| All learners | With or without disabilities | Universal design | • Title pages and use sequential headings.<br>• Design consistent graphics with adequate contrast.<br>• Provide clear navigation cues and logical flow of content.<br>• Make text large and clear.<br>• Give the learner control over progress through the tutorial by providing navigation options.<br>• Avoid flashing objects.<br>• Highlight important concepts. |
| Sensory-visual disability | Totally blind, legally blind | Screen reader magnification devices screen-magnification software large-print materials | • Label headings, graphics, navigation tools, and buttons with descriptive alt-text tags.<br>• Offer text-only options (e.g., transcripts).<br>• Avoid complicated tables and charts; screen readers may not be able to access these.<br>• Avoid background images.<br>• Avoid serif and italic fonts.<br>• Use high contrast between background, text, graphics, and navigation tools.<br>• Ensure interaction with screen readers. |
| Sensory-visual disability | Color blind | Grayscale screen | • Use black, gray, and white for optimal contrast.<br>• Avoid presenting information that is based solely on color recognition. |
| Sensory-hearing disability | Hard of hearing, deaf | Closed-captioning | • Avoid audio-only prompts.<br>• Provide real-time text captions for all audio, video, or other media.<br>• Offer text transcripts of the audio or video.<br>• Provide visual as well as audio notification of necessary cues such as navigation. |
| Motor disability | Paralysis, muscle weakness, traumatic brain injury | Alternative keyboard or pointing devices | • Ensure compliance with standard web-accessibility features.<br>• Provide tab navigation through the tutorial (avoid mouse-only navigation). |

[1]Adapted from Crow 2008 and Lewis and Sullivan 2012.

the next two sections will discuss how to craft the words you use and the graphics you develop for your tutorial. These best practices will apply to simple, stand-alone tutorials as well as to complex, multipart series of tutorials. The script will provide the structure that helps determine the graphic elements used, so it will be discussed first.

## Scripting

The script is the backbone of your tutorial. It can capture every word of the intended narrative or establish a basis for careful improvisation. It can provide a voiceover narration and can also be used for captioning or transcripts if you do not decide to provide narration. After you have determined the learning objectives of your tutorial and aligned the desired content with those objectives, your next task is to write the script. As noted in chapter 5, the cardinal rule to keep in mind is that your script is written to be heard, not written to be read. One way to test this is to read the script out loud to yourself as you write it (preferably in a quiet, private space!). Read sections out loud as they are written, and thoughtfully read the entire script to yourself when it is in draft format. This will help you detect run-on sentences, unintentional repetition, choppiness, or unclear language. Ask one or two colleagues (ideally someone unfamiliar with the project) to listen carefully as you read it to them and take notes about unclear points or record questions and observations that they have as they listen. It may also be useful to ask them to read it to you so that you can apply the same scrutiny. This sounds like a lot of reading out loud, but it's extremely helpful in order to catch verbal missteps early and avoid the need for late-stage corrections such as rerecording audio narration. Regina Koury et al. (2010) recommend that tutorial scripts be read aloud, edited to adjust complex phrases and pronunciation, and marked for pauses before attempting to record tutorial narration. Some guidelines for scripting effective narration are:

- Use short sentences. Long, complex sentences are difficult to read and difficult to understand. Narrators, and more importantly listeners, can get lost in the complexity and stop listening. Break long sentences, particularly compound sentences, into shorter ones. Short sentences also assist the narrator to breathe naturally so that the narration sounds more relaxed. Brief pauses help listeners absorb the material in smaller chunks (Shank 2011).
- The narration should refer directly to the images that are currently being displayed. If the script doesn't match the screen, it increases cognitive load and produces confusion for the learner, who will try to figure out what is happening and how to respond to it rather than focusing on the content that is being taught.
- Choose language that your targeted learners can readily understand. If you need to include terminology that may be new or confusing, provide background or clarifying definitions as part of the instruction. Scholarly language may sound impressive on paper, but it may be too stilted and confusing for effective narration. Learners engage more easily with language that sounds relaxed and conversational! Ruth Clark and Richard Mayer (2011) note that learners may engage more easily with a personalized, conversational tone in instruction but caution against using so much informal language or slang that it becomes distracting and sets an inappropriate tone for learning.
- Write narration in second person. Instruction is more memorable when you are addressed directly rather than indirectly. Compare these three sentences:
    1. In order to open the list of results, the learner will next click on the Results button.
    2. You will now click on the Results button to open the list of results.
    3. Next, click the Results button to open the list of results.
  The first example is written in third person and sounds a bit awkward. The second example is more direct and easier to follow than the first example. Sometimes second person uses "you" and sometimes the "you" is implied. In the third example, "you" is implied, which also results in clear, direct instructions. Clark and Mayer (2011) suggest that learners work harder to understand material that is presented by a conversational "partner" using less formal language.

- Use active voice. Active voice specifies who is doing an action in order to make the narrative clearer and often more concise. The subject of the sentence performs the action rather than having the action performed on the subject. Again, note the difference in the sentences below:
  1. Databases are searched by students and researchers in order to find journal articles. (Passive)
  2. Students and researchers search databases in order to find journal articles. (Active)

  Passive voice can sound vague and dull, but active voice clearly describes the intended action and is typically easier to grasp and follow.
- Test the readability of your narrative. Readability is an estimate of the effort it takes for your learner to understand your content. A high readability score means that the content requires less effort to read and is easier to understand. Even advanced learners exploring complex concepts appreciate content that is clearly presented and easy to understand (Shank 2012). The readability score is calculated by measuring elements of your text such as the average number of words per sentence and the average number of syllables per word. Be aware that readability doesn't measure the clarity or coherence of your writing! Asking someone with fresh eyes to critique your script can help identify problems that are not obvious to you or that cannot be diagnosed with a readability analysis.

In the Flesch Reading Ease system, levels of 60–100 are described as standard to very easy reading levels. Reading levels of 59 and below are described as fairly difficult to very difficult. Flesch Reading Ease scores can be measured in Microsoft Word when you proof your text for spelling and grammar. The spelling and grammar proof will also give you a percentage of sentences in passive voice and an estimated grade level that the narrative is appropriate for. This information can help you identify sentences written in the passive voice in order to revise them, as well as help you assess the readability of the text. The readability score is more accurate when a large block of text is assessed, so consider analyzing your entire script rather than short sections. The Flesch Reading Ease formulas, as well as other readability measures, can be accessed at http://www.readability formulas.com. Figure 6.3 shows the Flesch Readability Ease score for this chapter. As you can see, the Flesch Reading Ease score for this chapter is 34.5. That is considerably lower than you would hope to achieve for a tutorial, but is appropriate for a book geared toward professionals.

One way to begin to develop your script is to directly gauge the needs of your learners. In the development of a plagiarism tutorial, librarians and other members of an information-literacy committee formed a focus group to script the tutorial (Kellum, Mark, and Riley-Huff 2011). After the larger committee developed learning outcomes, the six-member focus group used brainstorming to develop messages around their outcomes and to produce slide-based storyboards. They tapped into principles of digital storytelling to "wrap" their message in a story with local relevance—a student who was tempted to plagiarize when feeling overwhelmed by an assigned paper. The script was developed over several drafts and revised due to known technology constraints that prompted minor changes. This is one of many possible examples of a typical script-development process. As you engage in more tutorial projects, you will come to know the level of scripting that works well for you—from a basic outline to a word-by-word script.

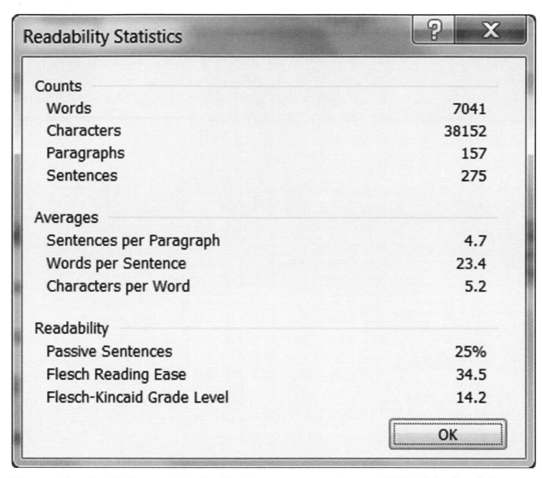

**Figure 6.3.** Readability statistics for this chapter generated using MS Word *Spelling & Grammar* function

For your first efforts, it is probably better to over-script than to under-script in order to avoid problems when you start to record narration or generate captions for your tutorial.

## Graphics, Videos, or Screencasts

Once you have the instructional content clarified and solidified in your script, it is time to start deciding how the tutorial will look. If you have the good fortune to work with an

**TIPS FOR WRITING SCRIPTS**

- Use short sentences.
- Refer directly to the images currently displayed.
- Choose language that is easy to understand.
- Address learners in the second person.
- Use the active voice.
- Test the readability of your content.

instructional or graphic designer, you may not need to produce graphics, but you will still need to know how to choose and use them effectively. What colors will you use throughout the tutorial? What graphics will be chosen or developed to illustrate the instructional points you wish to make? What fonts and font sizes will be used for the text? While it may be tempting to base these choices on personal preference, these choices affect the learning that can occur and should be chosen carefully in order to enhance that learning. However, this does not mean that your tutorial will be dull or that you won't have fun designing its look and feel!

You will recall that carefully chosen colors, text fonts, and adequate contrast among screen elements help provide accessibility. This section will provide information about how to use these concepts and tools when planning design elements such as screen backgrounds, colors, and fonts and when choosing or producing instructional objects that include graphics. The term *graphics* will be used to refer to almost any nontextual element added to your instructional material, such as line drawings, photographs, graphs, tables, screenshots, screencasts, animations, or infographics (Clark and Lyons 2010).

As you will remember from chapter 4, graphics that integrate with text or narration provide two channels in the brain (visual and verbal) for information to be processed and integrated into long-term memory. Since the capacity of working memory is limited, instructional designers try to improve learning by minimizing cognitive load, which can deplete the limited resources of working memory (Clark and Mayer 2011; Lewis and Sullivan 2012; Plass, Moreno, and Brünken 2010). Ruth Clark and Chopeta Lyons (2010) make a clear case that the visual aspects of your tutorial can either enhance or, in the worst case, interfere with learning. The instructional value of a graphic or visual depends on three aspects:

- The properties of the visuals themselves
- The instructional goals and content that are to be delivered
- The prior knowledge of your targeted learners

By now, you have spent a lot of time considering your targeted learners and refining the goals of your instruction and the content you intend to include. The first properties of instructional graphics you need to consider are their surface features—what they are intended to communicate and how the graphic will ultimately impact learning (Clark and Lyons 2010). The surface features of an image are the first characteristics you notice, such as whether the graphic is static, like a photo or table, or dynamic and involving movement, like a video or screencast. The second feature of a graphic to consider is its intended communication—what is it intended to convey? Four types of graphics—organizational, relational, transformational, and interpretive—are classified by Clark and Mayer (2011) as explanatory. These graphic types depict relationships among the instructional content elements and are useful for building deeper understanding. The third aspect, which has already been discussed in chapter 4, is to consider is how the graphic facilitates the psychological processes of learning. Graphics are particularly useful for supporting learner attention, activating prior knowledge, minimizing cognitive load, building mental models, and supporting transfer of learning and motivation. All three aspects of graphics should be considered in light of your learning objectives. For more detail about the surface, communication, and psychological functions of graphics and examples of the different graphics you might consider using, see table 6.2. For additional suggestions about visual examples to consider for communicating different types of knowledge, revisit table 4.2.

**Table 6.2.** Features of Instructional Graphics to Consider[1]

| CATEGORY | TYPES | DESCRIPTION | TUTORIAL EXAMPLES |
|---|---|---|---|
| Surface features | Static | Illustration, photograph, or model | Screenshot, line drawing, schematic |
| | Dynamic | Images plus motion—animation or video | Screencast, video tour, video interview |
| Communication functions | Decorative | Add humor or appeal | Avatar, cartoon character |
| | Representational | Realistic depiction of an object | Photo or video of information commons, screenshot of library website |
| | Mnemonic | Provide memory aid or retrieval cues for information | PARCA test showing the acronym and associated terms |
| | Organizational | Explanatory—depict qualitative relationships among content | Table, organizational chart, thesaurus, concept map |
| | Relational | Explanatory—depict quantitative relationships between multiple variables | Line graph or bar chart to communicate research results |
| | Transformational | Explanatory—how an idea changes over time or space | Illustrate a process like the scholarly publication cycle |
| | Interpretive | Explanatory—illustrate theory, abstract principles, or cause-and-effect relationships | Diagram of library service point or computer equipment |
| Psychological contribution to learning functions | Support attention | Draws attention to important elements | Highlight, callout, relevant text near graphic |
| | Activate or build prior knowledge | Engage existing models or provide mental models for new content | Refresh background information, provide overview of new content |
| | Minimize cognitive load | Avoid extraneous mental work | Line art vs. elaborate imagery, define individual components prior to teaching function of entire mechanism |
| | Build mental models | Help learners construct new understanding of content | Schematic such as a Venn diagram, flowchart of literature search process |
| | Support transfer of learning | Emphasize key features or promote deeper understanding | Apply database search skills to an unfamiliar database |
| | Support motivation | Make material interesting without introducing extraneous content | Illustrate content applied to relevant situations such as work scenarios |

[1]Adapted from Clark and Lyons 2010.

Color is an important dimension to consider when designing instructional graphics. Color can be used to create a particular impression, convey specific information (think of a road map), and highlight important points. Choosing a consistent color theme to use for fonts and backgrounds throughout your tutorial or tutorials provides a visual link between the elements. Choosing colors that work well together is an art, but there is also a science to those choices, particularly when you consider the possibility that some of your learners may be color blind. As noted earlier, for this reason, it is not advisable to convey information using color alone. When you think of a road map, you may realize that the type of road can be specified using color as well as line shape or thickness. Another example is when colors are used to demonstrate differences in a bar chart. Using patterns to show the differences between bars makes the information on the graph clear even when someone is viewing it in black and white.

If color is the only feature that conveys a certain piece of information, a color-blind or visually impaired learner may not receive the information. One way to check this is to print out your webpages or graphics in black and white, then evaluate them to determine whether visual information has been lost. This can also provide a visual flag for inadequate contrast. Red and green color blindness are the two most common types of color blindness, so using either color extensively or exclusively may present problems for your learners. This doesn't mean that you can't use those colors; it just means that you should not use them as the only way to communicate information. A red arrow is still useful because the shape of the arrow is communicating "look here." Red text is not useful because a person with red and green color blindness would not notice the difference between the red text and the surrounding text.

Contrast also affects the visibility of your graphics choices. Even if your color choices are excellent, a lack of contrast between elements will decrease visibility. Pale text on a pale background is difficult for learners with normal vision to read, as are dark text or graphics on a dark background. Using lots of bright colors together may not provide adequate contrast if their contrast values are very similar. The WebAIM Color Contrast Checker (http://webaim.org/resources/contrastchecker/), the WAVE Accessibility Checker (http://wave.webaim.org/), and other resources such as the MSF&W Contrast Ratio Calculator (http://www.msfw.com/accessibility/tools/contrastratiocalculator.aspx) assess the level of contrast of a webpage and its elements. Most contrast checkers assign a contrast ratio and indicate whether the graphics and fonts being assessed pass or fail the desired levels of contrast as specified by WCAG (see figure 6.4). The highest con-

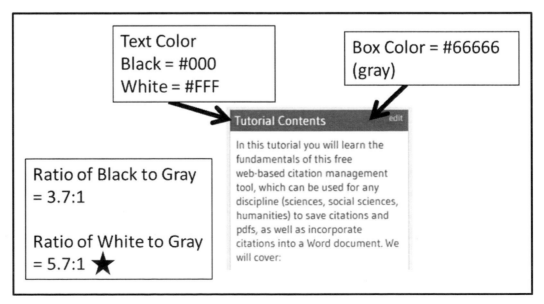

**Figure 6.4.**   Using the MSF&W Contrast Ratio Calculator to choose a text color

trast ratio is between black and white, but that combination can become tedious quickly! Practice finding other highly contrasting colors that work within your palette and then run them through the MSF&W Contrast Ratio Calculator to see what range of colors will work for your tutorial.

Because library tutorials often rely on screenshots to convey visual information, particularly about processes that are unique to your institution, such as how to search in your catalog or how to create an interlibrary loan account, it is important to make sure the screenshots make sense to your learners. Including too much information without specific visual signals can be confusing. For example, if you are demonstrating how to sign up for an interlibrary loan account, avoid taking a screenshot of the entire interlibrary loan webpage, which contains additional, distracting information (see figure 6.5), crop the screenshot so that it targets the information you want to draw attention to (see figure 6.6). Then use visual signals like arrows and a box to guide learners to the information they need. Visual cues like this are particularly helpful for less experienced learners or if the information you are covering is more complicated (Clark and Lyons 2010).

## Narration or Other Audio

Adding narration or other audio to your tutorial will increase its complexity and file size, so consider the necessity of using sound carefully before adding it. Clear, concise, thoughtful narration will add greatly to your tutorial, but murky, long-winded, or overly complex narration will not! Remember the discussion in chapter 4 about designing graphics, textual content, and audio content to help maximize learning. Text that is com-

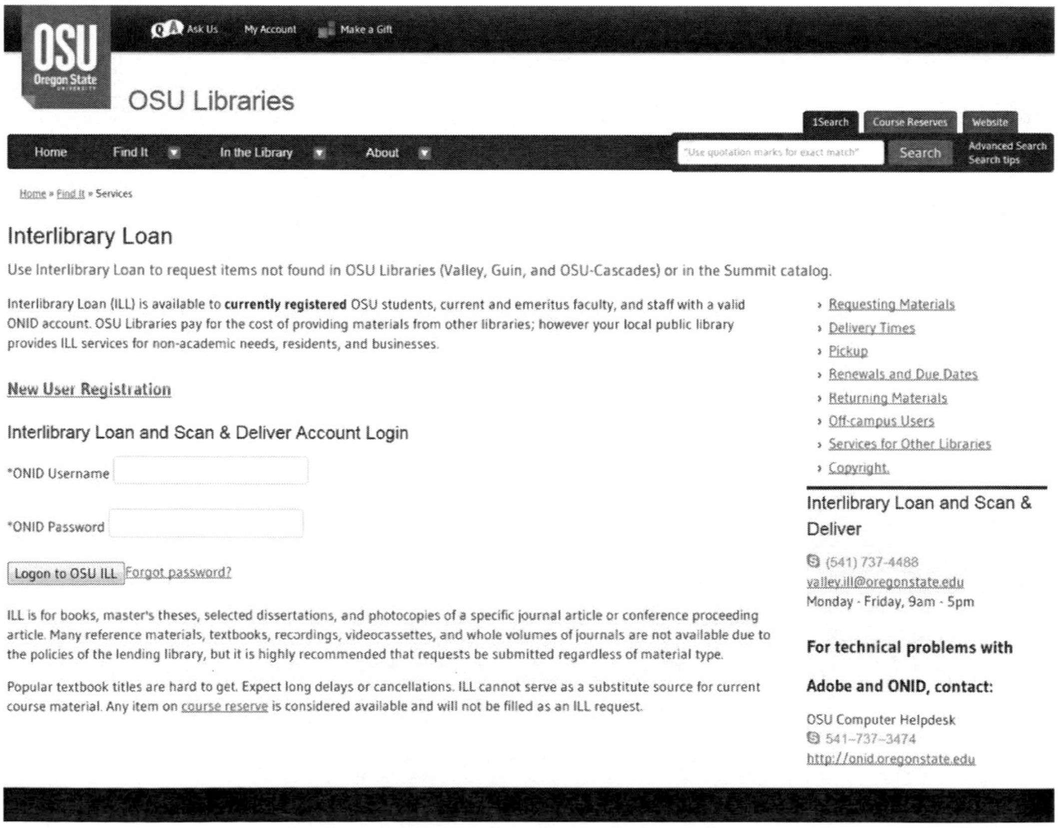

**Figure 6.5.** A screenshot of the entire interlibrary loan webpage

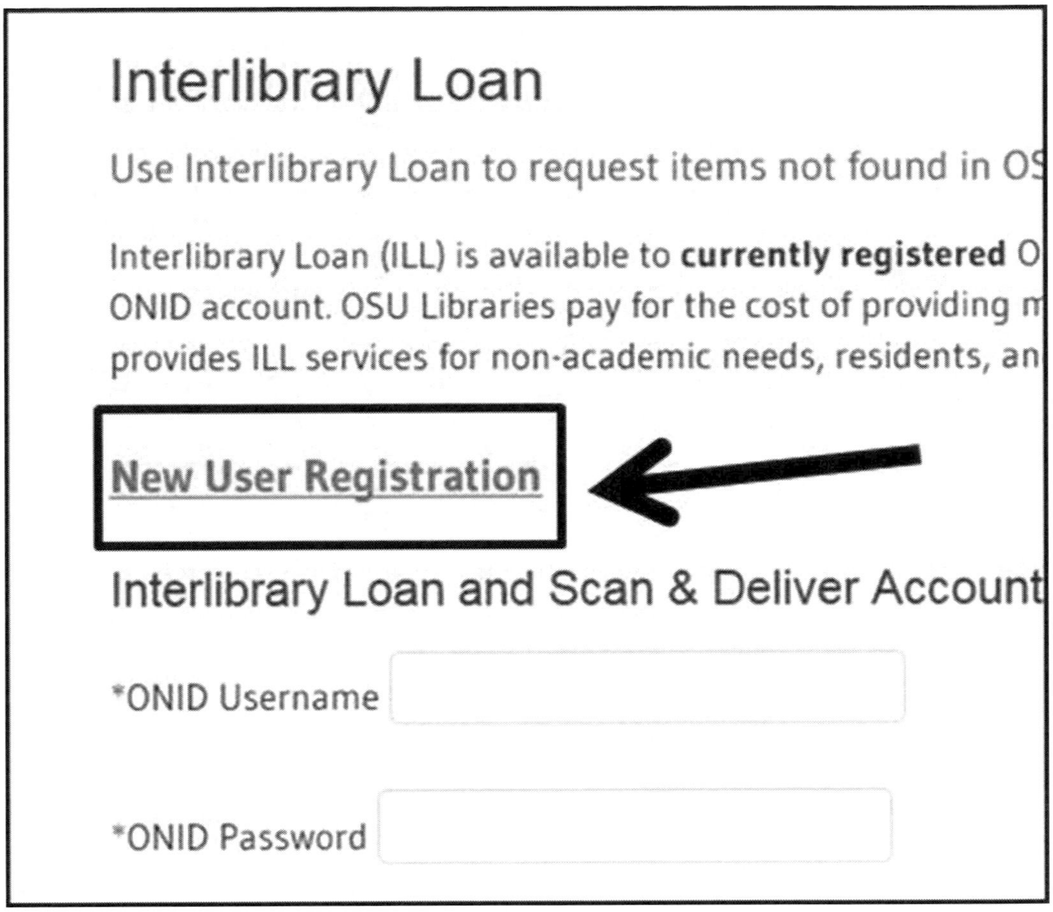

**Figure 6.6.** A targeted screenshot with focusing visual cues

bined with graphics in order to describe it should be placed close to the visual image that is being described. Using audio to describe visual elements may result in learning gains, but using text, audio, and graphics at the same time can be confusing and can increase the demand on the learner's visual-processing capability. When intended to enhance accessibility, recorded narration will most directly benefit visually impaired learners and should be supplemented with captioning, alternative text, or transcription for hearing-disabled learners. However, providing narration that mimics or repeats online text or captions can be distracting and increase extraneous cognitive load. Learners should have the option to use or disable narration and/or captioning so that they can make appropriate choices based on their abilities and preferred learning styles. Consider whether narration or music enhances the learning objectives of your tutorial or whether captions or other text will serve them as well or better and decide accordingly.

So when should you choose to include narration? Clark and Mayer (2011) recommend using narration rather than on-screen text to describe graphics when the graphics are the focus of the words and when they are presented simultaneously with the narration. This is particularly true when the presentation is either complex or fast paced and when the material being presented is familiar or brief. Clark and Mayer (2011) note that there may be technical reasons why it is not possible or advisable to include audio in a learning resource. These reasons may include cost, availability of needed equipment, and learners with limited bandwidth. They also note that in some situations, text should be used on-screen to make key points visually persistent in order to support retention of information.

If you decide that audio or narration will enhance your tutorial, it should be captured and delivered in the highest quality possible. It may not be possible to record your narration in a soundproof studio using professional equipment, but hopefully it is possible to find a quiet office (maybe after hours), a decent microphone, and a digital audio recorder to optimize the quality of your recording. If your department does not provide ready access to these tools, you may need to consider creative solutions such as borrowing equipment from your favorite instructional designer. If you are writing a grant to construct tutorials, consider including a request for necessary equipment as part of the grant. Reviews and recommendations on websites for electronics suppliers and large merchants like Amazon or Best Buy may help guide your purchases, or you may know an audiophile who will happily share his or her opinion.

Starting with good equipment and a high-quality recording will be extremely useful when it comes time to edit. Laurie Charnigo (2009) notes that use of a poor-quality microphone can cause audio problems necessitating additional editing steps in order to remove voice level fluctuations and audible breathing. Heidi Schroeder (2010) recommends using a good microphone and testing individual microphone quality, noting that in her experience, audio that initially sounded fine when being edited in Camtasia exhibited distracting flaws when converted to Flash files. She also recommends recording audio in a consistent environment in order to avoid different acoustics and hence very different audio quality. In addition, it is helpful to record short audio segments that can be easily rerecorded in case of mistakes rather than one long clip that must be rerecorded from start to finish in order to correct comparatively small problems.

While you might be tempted to speak slowly and deliberately in hopes that learners will be better able to process every word, researchers are finding that speaking quicker may actually be more helpful. Philip Guo, Juho Kim, and Rob Rubin (2014) note that students engaged more with videos when instructors spoke at rates of 160 words per minute (WPM) or above. They note that instructors who spoke quickly conveyed more energy and enthusiasm and recommend that instructors who are recording lectures be encouraged to speak quickly. They also recommend editing out filler words like *umm* and pauses. While this research was performed using recorded lectures, it has implications for tutorials too, which should be short, benefit from energy and enthusiasm, and can always be replayed if the audio moves quickly and needs to be reheard. In any case, obtaining the best quality sound that is possible will pay off—it may be necessary to compress and thus downgrade the sound quality slightly during editing, but it will not be possible to improve the quality of the original recording after it has been recorded—except by rerecording it.

One simple way to add audio to a tutorial is to record audio in a PowerPoint-based tutorial, which mirrors the process for adding audio in other tutorial-creation software. If your computer has an integrated microphone or if you can attach an external microphone, narration can be recorded slide by slide or in one fell swoop while advancing through the PowerPoint slides. While viewing the desired slide or beginning a series of slides, using PowerPoint 2010:

1. Click on the Insert tab
2. Choose "Audio"
3. Select "Record Audio"
4. Click on the Play button
5. Start recording your narration

Audio can be deleted and rerecorded as many times as necessary. PowerPoint also provides the option to insert audio from the web or an audio file from your computer. This is essentially how adding audio works in tutorial-creation software. You can record audio directly into your tutorial or insert audio from an external source and then adjust or synchronize the audio to the graphics or video displayed on the tutorial slide or video. After an audio clip is inserted, it can be edited by trimming it to match the duration of the slide by specifying the start and end times, adjusting the volume, and applying effects such as fading out to the playback.

The details of performing these functions differ from software to software, but typically there is a timeline or other visual means of adjusting the audio, video, graphics, and other elements like captions until they interact exactly as you wish them to. For example, Camtasia allows the capture of computer-screen activity while you are demonstrating a search strategy, and audio can be recorded simultaneously to simulate the narrative you might provide in the classroom. Or the audio can be recorded separately from the action of performing the search to allow you to follow a script more closely and pay more attention to the narrative quality.

The first method may feel more spontaneous and allows for synchronizing audio with the screen action on the fly, but it also may include accidental stutters or "*umms*" far too frequently. In some software, it is possible to easily edit out mistakes; in others it is not. Recording audio as a separate part of the process, either directly into the tutorial or by inserting individual audio clips, may reduce the number of mistakes and retakes. Separate recording also enables the use of audio-editing software like Audacity to correct and polish audio files for better quality. It may be easier to record directly into the tutorial after editing and polishing the screen-capture portion, especially if you are demonstrating a familiar topic or procedure.

Practice is definitely required in order to become more comfortable with the editing process. It may initially feel trickier to synchronize the audio and the screen action when clips are inserted into the tutorial during the editing process, but it allows more control and fine-tuning. If you are using software with a timeline feature, adjusting the audio to synchronize with screen action is done by moving the audio start and finish bars along the timeline's audio element until the audio clip begins and ends when you want it to. It is a good practice to allow for a brief pause at the beginning of the screen clip so that learners can do a visual scan and orient themselves to the page before the audio begins. Most software allows playback of individual slides to check the synchronization and to fine-tune it before moving on to the next slide or video. With practice, any of these three methods—recording audio while recording a screen capture, recording audio after editing the screen capture, or inserting and synchronizing audio clips while editing the screen capture—will become easier and smoother to execute.

Some designers prefer to have music playing in the background of a tutorial while captions or screen text explain the action and convey the desired information. Others find the added sound confusing, and the combination of elements may provide too much distraction for learners to absorb the desired content and skills. If you feel strongly about including background music, give your learners the choice to mute it or decrease its volume if they find it distracting.

## Last Steps: Editing and Publishing

Finally, you can begin to edit, assemble, and combine all the pieces you have created to form your finished tutorial. The steps of assembling the various pieces of your tutorial, as with every other part of the process, can range from fairly simple to very complex, depending on the type of software you are using, how many elements your tutorial contains, and how much editing you have done along the way. Chapter 4 discussed how to design a tutorial that follows a logical flow. Use the storyboards, outlines, or other organizing tools you created to direct you as you assemble the textual, visual, and audio components you have created. The design planning you did earlier should make the editing and assembly process much more straightforward.

The goal of editing is to eliminate distractions and to synchronize elements so that the purpose of the tutorial is clearly communicated. Remember to include focused graphics with guiding visual signals. If you have not already cropped your graphics and added in callouts or arrows, do this during the editing phase. While editing and synchronizing the audio or text with its graphical components, make sure to modify the sections of the tutorial that lag or feel overly rushed. Make sure to provide pauses for reflection or direct learners to review certain information if necessary. Add in the quizzing and other evaluation components you have created at the appropriate points in your tutorial, either as self-checks throughout the tutorial or at the end of the tutorial (quizzing and evaluation will be discussed in more detail in chapter 8). Check that you have used consistent navigational prompts throughout the tutorial. Do your best to catch as many inconsistencies as possible; however, chapter 7 will discuss how to do usability testing that will likely reveal more problems—particularly with issues like navigation—than you will see on your own.

As you assemble your tutorial, make sure to keep your learners in mind—especially focusing on the steps you can take to make your tutorial accessible for all learners. Use simple language, clear graphics, and remember to keep explanations succinct. The software that you use will dictate the final assembly steps, but after you have created and edited your textual, visual, and audio materials and have synchronized any audio and visual components, the last step is usually to publish your project in a file format that you can use on the web. Now you are ready to let others try out your tutorial!

## Key Points

Developing the components of a tutorial includes taking steps to make sure that the content is accessible for all learners. As you write your script, create graphics, and record audio components, follow the best practices for communicating in a clear and focused manner. Here are some key points to take away:

- Following accessibility guidelines helps learners on two levels: a more useful tutorial is created for all learners, and learners with special needs will also be able to understand the material with just a little extra effort on your part.
- Writing scripts that use direct and clear language makes learning easier and gives you a tool for recording audio and creating captions.
- Effective graphics use color and contrast and symbols to clearly signal to the learner the key information so that the learner can apply his or her knowledge in another context.
- Strategic use of narration or audio can help emphasize key points. The audio files themselves can be relatively simple to record and edit.

Now that you have a plan for developing your content, you are ready to see whether learners understand how to use your tutorial. Chapter 7 will guide you through the several usability options and methods for promoting your tutorial so that learners and instructors can use it.

## ⊚ References

Charnigo, Laurie. 2009. "Lights! Camera! Action! Producing Library Instruction Video Tutorials Using Camtasia Studio." *Journal of Library & Information Services in Distance Learning* 3, no. 1: 23–30.

Clark, Ruth Colvin, and Chopeta Lyons. 2010. *Graphics for Learning: Proven Guidelines for Planning, Designing, and Evaluating Visuals in Training Materials.* 2nd ed. Pfeiffer Essential Resources for Training and HR Professionals. Chichester, UK: Wiley.

Clark, Ruth Colvin, and Richard E. Mayer. 2011. *E-learning and the Science of Instruction: Proven Guidelines for Consumers and Designers of Multimedia Learning.* 3rd ed. San Francisco, CA: Pfeiffer.

Crow, Kevin L. 2008. "Four Types of Disabilities: Their Impact on Online Learning." *TechTrends* 52, no. 1: 51–55.

Guo, Philip J., Juho Kim, and Rob Rubin. 2014. "How Video Production Affects Student Engagement: An Empirical Study of MOOC Videos." *Proceedings of the First ACM Conference on Learning@Scale*, March 4–5: 41–50. http://dl.acm.org/citation.cfm?id=2566239.

Kellum, Karen Kate, Amy E. Mark, and Debra A. Riley-Huff. 2011. "Development, Assessment and Use of an On-Line Plagiarism Tutorial." *Library Hi Tech* 29, no. 4: 641–54.

Koury, Regina, Marcia J. Francis, Catherine J. Gray, Spencer J. Jardine, and Ruiling Guo. 2010. "Staying on Top of Your Game and Scoring Big with Adobe Presenter Multimedia Tutorials." *Journal of Library & Information Services in Distance Learning* 4, no. 4: 208–18.

Lewis, Joél P., and Stephen M. Sullivan. 2012. "Diversity and Accessibility." In *Trends and Issues in Instructional Design and Technology*, edited by Robert A. Reiser and John V. Dempsey, 348–57. Boston, MA: Pearson.

Plass, Jan L., Roxana Moreno, and Roland Brünken. 2010. *Cognitive Load Theory.* Cambridge and New York: Cambridge University Press.

Rose, David H., Ted S. Hasselbring, Skip Stahl, and Joy Zabala. 2005. "Assistive Technology and Universal Design for Learning: Two Sides of the Same Coin." In *Handbook of Special Education Technology Research and Practice*, edited by David Edyburn, Kyle Higgins, and Randall Boone, 507–18. Whitefish Bay, WI: Knowledge by Design.

Schroeder, Heidi. 2010. "Creating Library Tutorials for Nursing Students." *Medical Reference Services Quarterly* 29, no. 2: 109–20.

Shank, Patti. 2011. "Beginning Instructional Authoring: Learning How to Author." *Learning Solutions Magazine*, November 10. http://www.learningsolutionsmag.com/articles/791/beginning-instructional-authoring-learning-how-to-author.

———. 2012. "Beginning Instructional Authoring: Readability Statistics Help You Sound Human." *Learning Solutions Magazine*, May 10. http://www.learningsolutionsmag.com/articles/926/beginning-instructional-authoring-readability-statistics-help-you-sound-human.

Smith, Jared. 2014. "Accessibility Lipstick on a Usability Pig." *WebAIM Blog.* http://webaim.org/blog/accessibility-lipstick-on-a-usability-pig/.

WebAIM. 2013. "Constructing a POUR Website: Putting People at the Center of the Process." *WebAIM*, August 28. http://webaim.org/articles/pour/.

## ⊚ More Resources

Microsoft Word Readability Statistics. http://www.officetooltips.com/word/tips/viewing_document_and_readability_statistics.html.

MSF&W Contrast Ratio Calculator. http://www.msfw.com/accessibility/tools/contrastratiocal
culator.aspx.

WAVE Accessibility Checker. http://wave.webaim.org/.

Web Accessibility Initiative (WAI). http://www.w3.org/WAI.

WebAIM Alt-text Guidelines. http://webaim.org/techniques/alttext/.

WebAIM Color Contrast Checker. http://webaim.org/resources/contrastchecker/.

Web Content Accessibility Guidelines (WCAG) Checklist. http://www.w3.org/WAI/WCAG20/
quickref/.

# Implementation
## *Making Sure Your Tutorial Is Usable and Used*

JUST AS WITH THE OTHER INSTRUCTIONAL design principles, implementation does not fall cleanly into one stage of the tutorial-creation process. From an instructional design perspective, implementation includes the steps involved in getting a tutorial to your learners and into their learning process (Smith and Ragan 2005). Implementation begins as you try out parts of your tutorial on colleagues and student workers while the tutorial is being developed and continues through the process of collaborating with other librarians or instructors in order to incorporate your tutorial into a regular instructional workflow. You have already worked on designing and developing a tutorial that is useful. In this chapter, strategies involved in implementing a tutorial that is both usable and used by your learners will be discussed.

One component of implementing a tutorial involves being continuously on the lookout for feedback and suggestions for improvement. This chapter begins with a discussion of techniques to systematically seek out formative evaluation from a variety of stakeholders in order to help make your tutorial better and more usable. Another component of implementation involves letting people know that your tutorial exists. While the type of tutorial you create will influence the specific promotional path you take, having a promotional plan in mind will help make sure that the right audiences are aware of your tutorial at the right time. Finally, many of us create tutorials in the hopes that other librarians or instructors will be able to use them. Maybe your evening reference desk librarian colleagues could send tutorial links to patrons via chat reference, or perhaps graduate teaching assistants might assign your tutorial in an undergraduate composition class. Preparing a tutorial that doesn't serve only your own idiosyncratic instructional needs requires having directed discussions with others about how they might adopt and use a tutorial in their own context.

# ⑥ Formative Evaluation

Chapter 4 discussed how to design assessment and evaluation in order to measure how much your learners are learning. Now it is time to shift the evaluation lens onto your tutorial and think about some ways you can seek out formative evaluation of the tutorial itself in order to make improvements. Formative evaluation is the most iterative step of the implementation process, and to be truly useful, it should happen at various stages as you are creating your tutorial. Receiving feedback about learning outcomes, content ideas, draft scripts, and storyboards can help you spot problems before you spend a lot of time designing and developing your final product.

The goal in the initial phases of formative evaluation is to solicit input from others so that you can see whether your tutorial will be usable and useful for someone besides you or your project team. The field of user experience and usability is built around the principles of trying to make products more effective, efficient, and satisfying (i.e., more usable) for specific user groups (Barnum 2010). Ideally, this feedback will come from stakeholders you identified when conducting a needs analysis or a learning-environment analysis (see chapter 3). But it is also appropriate to solicit feedback from your peers and fellow coworkers at some of these stages. Another set of eyes is always helpful!

Usability testing at its simplest is checking whether or not your tutorial is usable by asking questions such as, Are the navigation elements findable? Does the language you used make sense to your audience? Do your users know what is expected of them? Are there clear ways to get help? The process of creating a usable tutorial began when you started making design decisions. Many of the elements that make a tutorial more usable were discussed in chapters 4 and 6, such as including content in the form of both textual and visual examples, connecting examples to the learning experience (i.e., no extraneous content), and developing navigational elements that are free of jargon and easy to see. If you are following those guidelines, you should be well on your way to creating a tutorial that is usable for your learners. However, it is important to actually check with them to find out whether or not your intentions match reality.

Several usability testing strategies can be used to learn more about your tutorial. Three methods for gathering formative evaluation will be discussed next:

- Rapid prototyping
- Formative usability testing
- Trials (aka beta testing)

All three of these methods fall under the larger umbrella of usability testing. These methods will be distinguished in the coming section by when you should deploy the various

**Table 7.1.** Characteristics of Usability Testing Methods

| | WHEN TO USE | NUMBER OF USERS | FIDELITY OF DESIGN | DEPTH OF THE TESTING SCENARIOS | NUMBER OF PROBLEMS REVEALED |
|---|---|---|---|---|---|
| Rapid Prototyping | Early—in the design and development stages | Few | Low–Medium | Few questions, somewhat realistic tasks assigned by the tester | Many |
| Formative Usability Testing | Middle—in the beginning of the implementation stage | Few | Medium–High | More questions, realistic tasks assigned by the tester | Some |
| Trials or Beta Testing | Late—at the end of the implementation stage | More | High | Highly realistic, realistic tasks initiated by the user | Few (hopefully) |

methods, the number of testers you should use, how close to completion the test tutorial should be, and how realistic and involved your testing scenarios should be (see table 7.1).

Whether or not you use all three usability (or formative evaluation) methods will depend on the amount of time you have, how much feedback you have been able to gather so far, and the overall scope of your tutorial project. Don't feel that all of these methods must be used in this exact order or your tutorial project will fail! Instead, begin by choosing at least one method that works best for your situation and try to get some second opinions from learners, other librarians, or instructors before finalizing your tutorial so that you can spot flaws before it's too late to do anything about them. As your usability skill set grows, add in more evaluation techniques and see how the additional input informs your end product.

## JUST ENOUGH USABILITY TESTING

If you don't have enough time to use all three usability testing methods, what formative evaluation information is essential to gather? Try to collect feedback from at least two to three typical users to find out if

a. the navigational elements make sense,
b. the language used is clear, and
c. the users understand the overall message or purpose of the tutorial.

Ideally, creating a realistic scenario to gather this information would be most helpful, but directly asking these questions can also be informative. With this level of information, you will gain valuable insights into how usable others find the tutorial.

## Rapid Prototyping

One relatively fast and easy way to get feedback early on is through the use of rapid prototyping. Rapid prototyping is intended to be used early in the design and development phases to make sure that the main functions and ideas about your tutorial are on track (see figure 7.1). Rapid prototyping is an iterative, three-step process (Cerejo 2010). Rapid prototyping involves

- creating the prototype;
- getting feedback; and
- refining the prototype.

When creating a prototype, the key is to focus on making the main functions of your tutorial usable. This means making sure your users are able to move around in your tutorial, understand the terms used, and have a sense of the overall purpose of your tutorial. Design experts recommend focusing a rapid prototype on the "20% of the functionality that will be used 80% of the time" (Cerejo 2010). This means that a rapid prototype does not have to match the final look and feel of your tutorial, or as usability experts say, it can be fairly low fidelity (Cerejo 2010). In other words, this isn't an evaluation method used to determine whether or not you have the perfect color scheme or if you have found the staff member with the best recording voice, but it is meant to make sure users understand how to work their way through your tutorial at the most basic level

Create your prototype with tools that are simple for you to use and that you can easily adjust. Rapid prototyping is meant to be a fast process that could be done with pencil-and-paper sketches or rough web designs of your tutorial. For many librarians, LibGuides can be used as a way to develop a rough sketch of a tutorial quickly by displaying and arranging content without spending a lot of time styling the tutorial. For other librarians, PowerPoint might be the simplest way to quickly create a sketch of the tutorial content and layout. Because rapid prototyping is meant to be used early and often in the

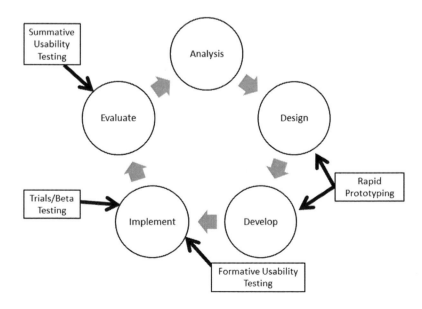

**Figure 7.1.**   Incorporating formative evaluation into the ADDIE cycle

tutorial-design process, this could also be a good time to repurpose your storyboards (see chapter 4) as a testing tool.

One of the keys to creating a simple prototype is to test one or two questions about your tutorial at a time. The rapid prototyping technique can be helpful for testing the language you use, basic layout decisions, or navigational options—but don't try and test all of those things at once. Breaking your questions into smaller chunks will help you make revisions more quickly. In this Zotero tutorial (see figure 7.2), users' ability to navigate using two navigational options—a table of contents menu or a pull-down menu—was tested using a basic LibGuides page. The LibGuides page was only populated with some of the tutorial content, but enough choices were provided in both the table of contents and the pull-down menus to help the designer determine how users preferred to move through the tutorial.

When gathering feedback using rapid prototyping, you only need to gather input from a small subset of your stakeholders. Feedback from two to three people will likely be sufficient to demonstrate general trends or issues with your tutorial. Again, rapid prototyping is a tool for gathering rapid feedback and making quick changes, so scheduling lengthy sessions with a wide audience of stakeholders isn't necessary. However, do try to include somewhat diverse stakeholders in your sample. Refer back to your learner analysis (chapter 3) and try to include at least one member of your intended audience in addition to fellow librarians, student workers, or volunteers who may be close at hand.

During the prototyping testing session, give the users guidance as to the type of feedback you are looking for. This can range from directly asking them about the particular feature you want information on to providing a scenario based on a realistic use of the tutorial (see sidebar). Remind the users that this is just a prototype, you are testing a few key elements, and the design is still flexible. At this stage of the formative-evaluation process, setting appropriate expectations and providing structure for the users' feedback helps you learn what you need in order to move forward without addressing extraneous suggestions over which you may have limited control.

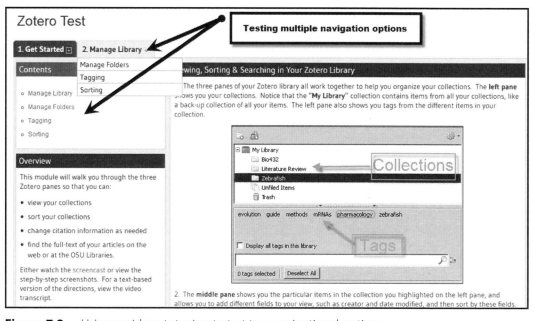

**Figure 7.2.** Using rapid prototyping to test two navigational options

Keep the rapid prototyping process simple by taking handwritten or typed notes of users' responses. Take what you have learned from the feedback and make changes to your tutorial accordingly. Because rapid prototyping is not intended as an approach for evaluating the final version of your tutorial, the changes identified should be relatively easy to make. If the needed changes are fairly major, the rapid prototyping approach means that all you need to do is erase your sketch or delete several online modules rather than reconfiguring the entire architecture of your tutorial.

After making the identified changes, try out your revision with some of the same testers you used in the first round. Ask them the same questions as before so that you can reevaluate their experience with the changes in place. During this iteration, you may also choose to add in a new, additional question or two based on another aspect of the tutorial that you wish to evaluate. Again, rapid prototyping is an iterative process, so don't be afraid to repeat the three phases of creating the prototype, getting feedback, and making changes several times until you are satisfied that the main functions of the tutorial are clearly usable.

Despite the intended ease of rapid prototyping, it does take some practice to become proficient at it. Not all of us are able to express a design idea quickly using paper and pencil or LibGuides. If you find yourself spending too much time creating and redesigning an early stage prototype, then this approach might not work best for you. It may be more helpful for you to get feedback on an outline or to discuss content ideas with a colleague. The main keys of rapid prototyping are to get input from others, take the feedback that is useful and realistic, and let the rest go (Cerejo 2010).

## Formative Usability Testing

Another type of formative evaluation is formative usability testing. This is the type of formative evaluation that is likely the most familiar to you, because librarians have been doing this kind of usability testing since the earliest days of the web. Hopefully, many of your library websites have undergone formative usability testing. Formative usability testing overlaps with rapid prototyping because the goal of both methods is to learn how people use the main functions of your tutorial and whether they understand the purpose of the tutorial. Like rapid prototyping, formative usability testing is also meant to be an iterative process. However, formative usability testing should be used at a different stage of your tutorial-creation process than rapid prototyping, requires different users and testing scenarios, and uses a more mature version of your tutorial design.

## Who to Test

Formative usability testing places much greater emphasis on gathering feedback from stakeholders who more closely match your final user group. While it can be easy to simply grab several available library student workers or library volunteers for rapid prototype testing, in order to find out how your tutorial will work for your intended audience, you will need to include members of that audience in your usability testing. Luckily, usability experts have found that five to ten people representing the target user group are sufficient in order to gather meaningful usability information (Barnum 2010; Tullis and Albert 2013). While this is an increase from the number of people needed for rapid prototype testing, you don't need to feel pressured to test your entire target user group. However, depending on when you want to do your formative usability testing, you will likely need to have some incentives for your volunteer users in order to get enough participants, so make sure to include that time and expense in your budget and planning cycle.

Because you want users who are representative of your target user group, it is a good idea to screen potential testers using a brief questionnaire prior to participating in your usability testing (see table 7.2). Compile a list of the characteristics that represent your user group and then craft the questionnaire based on these characteristics. For example, if you are creating a tutorial intended for first-year students with no previous university library experience, you may want to create screening questions such as, What is your academic standing? Have you received library instruction at this university library or another university library? The more closely your users match your target user group, the more meaningful your results will be.

## What to Test

To learn the most from formative usability testing, be prepared to test a medium- to high-fidelity version of your design. You should be closer to implementing your tutorial at this stage, and you should have moved beyond pencil-and-paper sketches or incomplete LibGuides modules to a fairly robust version of your tutorial. While you may not have worked out all of the finishing touches for your tutorial, you want your users to have a realistic sense of what it will feel like to interact with your tutorial. This is an appropriate time to see whether your users can navigate through your tutorial, as well as to test whether or not they understand the language you are using and if your quiz questions make sense. According to Thomas Tullis and William Albert (2013) the most important things to learn from formative usability testing are

- What works well for users?
- What are the most significant usability issues preventing users from learning from your tutorial?
- What frustrates users?
- What are the most common mistakes?

Use these four guiding questions as you create your test scenario. Your test scenarios should now represent realistic tasks for users of your tutorial. However, while testers may need to learn something from your tutorial in order to adequately evaluate it at this stage, their learning is not the focus of formative evaluation. The focus should be on checking that your tutorial is effective, efficient, and satisfying for these users (Barnum 2010). To

**Table 7.2.** Steps for Conducting Usability Testing Synchronously or Asynchronously

| SYNCHRONOUS USABILITY TESTING (IN PERSON OR ONLINE) | ASYNCHRONOUS USABILITY TESTING (ONLINE) |
|---|---|
| 1. Create questions based on research questions that you need to answer. | 1. Create questions based on research questions that you need to answer. |
| 2. Find comparator tutorials to include so that you get a broader range of observations. | 2. Find comparator tutorials to include so that you get a broader range of observations. |
| 3. Create tasks to address those questions from your tutorial and comparator tutorials. | 3. Create tasks and images to address those tasks and comparator tutorials using an online survey tool. |
| 4. Solicit 6–8 participants matching your real user group. Screen them using a brief questionnaire to make sure that they match the characteristics you want. | 4. Solicit 6–8 participants matching your real user group. Screen them using a brief questionnaire to make sure they match the characteristics you want. |
| 5. Schedule a time and place for participants to do the usability tasks. | 5. Send the link for the online usability test (if using a survey) or the test prompts (if participants are recording their screen movements) and provide a deadline for participants to do the usability tasks. |
| 6. Conduct the usability test:<br>a. Provide a computer.<br>b. Record screen movements and audio using software or take notes.<br>c. Give introductory comments—explain the purpose of the task, ask users to think aloud, make them feel comfortable, give them an idea of how long this test should take.<br>d. Provide the tasks on a printed sheet so that users can read the tasks as well as hear them.<br>e. Start with an easy task. | 6. Conduct the usability test:<br>a. Provide a link to the usability test or the list of test prompts.<br>b. Use survey software such as Qualtrics that allows you to track where users click on an image or recording software like BB Flashback Express or QuickTime.<br>c. Give introductory text—explain the purpose of the task, give users an idea of how long this test should take.<br>d. Provide the task questions.<br>e. Start with an easy task. |
| 7. Ask follow-up questions after the test is finished:<br>a. What worked well?<br>b. What was frustrating?<br>c. Other feedback | 7. Ask follow-up questions after the test is finished:<br>a. What worked well?<br>b. What was frustrating?<br>c. Other feedback |
| 8. Analyze the data:<br>a. What worked well?<br>b. What were common mistakes?<br>c. What prevented users from working with the tutorial as well as they should have? | 8. Analyze the data:<br>a. What worked well?<br>b. What were common mistakes?<br>c. What prevented users from working with the tutorial as well as they should have? |
| 9. Revise the tutorial based on what you learned. | 9. Revise the tutorial based on what you learned. |
| 10. Repeat. | 10. Repeat. |

achieve these goals, create test scenarios that address specific research questions (Rees 2013). For example, using the Zotero tutorial described earlier and shown in figure 7.2, some usability research questions might be:

1. Are users able to understand the terminology used to describe Zotero functions such as tagging, sorting, libraries, and collections?

2. Are users able to navigate through the interface in order to move back to the tutorial homepage, to the next consecutive section of the tutorial, or to other, nonconsecutive sections of the tutorial?

Based on these research questions, some formative usability test scenarios could be:

1. "Now that you have some articles in your Zotero library, you would like to be able to display those articles from the oldest article published to the newest article published. Where would you click to learn how to do this?"
2. "You have finished learning how to use tags to manage your library. Where would you click to return to the main Zotero tutorial homepage?"

The first question is primarily focused on terminology issues and is trying to gauge whether users will be able to understand what the "sort" label means in the tutorial. In order to determine this, the scenario does not directly ask users to "sort" the articles in their library so as to discover whether the term *sort* has meaning for users or not. A more familiar usability scenario for many librarians involves asking users to find a book in the library. As John Kupersmith (2012) demonstrated in his classic document "Library Terms That Users Understand," the term *library catalog* is unfamiliar for many users, so asking them to find a book in the library often requires them to navigate websites filled with unknown jargon.

The second scenario question is designed to help determine whether users will be able to navigate through the tutorial by asking users to try and get back to the beginning once they have finished a module within the tutorial. Because this tutorial was created using LibGuides, there is a substantial amount of extraneous material on the page, such as the library's homepage, a search box, bread crumbs, and drop-down menus that could lead users astray. Observing how users navigate through the variety of navigational cues on this page can help the designer learn whether the page is too cluttered or whether sufficient visual signaling is in place to direct users back to the tutorial homepage. Learning about these navigational and terminology roadblocks through realistic scenarios can help you make changes to your tutorial before it is widely implemented.

It can also be helpful to ask your usability testing participants to evaluate a tutorial you didn't create. Providing this second tutorial achieves several outcomes: it can allow users to respond to different navigational and terminology choices; it can give you a better understanding of how users navigate in a wider variety of situations; and it can help users be more truthful about their overall experience if they don't feel like they are just critiquing tutorials they know that you made (Rees 2013). Check and see whether there are other libraries that have tutorials with design elements that you are interested in comparing, different ways of wording similar terminology to your tutorial, or alternative navigational strategies. You may even have found some interesting tutorials during the initial phases of your tutorial project when you were gathering ideas—this would be a good time to reexamine them. While including a tutorial from another library isn't a requirement, it can certainly help you generate some new ideas and gain new perspectives.

## How to Test

Once you have identified users to help test your tutorial and have crafted testing scenarios that reflect your research questions, the next step is administering the actual formative usability test, as shown earlier in table 7.2. Best practices for formative usability testing suggest (Barnum 2010; Rees 2013; Tullis and Albert 2013):

- Beginning the test by making users feel comfortable so they are able to behave as naturally as possible during the test.
- Starting by letting the users know that you are testing the tutorial—not them!
- Giving the users an idea of how long the test will take and sticking to this time-table.
- Starting the test with a warm-up scenario that doesn't involve your tutorial and is more general and achievable, for example, asking them to find a tutorial on a hobby of their choice or finding a specific piece of information on your university's website. A warm-up task makes the user feel more comfortable and gives you a chance to watch how the user navigates other interfaces.
- Providing a copy of the test-scenario questions so that users can either read or listen to you, depending on their preference.
- Asking the users to think aloud while they are navigating and making choices so that you understand how they make decisions.
- Recording the user's actions and thoughts either using screen-recording software such as Camtasia or QuickTime, video-recording equipment, audio-recording equipment, or by taking notes.
- Resisting the urge to redirect users or show them the "right" way to do the task.
- Asking follow-up questions to find out about users' overall experience, including frustrations or things they enjoyed or to better understand specific choices that they made.

While some companies have special rooms or laboratories dedicated to usability testing, most libraries don't have that luxury. However, the field of usability testing has become increasingly flexible in recommendations for how usability testing can be administered (Barnum 2010). You probably visualized most of the best-practice steps for the formative usability test described above taking place in a quiet office somewhere in your library. Traditionally, formative usability testing only took place in person, but it has now expanded to online or remote testing as well. Either in person or online formative usability testing can be effective. When testing something like an online tutorial, the main requirements are that users have access to a computer, a way of recording how they interacted with the tutorial, and a way to provide open-ended feedback.

Choosing whether to do your formative usability testing online or in person will depend on where your target user group is located, how difficult it is to schedule in-person meetings, and how much follow-up questioning you feel is necessary. Helpful usability results can be obtained from a range of methods, so feel free to experiment with a range of in-person or online testing, including synchronous or asynchronous testing, in order to see which route works best for you. Again, the most important thing to keep in mind at this stage of formative evaluation is to get feedback from users who are representative of your target user group.

Online usability testing offers great flexibility in terms of when and where you schedule your usability sessions. Online usability testing can also feel more natural for users as they can use their own computers in environments that are more comfortable for them. A wide range of technologies are available that allow users to do formative usability testing from their own computers. One of the simplest methods of asynchronous online testing is through the use of online survey tools. Survey tools like Qualtrics provide the option of uploading images such as screenshots that can be transformed into a clickable heat map. Ask users to click on the screenshot in response to your testing-scenario questions, such as those asked in the Zotero tutorial example above. The survey results show the compilation of where users chose to click based on the scenarios—the larger the heat map circle, the more users clicked on that option (see figure 7.3). Alternatively, if your survey tool doesn't provide a heat map option, you can still upload tutorial screenshots and then ask users to respond to multiple-choice questions based on the testing scenario.

Another asynchronous option is to ask users to record their screen movements using free tools like BB Flashback Express for PCs or QuickTime for Macs. Users can follow your testing-scenario prompts and then send the file to you through file-sharing programs like Google Drive or Dropbox. For either asynchronous method, always make sure to include space for open-ended responses in order to allow users to describe what they found confusing, what they liked, and any additional feedback they may have.

Using an online survey is an asynchronous way to solicit formative usability feedback. Synchronous remote usability testing can also be used if it is inconvenient for your users to travel to your library. A range of conferencing tools like Google Hangouts, GoToMeeting, Skype, and Adobe Connect can be used to share screens and conduct the usability interview. Several of these conferencing tools have the ability to record built in; others require a secondary recording option to capture the shared screen.

Remember, formative usability testing is meant to be an iterative process. Online formative usability testing can serve as a convenient way to test a somewhat less mature iteration of your design. If you feel you need to ask more in-depth clarifying questions,

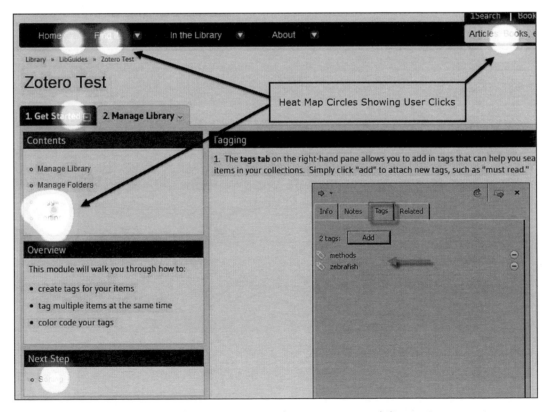

**Figure 7.3.**   Using a Qualtrics heat map to record responses to usability testing scenarios

a second round of usability testing done either in person or via a synchronous online meeting tool may be helpful after you have made changes based on the first round of formative usability testing.

## What You Can Learn

Interviews with PRIMO award–winning tutorial creators illustrate some useful lessons that can be learned from formative usability testing. While working on their tutorial project, a team from California State University, East Bay, and the University of California, Irvine, were able to improve navigation and layout features as a result of usability testing. They also discovered some technology constraints: because their tutorial had been designed using Adobe Flash, users with mobile devices were unable to interact with the tutorial. As a result of usability testing, they were able to fix these problems (Bussmann, Plovnick, and Palmer 2013).

As a result of their usability testing, a team from Menlo College realized that their tutorial's quiz questions were unnecessarily confusing, navigation could be improved, and less explanatory text should be displayed (Smith and Velarde 2013). Hopefully, as you move through several iterations of formative evaluations, the number of problems that your users encounter will decrease, and a better tutorial design will emerge.

## Trials (aka Beta Testing)

Trials, or beta testing, are the next step on the formative evaluation continuum. A trial can be used late in the implementation stage (see table 7.1) as a way to release a nearly or completely finished version of your tutorial on a smaller scale, for example, just to one section of a larger class. A trial will involve more users than the previous types of evaluation because it should mimic a more realistic learning situation; however, the feedback you gather from each individual user will likely be less detailed than the information you gathered during formative usability testing. During a trial, users should be interacting with the tutorial in the same way and in the same environment that you intend learners

---

### EXAMPLES OF REACTION-EVALUATION QUESTIONS[1]

- What did you like best about this tutorial?
- What did you like least about this tutorial?
- Would you recommend this tutorial to someone else?
- Was the purpose of the tutorial clear to you?
- Did you like the way the tutorial looked?
- Was it easy or difficult to navigate through the tutorial?
- Do you feel like taking this tutorial was a good use of your time?
- Is there anything else you would like to tell us about this tutorial?

Note
1. Adapted from Hodell 2006, 81.

to interact with the tutorial when it is finished. This means you won't be giving users test scenarios but rather that users should have an authentic reason of their own that drives their experience with your tutorial.

Because users will be interacting with the tutorial in a more realistic way during a trial, this is an appropriate time to assess how well users are able to learn from your tutorial. Again, this assessment is not focused on the users' ability to learn as much as on whether or not your tutorial is able to fulfill the goal of providing a learning experience. Donald Kirkpatrick (2006) recommends starting this part of the evaluation process with users' reactions to a tool or instructional experience, such as a tutorial. These reactions are primarily a measurement of user satisfaction with their learning experience. As a result, evaluation at this stage is more superficial with a focus on simple questions such as what did you like best or least about this tutorial (see sidebar).

It is important to solicit this type of feedback right after users have interacted with your tutorial because reaction questions are designed to measure users' initial impressions (Hodell 2006). Initial impressions are important, because if users have negative initial impressions, this will prevent them from engaging further with the tutorial or recommending it to others. Conversely, positive initial impressions can lead to a greater willingness to engage further with the tutorial or recommend it to others. While reaction-evaluation questions should not be the only measurement of learning, they can help predict willingness to continue learning.

To gather more than just trial participants' initial impressions of your tutorial, the next stage of evaluation focuses on behaviors that demonstrate learning. Chuck Hodell (2006) recommends doing this by giving participants tasks that measure whether learners can translate what they have just learned into behaviors that show an increase in knowledge or skills. These evaluation tasks should mirror the learning objectives that you established for your tutorial (see table 7.3). Break your learning objectives down into the behavior you want the learners to be able to display, create a condition or context for the learners to demonstrate that behavior, and specify to what degree they need to demonstrate the behavior in order to signify that learning has occurred as a result of the using the tutorial.

During this stage of formative evaluation testing, focus groups can be a useful way to gather feedback not just from potential learners but also from instructors or other librarians who might be assigning or distributing your tutorial (Piskurich 2006). Librarians from the University of Illinois, Chicago, who built a tutorial tailored for health sciences students held focus groups with faculty in the health sciences. Disciplinary faculty were able to apply their subject expertise in order to help improve the content, provide useful

**Table 7.3.** Example Strategy for Evaluating Learning[1]

| | OBJECTIVE | EVALUATION TASK |
|---|---|---|
| **Behavior** | Users will recall the steps of downloading an e-book using the vendor software in order to add e-books to their own personal e-reader device. | Recall the steps of downloading an e-book using vendor software. |
| **Condition** | The learner is given a range of downloading steps. | The learner is given a range of downloading steps in a sequence-order quiz question at the end of the tutorial. |
| **Degree** | All the steps are in the correct order. | Arrange all the steps in the correct order. |

[1]Adapted from Hodell 2006, 82.

feedback on terminology that was unclear, and in some cases, give the difficult feedback that they wouldn't include the tutorial in their classes (Appelt and Pendell 2010). Creating a tutorial that will be used is one of the most important goals to achieve through evaluation. Some strategies for encouraging the use of your tutorial will be discussed later in this chapter.

Ideally, if you have been gathering formative evaluation throughout all the stages of your tutorial development, the number of problems revealed during a trial will be relatively few. Just as with the previous methods of testing, use the feedback you received from trials as a way to make improvements to your tutorial. Finally, trials can also be part of your dissemination strategy, as the feedback you receive from a trial can be used to promote your tutorial to other librarians or instructors. Strategies for promoting your tutorial will be the focus of the next section.

## ◎ Promoting Your Tutorial

After evaluating your tutorial and making changes based on the feedback you have gathered, you should now be ready to release your tutorial. The next step in the implementation phase focuses on ensuring that learners actually use the tutorial you have carefully designed, developed, and evaluated. Promoting your tutorial to the right audiences with messages tailored for them will help ensure that your tutorial doesn't just sit on a virtual shelf gathering dust. The next section will discuss a range of promotional strategies to help provide you with options that you can personalize in order to match the needs of your own audience. Creating a thoughtful promotional plan will increase the likelihood that your tutorial will reach your intended users.

Successful promotion begins with knowing who your user group is. The information you gained from the learner analysis and learning-environment analysis discussed in chapter 3 can also be used to help guide your promotional efforts. Once you know who your audience is and what their needs are, you can better communicate why your tutorial will be useful to them in the manner that is most meaningful to that audience.

Some basic definitions can help guide this discussion of promotional strategies. For those of us who are not involved in marketing and promotions on a regular basis, it can be easy to conflate marketing with promotions. Marketing emphasizes doing market research and satisfying customer needs by providing a particular product (ACRL, 3M Inc., and Reynolds 2003; Garoufallou et al. 2013). Promotion is a subset of the field of marketing that focuses on the messages and vehicles (or techniques) used to let your audience know about a product—in this case, your tutorial.

In 2003, the Association of College and Research Libraries (ACRL) provided a marketing plan for libraries that emphasized using the benefit, message, target audience approach in order to promote libraries and their services (ACRL, 3M Inc., and Reynolds 2003). The benefit, message, target audience approach provides a helpful framework for building a simple promotional message that you can repurpose for different circumstances (see table 7.4).

To craft your promotional message using this technique, consider returning to your learning objectives. Learning objectives can provide a springboard for framing the benefits that learners will receive from using your tutorial. In a slight modification of the ACRL approach, next consider your target audience. Are you promoting this tutorial directly to students or library patrons? Alternatively, are you promoting this tutorial to

**Table 7.4.** Creating a Promotional Message Based on Tutorial Benefits and the Target Audience

| TUTORIAL TOPIC | BENEFIT | AUDIENCE | MESSAGE |
| --- | --- | --- | --- |
| Using e-book downloading software | Patrons will be able to load e-books onto their own device by themselves. | Library patrons | Get library books on your e-reader whenever you want, wherever you are! |
| Learning the difference between primary and secondary sources | Undergraduate students will be able to find more appropriate sources for their research paper. | Teaching faculty | Give your students the information and assistance they need to find better sources. |
| Using Zotero to create a bibliography | Researchers will manage sources more easily, efficiently, and accurately when using a free online tool. | Undergraduate students, graduate students, and faculty | Create bibliographies effortlessly using Zotero, a free online source management tool. |

instructors who might assign the tutorial to their students? Knowing the target audience for your promotional message will help you create a message that is relevant and appropriate for that audience. A promotional message targeted to students will have a different emphasis and tone than a message targeting faculty (see table 7.4 for some examples). Your promotional message should be fairly brief and direct. While this message does not need to be ready to put on a poster or banner, it should encapsulate the main benefit of your tutorial in an appealing way. Promotional messages can serve as the theme for an elevator speech, a faculty development presentation topic, or even a poster.

Once you have your core message in place, choose what language or tone to use in your promotional messages based on where your audience is in terms of their learning need or exposure to your tutorial. The awareness, interest, desire, action (AIDA) cycle provides four strategies for how to modify the language of a core promotional message (Boundless 2014). Each of the four parts of the AIDA cycle emphasizes a different need that the target audience has at a particular time, and the messages evolve to respond to that need (see table 7.5 for example messages). The AIDA model posits that when your tutorial is first released, the most important strategy is to create messages that promote

## AIDA CYCLE

- *Awareness*—The tutorial is new; use simple messages with eye-catching graphics.
- *Interest*—The tutorial is underused; provide more information about what the tutorial is for and what problem it solves.
- *Desire*—The user is trying to decide whether using the tutorial is worth the effort; include information on how the tutorial works, possibly include testimonials.
- *Action*—The user needs a small push to actually try out the tutorial; use active language.

**Table 7.5.** Using the AIDA Cycle to Create a Message That Matches the Audience's Needs[1]

| | MESSAGE | AWARENESS | INTEREST | DESIRE | ACTION |
|---|---|---|---|---|---|
| **Example 1** | Get library books on your e-reader whenever you want, wherever you are! | E-books—anytime, anywhere! | Want to learn how to get library e-books on your own? Find out how! | You're three minutes away from knowing how to get library e-books! | Click here to learn how to get library e-books on your own e-reader. |
| **Example 2** | Give your students the information and assistance they need to find better sources. | The library has tutorials to help your students become better researchers today. | Did you know that the library has high-quality tutorials for use in your class? | Assign two-minute library tutorials; get excellent research papers! | Link here to add library tutorials to your course page today. |
| **Example 3** | Create bibliographies effortlessly using Zotero, a free online source management tool. | Create bibliographies in a snap using Zotero! | Wonder how the research pros make their bibliographies? Learn how. | Watch the most popular library tutorial so you too can create bibliographies like a pro. | Start the Zotero tutorial now and create a flawless bibliography within minutes. |

[1]Adapted from ACRL, 3M Inc., and Reynolds 2003.

awareness. Once the tutorial has been released, messages promoting interest, desire, and action help the audience understand what the tutorial is for and whether it is worth their time and effort and pushes them to take the next step and actively engage with the tutorial.

After creating a range of possible promotional messages, it is time to choose some vehicles, or methods, for communicating your messages. Promotional vehicles can be categorized in a number of ways (Schewe and Hiam 1998). Some corporate vehicles that can be applicable for promoting tutorials are

- *advertising*—broadly targeting all potential users;
- *direct marketing*—targeting a more specific user group; and
- *personal selling*—talking directly to potential users and providing more detailed descriptions of the tutorial.

While the terminology used for these vehicles is connected to concepts of selling things, the principles behind these terms have utility for librarians. You likely have used some combination of these vehicles before, whether it was putting up a poster in your library's lobby in order to broadly advertise a service or event to anyone who might happen to walk by, handing out a bookmark to promote a new service to interested patrons at the reference desk, or talking to an instructor you thought might be interested in a new database. See table 7.6 for more promotional vehicle ideas; using a variety of examples from each of the vehicle types can help create a strong promotional campaign. Some of these promotional vehicles require more effort than others, while some of these methods are probably tasks you were planning to do anyway, such as meeting with faculty or providing

**Table 7.6.** Types of Promotional Vehicles[1]

*Use a variety of examples from each vehicle type to create a strong promotional campaign.*

| VEHICLE | EXAMPLES |
|---|---|
| **Advertising** | • Posting on Twitter accounts<br>• Posting on Facebook<br>• Promotional blurb and link on the library's homepage<br>• Descriptive text and link from a tutorial page on the library's website<br>• Poster in the library lobby |
| **Direct Marketing** | • Promote in person in classes or workshops<br>• Integrating in a specific course<br>• Featured in a newsletter to all instructional designers on campus<br>• Promote from within the learning management system<br>• Flyers posted in departments<br>• Bookmarks with tutorial links handed out at the reference desk |
| **Personal Selling** | • Highlight at faculty meetings and workshops as a pedagogical tool<br>• Call for partners willing to do trial or beta testing<br>• Word-of-mouth promotion with instructors |

[1]Many of these examples were gleaned from the PRIMO Interviews, http://www.ala.org/acrl/aboutacrl/directoryofleadership/sections/is/iswebsite/projpubs/primo/site.

classroom demonstrations. The key is to use the vehicles in combination with each other for the greatest effect.

Other promotional methods may be outside of your traditional comfort zone. If so, this may be a good time to delegate or ask for support from colleagues who have strengths in other areas, such as graphic design or social networking. If you have already prepared a variety of messages, this will make it simpler to explain your vision to others and translate your promotions across a variety of platforms.

Using the AIDA cycle to create multiple messages and choosing several promotional vehicles for those messages helps provide the basis for a promotional campaign. Promotional messages usually need to be delivered more than once in order to be successful. Few libraries have marketing or promotions coordinators, and the thought of organizing a tutorial promotional campaign in addition to your already full schedule may feel daunting. Creating a campaign schedule and adding it to your calendar may help reduce the anxiety involved in planning a sustained promotional effort. Breaking your tutorial promotional campaign into smaller chunks, like those presented in the sidebar, may make a promotional campaign feel more doable. Be sure to include time between the events on your promotional campaign calendar or your audience may start to tune you out. Also, return to different parts of the AIDA cycle as necessary in order to create interest or desire if you need to generate more use of your tutorial over time.

While the types of messages and vehicles described in this section are meant to represent promotional ideas that could be deployed at a wide range of libraries, it is important to remember that the best strategies for you will depend on your individual context. Perhaps you have had specific faculty partners working with you on this tutorial since the idea began germinating, and you have no need to promote the tutorial to the general population. However, many tutorial projects do require some promotional activities in order to reach their intended audience. Whether that involves promoting the tutorials primarily to your fellow librarians or to a specific population of students depends on your individual

## SAMPLE SCHEDULE FOR A PROMOTIONAL CAMPAIGN FOR A CITATIONS 101 TUTORIAL

**Late summer**
- Post Facebook and Twitter messages.

**One week before term starts**
- Give faculty development presentation.
- Meet with individual faculty.
- Remind reference desk librarians about the tutorial.

**Start of term**
- Post message on the library's website.
- Demonstrate in classes.

**Midterm**
- Put posters up in the library lobby.

**Late term**
- Write a brief article in faculty newsletter; include some testimonials.

context. Successful promotional campaigns are often idiosyncratic. What works really well at one institution may not play well at another campus or in another town. Don't beat yourself up for not trying every new promotional idea you hear about. Know your culture and what resonates well with your target user group, but also be willing to try new things and push that boundary a little bit. Finally, promotional activities do cost time and money, so assess what messages and vehicles are the most effective so that you can make good use of limited resources.

## Tutorial Adoption by Other Librarians and Instructors

For many tutorial creators, a crucial measure of implementation success is whether or not other librarians or instructors use the tutorial. Classic tutorials such as *TILT* (*Texas Information Literacy Tutorial*), the University of Washington's *Research 101*, and the University of California, Irvine's, *Begin Your Research* tutorial have had fantastic implementation rates because they have been used by other librarians all over the world. Your goal may not be to create a tutorial that is used quite so ubiquitously, but you may hope that at a minimum your local colleagues will use it. Asking colleagues to incorporate a new tool into their instructional workflow takes work and isn't just a matter of letting them know that the tutorial exists. The following section will draw on the work done in the fields of instructional design and change process research in order to help provide some strategies to create buy-in among your colleagues for using your tutorial.

While promoting your tutorial to your colleagues (who may include other librarians at your institution, librarians at branch campuses, or other teaching faculty) is the first step in diffusion or dissemination, this cannot be the last step in implementing your tutorial. The previous section discussed promotional methods that can be effective for both learners and instructors. Use these promotional methods to promote awareness and interest of your tutorial, but continue working with your colleagues to move toward adoption—the next phase of implementation.

Instructional designers Patricia Smith and Tillman Ragan (2005) define adoption as making full use of a new tool or technique after a thoughtful analysis of how it will work in your own context. However, educational researchers Gene Hall and Shirley Hord have found that for classroom teachers "introducing new practices alone seldom results in new practices being incorporated into ongoing classroom practices" (2011, 52). A variety of professional development activities are required to support any suggested changes, from learning new skills to understanding what support is available for the tool. If a change is introduced without the necessary support system or buy-in, the new tool is likely to be ineffective. Instead, Hall and Hord (2011) use the metaphor of building a bridge to encourage incremental and guided support so that the suggested (or required) change doesn't feel like walking off a metaphorical cliff.

The following professional development activities may be helpful as a way to create buy-in and demonstrate support as colleagues consider adopting your tutorial into their instructional practice. These professional development activities are based on the Concerns-Based Adoption Model (CBAM), which was developed for use by K–12 classroom instructors but which also has value for other types of instructors. There are three parts to CBAM (Hord et al. 1987):

- Stages of concern
- Innovation configurations
- Levels of use

Components of each of these three elements can be adapted for use in your professional development context.

The first part of CBAM, stages of concern, explores the affective aspects of change. There are four stages of concern:

- *Unconcerned*—the stage people are in before they know anything about the coming change
- *Self-concerns*—reflects concerns about how the change will affect you as an individual
- *Task concerns*—happens when people are worried about how they will get all of the work done
- *Impact concerns*—focuses on how students are using the tool

If the use of a new tutorial is causing some anxiety at your institution, the stages of concern could be used as a way to guide a discussion-based professional development activity to elicit how your colleagues are feeling about the transition to using the new tutorial. Or depending on your workplace culture, perhaps a more anonymous approach may be more effective. Colleagues could post sticky notes describing their personal experiences or feelings related to using the new tutorial on a whiteboard under headings for the four stages. Alternatively, an online forum such as a wiki or shared document could be used as a sounding board to gather input. Allowing colleagues an outlet for processing their concerns can help them feel like their voices are being heard and will hopefully lead to higher rates of buy-in.

The next element of CBAM that can help encourage ownership over the process of adopting the new tutorial is called innovation configurations. Innovation configurations can be used as a way to discuss and visualize the intended uses for a particular innovation—in this case, a tutorial. Within the K–12 educational setting, innovation configuration maps help educators use recommended innovations or tools in a consistent way, as many of these educators are trying to meet a common set of standards. Within libraries, the desire for consistent use of tutorials may not be as strong, but it can still be helpful to clarify the intended uses for the tutorial in order to get everyone on the same page initially.

Innovation configuration maps (see table 7.7) can be used as an activity at professional development training in order to help develop a shared vision for how the tutorials could be used. Innovation configuration maps are similar to rubrics in that they try to provide a consistent way to think about a shared experience. However, unlike rubrics, they are not used to evaluate students but rather to create a common understanding of the intended instructional purpose of the tutorial. During your professional development training, divide librarians into small groups and ask them to use action verbs to describe several instructional components of the tutorial and variations of those components that range from the "ideal use of the tutorial" to "unacceptable use of the tutorial" (see table 7.8 for examples). Bring the small groups back together to discuss the range of ideas, and then create a common map together. Keep this map somewhere so that you can refer back to it or use it when training new hires to help them understand the instructional purpose of the tutorial.

The last element of CBAM is levels of use. The idea behind levels of use is that while many of your colleagues may have adopted your tutorial into their instructional activities, not all of them may be using the tutorial to the same degree. On one extreme end of levels of use are those who are not using the tutorial at all. However, a more common

**Table 7.7.** Creating an Innovation Configuration Map to Help Manage Implementation[1]

|  | Module 1 | Module 2 | Module 3 |
|---|---|---|---|
| **Ideal use of the tutorial** |  |  |  |
| **Acceptable use of the tutorial** |  |  |  |
| **Less-than-ideal use of the tutorial** |  |  |  |
| **Unacceptable use of the tutorial** |  |  |  |

[1]Based on Richardson 2004.

**Table 7.8.** Sample Completed Innovation Configuration Map for a Citations 101 Tutorial

|  | COMPONENT 1—BROAD STUDENT REACH | COMPONENT 2—ENSURES INDIVIDUAL ACCOUNTABILITY | COMPONENT 3—PROVIDES FEEDBACK AND ASSISTANCE |
|---|---|---|---|
| **Ideal use of the tutorial** | Assigns the Citations 101 tutorial to all first-year writing classes, both on-campus and distance learners. | Requires all first-year students in writing classes to answer the tutorial quiz questions after logging in with a unique student ID. | After assigning the Citations 101 tutorial, the instructor references the material in class and suggests resources for getting more help. |
| **Acceptable use of the tutorial** | Assigns the Citations 101 tutorial to 90 percent of the first-year writing classes. | Requires all first-year students in writing classes to answer the tutorial quiz questions, but does not require a unique log-in. | After assigning the Citations 101 tutorial, the instructor emphasizes resources for getting more help. |
| **Less-than-ideal use of the tutorial** | Only assigns the Citations 101 tutorial to the distance learners. | Requires most first-year distance learners in writing classes to answer tutorial quiz questions, and does not require a unique log-in. | After assigning the Citations 101 tutorial, the instructor does not refer to any of the content covered in the tutorial. |
| **Unacceptable use of the tutorial** | Does not assign the Citations 101 tutorial to any first-year writing classes. | No tutorial quiz questions are assigned. | The instructor neither assigns the tutorial nor refers to the content covered in the Citations 101 tutorial. |

middle level describes instructors who are using the tutorial but who aren't very familiar with it yet. Hall and Hord (2011) call this middle level "mechanical use." Instructors at this level are primarily concerned with the bare-bones details needed to work with the tutorial and are unable to think about the tutorial in a big-picture way or as part of their larger instructional goals. Being at this mechanical-use level can result in using the tutorial inefficiently, making mistakes in administering it, or feeling frustrated over the need to use the tutorial.

Paying attention to the needs of instructors who are at the mechanical-use level is important for a variety of reasons. These instructors may be more inclined to become disillusioned and stop using the tutorial altogether. If the users at this level are faculty instructors, this becomes especially problematic because researchers have found that students are more likely to use library tutorials when they are required for a class (Appelt and Pendell 2010; Michel 2001). Also, because mechanical users typically either are first-time users or do not yet have ownership over the use of the tutorial, they are not good candidates from which to solicit summative feedback about the tutorial as they are unlikely to have nuanced opinions or insights.

On the other end of the levels of use spectrum are those instructors who have fully integrated the tutorial into their instructional program to the point that the use of the tutorial is routine. Or perhaps these instructors have gone one step further and have adapted the tutorial for their own needs. They could be using the tutorial in a hybrid or flipped class or may be using several modules from the tutorial but not the entire tutorial to support their instructional goals. While these instructors' use of the tutorial may not match the initial intended use for the tutorial as mapped out in an innovation configuration map, this should not be too big a concern as librarians tend to be less bound to meeting specific standards and are more focused on creating an authentic learning environment for their learners. In addition, the adaptations these instructors make can serve as a form of user feedback to help shape future iterations of the tutorial.

## ◎ Key Points

Implementing a tutorial requires not only posting your tutorial on a web server but also evaluating how usable your tutorial is, how you will promote your tutorial, and how you will encourage other colleagues to use your tutorial. Here are some key points to take away:

- Solicit feedback from several users who match your intended audience. Provide them with realistic scenarios, and observe any difficulties or frustrations that they may have as they try to complete sample tasks. Be prepared to make changes to your tutorial based on their feedback.
- Successfully promoting your tutorial will involve combining a variety of techniques targeting specific and general audiences. Create clear promotional messages to help your audiences understand how your tutorial will benefit them.
- Encouraging other colleagues to use your tutorial may require some work to develop buy-in. Planning thoughtful professional development activities that are responsive to their concerns will provide a foundation for authentic use of your tutorial by others.

Now that you have an understanding of the elements that go into implementing your tutorial, you are ready to undertake summative evaluation of your tutorial. Chapter 8 will guide you through how to measure your learners' overall ability to meet the learning objectives for your tutorial and how to gauge the effectiveness of your tutorial.

## ◎ References

ACRL, 3M Inc., and A. B. Reynolds. 2003. "Strategic Marketing for Academic and Research Libraries." American Library Association, Association of College and Research Libraries. http://www.ala.org/acrl/sites/ala.org.acrl/files/content/issues/marketing/ParticipantManual.pdf.

Appelt, Kristina M., and Kimberly Pendell. 2010. "Assess and Invest: Faculty Feedback on Library Tutorials." *College & Research Libraries* 71, no. 3: 245–53.

Barnum, Carol M. 2010. *Usability Testing Essentials Ready, Set . . . Test*. Burlington, MA: Elsevier Science.

Boundless. 2014. "AIDA Model." *Boundless Marketing*, June 1. https://www.boundless.com/marketing/textbooks/boundless-marketing-textbook/integrated-marketing-communication-12/introduction-to-integrated-marketing-communications-81/aida-model-406-4060/.

Bussmann, Jeffra, Caitlin Plovnick, and Cathy Palmer. 2013. "April 2013 Site of the Month." American Library Association, Association of College and Research Libraries. http://www.ala.org/acrl/aboutacrl/directoryofleadership/sections/is/iswebsite/projpubs/primo/site/2013april.

Cerejo, Lyndon. 2010. "Design Better and Faster with Rapid Prototyping." *Smashing Magazine*, June 16. http://www.smashingmagazine.com/2010/06/16/design-better-faster-with-rapid -prototyping/.

Garoufallou, Emmanouel, Rania Siatri, Georgia Zafeiriou, and Ekaterini Balampanidou. 2013. "The Use of Marketing Concepts in Library Services: A Literature Review." *Library Review* 62, no. 4/5: 312–34. doi:10.1108/LR-06-2012-0061.

Hall, Gene E., and Shirley M. Hord. 2011. "Implementation: Learning Builds the Bridge between Research and Practice." *Journal of Staff Development* 32, no. 4: 52–57.

Hodell, Chuck. 2006. *ISD from the Ground Up: A No-Nonsense Approach to Instructional Design.* Alexandria, VA: ASTD Press.

Hord, Shirley M., William L. Rutherford, Leslie Huling-Austin, and Gene E. Hall. 1987. *Taking Charge of Change.* Alexandria, VA: Association for Supervision and Curriculum Development.

Kirkpatrick, Donald. 2006. *Evaluating Training Programs: The Four Levels.* San Francisco, CA: Berrett-Koehler Publishers.

Kupersmith, John. 2012. "Library Terms That Users Understand." eScholarship, University of California, February. http://escholarship.org/uc/item/3qq499w7.

Michel, Stephanie. 2001. "What Do They Really Think? Assessing Student and Faculty Perspectives of a Web-Based Tutorial to Library Research." *College & Research Libraries* 62, no. 4: 317–32.

Piskurich, George M. 2006. *Rapid Instructional Design: Learning ID Fast and Right.* 2nd ed. San Francisco, CA: Pfeiffer.

Rees, Damian. 2013. "Improving Your Website Usability Tests." *Smashing Magazine*, January 8. http://www.smashingmagazine.com/2013/01/08/improving-your-website-usability-tests/.

Richardson, Joan. 2004. "Taking Measure." *Tools for Schools*, October/November, 1–8. http://learningforward.org/docs/tools-for-learning-schools/tools10-04.pdf.

Schewe, Charles D., and Alexander Hiam. 1998. *The Portable MBA in Marketing.* 2nd ed. The Portable MBA Series. New York: J. Wiley.

Smith, Linda K., and Lisa Velarde. 2013. "December 2013 Site of the Month." American Library Association, Association of College and Research Libraries, http://www.ala.org/acrl/aboutacrl/directoryofleadership/sections/is/iswebsite/projpubs/primo/site/2013december.

Smith, Patricia L., and Tillman J. Ragan. 2005. *Instructional Design.* 3rd ed. Hoboken, NJ: J. Wiley & Sons.

Tullis, Thomas, and William Albert. 2013. *Measuring the User Experience: Collecting, Analyzing, and Presenting Usability Metrics.* 2nd ed. Burlington, VT: Elsevier Science.

## ◎ More Resources

Gagné, Robert M. 2005. *Principles of Instructional Design.* Belmont, CA: Thomson/Wadsworth.

"Remote Usability Testing—Remote Usability and UX Research Tools." 2014. Remote Research. http://remoteresear.ch/tools/.

# CHAPTER 8

# Evaluation

## *Measuring the Impact of Your Tutorial to Guide Decision Making*

THE LAST ELEMENT OF THE ADDIE cycle is evaluation. However, as you have learned, the ADDIE model is iterative, and in reality, many of the activities that help contribute to a meaningful evaluation process should already be under way. In chapter 4, learning objectives were designed, and the elements that help frame an assessment strategy were outlined. In chapter 7, the steps involved in gathering feedback and determining whether or not a tutorial is useful and usable were discussed. Because different institutional contexts call for different evaluation needs, this chapter will examine some more options for evaluating tutorials, with a particular emphasis on assessment of learning due to the learner-centered nature of most library tutorials.

*Evaluation* is a term that can mean different things in different contexts. Even educators don't always share the exact same definitions for *evaluation*. For example, e-learning instructional designer William Horton takes a broad view, saying that "evaluation means assigning a value to something. It answers questions about the value of your e-learning course or project" (2001, 1). Other instructional designers focus on the importance of evaluation for guiding decisions and note that evaluation can be informed by assessment data such as test scores (Gagné et al. 2005). And library administrator Susan Sharpless Smith takes a more strongly programmatic view of evaluation, describing it as "the process of judging the effectiveness and worth of . . . educational programs and products" (2010, 185). While each of these definitions is somewhat different, they all point to the importance of using evaluation information to measure the effectiveness and impact of a tutorial in order to make decisions.

This chapter will begin with an overview of evaluation options so that you can determine an overall evaluation strategy. As noted earlier, this chapter will primarily focus on gathering learning-assessment data as a way to determine the value of a tutorial. *Assessment* is another term that sometimes has a variety of definitions. However, in this book, *assessment* will be defined as the activities that are used to measure student learning. The nuts and bolts of gathering assessment data within the tutorial context will be discussed, including various approaches to gathering assessment data, from choosing the types of questions to include on tests to writing those questions. These assessment techniques will help provide you with a solid understanding of the impact that your tutorial has on learning so that you can evaluate the overall effectiveness of your tutorial.

There are many different ways that tutorials can be used and the learning resulting from the use of those tutorials assessed. Tutorials can be used in a hybrid or flipped instructional environment where the tutorials are used in addition to in-person instruction. Depending on the size of the audience, the assessment for these situations may be performed either manually or automatically. Alternatively, some librarians create tutorials that replicate an entire class session or in-depth topic, but as was discussed in chapter 4, online library tutorials fit that mold less frequently. Again, depending on the size of the audience, the assessment for these tutorials may be done manually or automatically. Some tutorials are created in order to address a single point-of-need issue, and learners are self-directed in their exploration for additional information. As a result, the assessment of this kind of learning experience will serve primarily to engage the learner and to provide self-checks of learning or reinforce concepts. Feedback in this context is generated automatically. Finally, some tutorials have no direct assessment of learning. While the core principles of evaluation discussed in this chapter can be used in a wide variety of contexts, the main use case for evaluation that will be discussed is when a tutorial is used by many learners over a wide range of times, and as a result, the assessment of learning needs to take place within the tutorial platform itself and responses must be gathered automatically, and the corresponding feedback must also be given automatically.

## Evaluation: Choosing the Right Strategy for Your Situation

The instruction you provide via tutorials is likely to be part of a larger, programmatic instructional effort. Perhaps your library's instruction department is trying to reach all first-year students at your university. Or the instruction delivered via tutorials may be one component of a larger institutional goal. Maybe your university has the goal of graduating students with specific critical-thinking skills. Alternatively, you may just be experimenting with creating a few pilot tutorials and want to see how they are received on a very local level. If you intend to create tutorials on a regular basis, drafting a plan for gathering data on the impact of your tutorial will help ensure that your work is valued by your learners, your colleagues, and your administrators. Continuous and intentional evaluation of your tutorial is important because the information you gather provides the justification for the resources you have invested in creating the tutorial and demonstrates whether the investment was worthwhile or whether changes need to be made (Horton 2001). Information gained from a systematic evaluation can be used to help make better decisions about a tutorial. For example, you may need to consider whether you need to assign or hire more people to work on specific aspects of your tutorial, or you may need different tutorials for different audiences, or you may need to place your tutorial on a more highly visible part of your website.

Evaluation is a process that can involve a variety of components depending on how you will be using the information gathered in your evaluation. An evaluation process used to meet expectations of an external audience, such as an accreditation body, will be quite different from an evaluation process meant to explore and report to a local administrator as to whether there is a need for newer software to help create more tutorials. Because your evaluation needs may not be the same as a librarian at another institution, one helpful starting point for considering how and what you may need to evaluate is to use Donald Kirkpatrick's (2006) four levels of evaluation (see table 8.1). Kirkpatrick's four levels of evaluation are

- reaction,
- learning,
- application, and
- programmatic results.

Kirkpatrick's levels of evaluation were first discussed in chapter 7 and are a frequently used method for evaluating training programs. The levels are useful because of their flexibility within a variety of contexts. Often, evaluation data is only gathered for some of these four levels, so depending on who the audience is for the evaluation information you gather, you can use the combination of Kirkpatrick's evaluation levels that work for you. A good evaluation process should not only be flexible but should be easy to implement, be able to reliably measure results, be suitable and repurposable for various types of tutorials, and shouldn't be too resource intensive (Horton 2001). The next sections will guide you through the four levels of evaluation in order to help you determine the types of evaluation that will best meet your needs.

**Table 8.1.** Kirkpatrick's Four Levels of Evaluation and What They Measure[1]

| LEVEL OF EVALUATION | WHAT IS MEASURED? | TIMING |
| --- | --- | --- |
| 1—Reaction | Did the learners like the tutorial? | Immediately after completing the tutorial |
| 2—Learning | Do the learners know more than they did before? | 0–6 weeks after completing the tutorial |
| 3—Application | Can the learners apply what they learned in a realistic situation? | 1–6 months after completing the tutorial |
| 4—Programmatic Results | Have the tutorials impacted programmatic or institutional learning goals? | 1–3 years after implementation of the tutorial(s) |

[1]Levels of Evaluation model from Kirkpatrick 2006.

# ⊚ Measuring Reaction: Level 1

Kirkpatrick's first level of evaluation gauges learners' reactions to the tutorial. Because this type of evaluation was already covered in chapter 7, this section will just briefly touch on the value of evaluating learners' reactions to a tutorial. The reason this type of evaluation was discussed in chapter 7 is because in order to implement or release a tutorial, you need to evaluate learners' impressions of the design of the tutorial. Kirkpatrick calls this type of evaluation a "customer satisfaction measurement" (2006, 21). Examples of questions to ask in order to learn about learners' reactions (level 1 evaluation) to your tutorial are provided in chapter 7. These questions focus on whether or not learners like the tutorial, whether the tutorial was visually pleasing, and whether learners would recommend the tutorial to someone else. Many of these questions can be asked as part of the usability studies you do before releasing the tutorial.

In addition to asking questions in a direct way through usability-study interviews or surveys, unobtrusive measurements of learners' reactions can be collected via web analytics (Horton 2001). For example, rate of progress through the course, completion rates, and the number of pages within the tutorial that learners accessed can be measured in order to get another view of the reaction to the tutorial. However, these quantitative measurements may need to be combined with qualitative measurements, such as conversations with learners about specific usage behaviors, in order to get a more complete understanding of the reaction to the tutorial.

The evaluation data you collect from usability studies, web analytics, or through guided conversations with a sample of your users can be used to make cosmetic as well as structural changes to your tutorial design (see table 8.2). Demonstrating that learners like your tutorial can also help inform whether or not you use a similar design for future tutorials. You can use this information to help convince administrators to allocate more money for designers or design software if you find that particular features of your tutorial don't appeal to learners in terms of aesthetics or navigation. However, simply gathering information about learners' reactions to your tutorial does not help you evaluate whether or not your learners have gained new skills because of engaging with your tutorial.

# ⊚ Measuring Learning: Level 2

The second level of evaluation in Kirkpatrick's (2006) model focuses on learning, particularly learning that is demonstrated through an increase in knowledge, skills, or a change in attitude. Measuring the skills or knowledge gained through interacting with your tutorial is highly relevant for determining the impact of your tutorial. The information that

---

### REACTION (LEVEL 1) EVALUATION QUESTIONS

- Can learners use the tutorial?
- Do learners like the tutorial design?
- Are more resources needed in order to improve the design?

**Table 8.2.** Kirkpatrick's Four Levels of Evaluation as a Guide for Making Decisions[1]

| LEVEL OF EVALUATION | WHAT IS MEASURED? | DECISION-MAKING PROMPTS |
|---|---|---|
| 1—Reaction | Did the learners like the tutorial? | • Are cosmetic design changes needed?<br>• Are navigational design changes needed?<br>• Are more resources warranted? |
| 2—Learning | Do the learners know more than they did before? | • Are learning objectives realistic?<br>• Are content changes needed?<br>• Does your assessment match your learning objectives?<br>• Was your tutorial worth the investment of resources?<br>• Does your tutorial need more resources? |
| 3—Application | Can the learners apply what they learned in a realistic situation? | • Are your tutorials meeting your learners' needs?<br>• Are your tutorials offered at the right time?<br>• Do you need more or fewer tutorials? |
| 4—Programmatic Results | Have the tutorials impacted programmatic or institutional learning goals? | • Are your tutorials meeting your learning objectives?<br>• Do your learning objectives map to higher-order standards?<br>• Should you keep offering your tutorials?<br>• Is major reworking required?<br>• Do administrators understand the value of your tutorials? |

[1]Levels of Evaluation model from Kirkpatrick 2006; Decision-making prompts adapted from Horton 2001.

you can collect through level 2 evaluations is meaningful but does not have to be pulled together in an extremely resource-intensive manner as much of it can be gathered in an automated way through online surveys and quizzes or other online tools (Horton 2001).

The definition given for *assessment* at the beginning of this chapter was the measurement of learning, which mirrors the intention of performing level 2 evaluations. Because assessing learning is so important for evaluating the overall effectiveness of tutorials, and because having a positive impact on learners is at the heart of library instruction and outreach efforts, techniques for measuring learning will be the primary focus of the rest of this chapter. Designing effective assessments is a new skill for many librarians. Just as few librarians started their library careers knowing how to create tutorials, few librarians are experts in developing assessment or quiz questions. This section will compare designing learning assessments for tutorials to designing in-class assessments and then will walk through the process of creating meaningful questions and quizzes to assess the knowledge and skills your learners have gained based on interacting with your tutorial.

## How Is Assessment Different in the Tutorial Environment?

Assessment of in-class learning often takes place online—online surveys are given, clickers are used, or entire tests are completed virtually—so what is different about conducting an assessment of learning with an online tutorial? If you are using tutorials as part of a hybrid learning experience where the tutorials are used to supplement in-class experiences, the answer may be "not much." Some instructional designers recommend thinking about what you do to assess learning in the classroom and then see whether those approaches will work in an online context (Horton 2001). While that approach can certainly help to jump-start the assessment brainstorming process, there are important contextual differences that require somewhat different strategies when planning an assessment of learning for an online tutorial.

Different instructional considerations that impact designing for the tutorial environment were described in table 4.1. Some of the differences included interacting with learners asynchronously, having fewer overall opportunities for interaction, and the potential for more online distractions. Some of those same distinctions between the in-person versus the tutorial environment arise when thinking about conducting an assessment of learning. In addition to the differences already mentioned, the ability to give interactive feedback is more limited, a higher degree of trust is required as the instructor is not directly monitoring learners, and the opportunities for using assessment techniques that authentically match the learners' environment are fairly limited. Because of these differences, and especially because tutorials are usually meant to serve a large number of learners asynchronously, objective assessments, such as multiple-choice questions, are the norm for most tutorials.

However, some of the differences between the in-person and the tutorial environment also result in an assessment of learning that can be much more scalable. Many learners can take the same online assessment at any time, from wherever they are. And assuming that you can use an e-learning authoring tool to give automatic feedback based on the learners' responses (see chapter 4), learners can instantly find out whether they are on the right track and make adjustments accordingly. Most e-learning authoring tools also allow for branching based on learner responses, so learners can advance to new material or go back to review previous material depending on their responses. This would be much harder to replicate in an in-person class.

Chapter 1 introduced the idea that tutorials are more conducive to helping learners gain certain types of knowledge than others. Declarative, conceptual, and procedural knowledge (see table 1.1) are the most appropriate types of knowledge to address using a tutorial, in part because these types of knowledge can be assessed using tools that are embedded in the tutorial itself. For example, measuring learners' understanding of library-specific terminology (declarative knowledge) can be done easily with a matching exercise in a tutorial. In contrast, measuring learners' ability to apply metacognitive skills (cognitive strategies), such as brainstorming or note taking, is not very realistic in the tutorial context because application of this skill cannot be truly assessed with a system that only provides automatically generated feedback. However, if you are able to have more direct contact with your learners and can manage the volume of responses, you could design an online assessment that involved scanning in a representation of their work, which you would then need to manually grade.

Learning to create effective learning assessments for the tutorial environment takes some practice. While you probably won't be able to just use the same learning assessments that you use in your in-person classes, you will be able to use the same underlying principles that you learn about creating assessments for tutorials for designing in-class assessments.

## Designing Assessments for Both You and Your Learners

Before talking about the nuts and bolts of creating learning assessments, it is important to think about which of your assessments provide information primarily for you and which of your assessments provide information for your learners. Once you have made this distinction, you can then structure your assessments in order to meet both your needs and your learners' needs. There are two main goals when performing assessments: determining whether learners have gained new skills because of what you have taught and diagnosing whether there are gaps in learners' understanding (Gagné et al. 2005). These goals are at the core of formative evaluation, the process of collecting information both so that you can improve the effectiveness of your instruction and so that learners can improve their learning (Dick, Carey, and Carey 2004). In other words, formative evaluation acknowledges that changes will need to be made either by the instructor, the learner, or both. Formative evaluation was initially discussed in chapter 4, primarily as a way to provide structured feedback to learners, and then in chapter 7 as a way to gather information from learners about how usable a tutorial is in order to create a more effective tutorial. In this chapter, formative evaluation is discussed as a way to gather information about the impact a tutorial has on learning and whether the learning outcomes have been achieved.

Kirkpatrick's level 2 evaluation typically focuses on just the first assessment goal—determining whether or not learning happened. And this type of evaluation usually is only measured at the end of a learning experience. In contrast, the second goal of learning assessments—diagnosing gaps in understanding—requires that information be collected along the way so that learners (and sometimes instructors) can make adjustments. Combining both diagnostic information and measurements of skill or knowledge gains throughout a tutorial can provide a richer learning experience by making users more responsible for their own learning. At the same time, diagnostic assessments can provide the instructor with more evaluation information to help improve the instruction experience. Including diagnostic assessments throughout tutorials also can be helpful because of the limited options for feedback and interactivity within the tutorial environment. Ideally, diagnostic assessments would be gathered throughout the tutorial at the end of modules or sections. If you only give feedback at the very end of the tutorial, learners don't have opportunities to make adjustments and improve their learning (Mager 1997).

Another way that diagnostic assessments can be used is to provide self-checks for the learner either in the form of quizzes or metacognitive reflections. You may not choose to collect or save the data from these types of self-checks. If you do not need the information from these self-checks either to give the learners a grade or to inform a larger evaluation strategy, then it is fine to simply include diagnostic self-checks as a way to

### FORMATIVE ASSESSMENT EXAMPLES

- Pretests
- One- to two-question multiple-choice quizzes
- Self-reflection prompts
- Brief application exercise ("now try it yourself")

prompt deliberative practice or reflection. Note that if all of the self-checks are quizzes, be careful not to overuse them. A meta-analysis performed by the U.S. Department of Education found that online quizzes didn't influence the amount of learning (Means et al. 2009). However, self-checks in the form of metacognitive prompts were found to increase learning, so consider including a variety of types of diagnostic assessments that engage learners throughout the tutorial.

The purpose of your tutorial will determine whether or not you need to provide a grade or a score for your tutorial. If your tutorial is connected to a class or a credential, then proof of proficiency or completion likely will be needed. If your tutorial is designed for self-directed learners at their point of need, a recorded score probably won't be required. Regardless of whether or not you need to provide graded feedback to your learners, you may want to collect assessment information that you can compare over time to show a change in learning based on the use of your tutorial. Pre- and posttests are commonly used to demonstrate this type of cause-and-effect relationship. Pre- and posttests can use questions that look at changes in attitude, as well as questions that gauge changes in knowledge or skills (Dick, Carey, and Carey 2004).

Before drafting a thirty-question pre- and posttest for your tutorial, step back and consider the purposes for your assessment (see table 8.3). Is the assessment experience just intended to provide a self-check for the learner? In that case, one to two questions early enough in the module to allow the learner to make any needed adjustments should suffice. If the assessment experience is meant to inform both the learner and the instructor so that adjustments can be made, a rough rule of thumb is that around three questions should be used for each learning objective (or content area) in order to make sure the learner actually demonstrates understanding of the content and didn't either make an unfortunate mistake or get lucky (Gagné et al. 2005). These questions should be included at the end of a module or section.

Summative evaluations (which will be discussed more in the "Measuring Programmatic Results: Level 4" section later in this chapter) inform both the learner and the instructor, but typically only the instructor can make any meaningful changes based on

**Table 8.3.** Number of Questions to Include throughout the Tutorial Based on the Type of the Assessment

| TYPE OF ASSESSMENT | WHO WILL USE THE INFORMATION? | TYPE OF FEEDBACK GIVEN | HOW MANY QUESTIONS TO INCLUDE | WHERE TO PLACE THE QUESTIONS |
|---|---|---|---|---|
| Formative self-checks | Learner | • Automated if using objective questions <br> • None if using metacognitive prompts <br> • Ungraded | 1–2 questions | At logical points throughout a module |
| Formative quizzes | Learner and instructor | • Automated if using only objective questions <br> • Typically ungraded | No more than 3 questions | At the end of a section or module |
| Summative evaluation | Learner and instructor, but primarily the instructor | • Automated if using only objective questions <br> • Typically graded | No more than 3 questions per learning objective covered in the tutorial | At the end of the tutorial |

the information gathered because the evaluation is done at the very end of the tutorial. Again, approximately three questions per learning objective should be included. However, in addition to creating questions based on the number of learning objectives, you should also create enough questions to cover the reasonable range of conditions in which learners could apply what they have learned (Mager 1997). For example, if learners need to be able to apply the same concepts in multiple databases, then make sure to include questions based on scenarios in more than one database. However, don't try to include every possible scenario and make your evaluation unnecessarily long. Use a few of the most common and relevant conditions in order to get a realistic sense of learners' knowledge and skills. The next section will talk about how to create questions that help you effectively measure whether or not learners can meet the learning goals that you set for them.

## Measuring Learning: A Return to Learning Objectives

Because the ADDIE model has been used throughout this book, you have already done much of the work required to design a tutorial that can effectively measure learning. The first step was thinking about the type of knowledge that could be conveyed best in the tutorial setting. The next step was creating specific learning objectives for your tutorial. These learning objectives will now help guide you as you create effective assessments of learning (more commonly known to learners as quizzes or tests).

When you designed your learning objectives (see chapter 4), you defined not only what content you wanted your learners to know but also the context, conditions, and degree to which they should learn the content so that you could assess their learning. Instructional designers call learning assessment that is directly measured against specific learning outcomes objective referenced (Dick, Carey, and Carey 2004; Gagné et al. 2005; see figure 8.1). Objective-referenced assessment can be highly effective because it provides a clear link to the content that you have designed rather than falling into the trap of being tangential or testing something that you didn't actually cover (Mager 1997).

The learning verbs you used to create your learning objectives now act as helpful guides for choosing appropriate learning assessments. In chapter 4, the highly regarded Revised Bloom's Taxonomy of Learning Verbs (Anderson and Krathwohl 2001) was

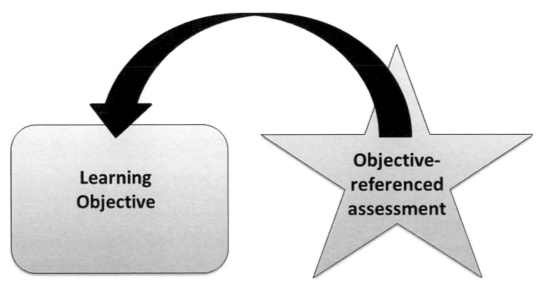

**Figure 8.1.** Objective-referenced assessment is directly linked to learning objectives

used as a guide for writing learning objectives. These verbs belong to a hierarchy of cognitive processes (remembering, understanding, applying, analyzing, evaluating, and creating) that are very similar to the knowledge types that have been discussed as a guide for creating tutorials throughout this book. Sometimes instructional designers refer to *learning domains* as another way of categorizing different kinds of learning (Dick, Carey, and Carey 2004, 149). But the idea behind all of these categories is the same: to indicate that not all types of learning objectives can be evaluated using the same assessment techniques. As a result, it is important to design assessments in order to match the appropriate learning category (which will continue to be referred to as *knowledge types* for consistency).

As noted earlier, objective assessment questions, or those that have a defined set of answers, such as multiple-choice or matching questions, are the easiest and most scalable types of assessment questions to use in a tutorial because responses can be automatically collected and feedback can also be given automatically using online tools. Fortunately, the knowledge types that are most appropriate for tutorials—declarative, conceptual, and procedural—can be evaluated using objective assessment questions. While problem-solving knowledge is usually best assessed using subjective questions or scenarios, such as a live demonstration or a simulation, well-written objective questions can also measure problem-solving knowledge gains.

The range of types of assessment questions that you create will likely be determined by the e-learning authoring tool or survey tool (e.g., Captivate, Camtasia, or SurveyMonkey) that you use. Commonly used learning-assessment question types include

- true/false (or yes/no),
- short answer/fill in the blank,
- hot spot,
- matching,
- multiple choice,
- sequencing, and
- simulations,

To choose the question type that works best for your learning objective, begin by recalling what type of knowledge is covered by your learning objective. Next, match your learning verb to the appropriate type of question. Table 8.4 provides knowledge types, along with examples of learning verbs and the appropriate corresponding question type. So, for example, if a learning objective addresses conceptual knowledge and uses the learning verb *locate*, appropriate question types would include short answer/fill in the blank, hot spots, matching, and multiple choice.

As you can see, there are multiple appropriate question types for all of the knowledge categories. Having multiple question types can create a more engaging experience for your learners. A more detailed guide to choosing between appropriate question types is given in table 8.5. Choosing question types often involves balancing learner engagement, the technological capabilities of your e-learning authoring tool, appropriate knowledge types, and the context of your learning objective. Perfecting this balancing act takes some practice.

**Table 8.4** Matching Knowledge Types and Learning Outcomes to Appropriate Testing Strategies

*Asterisks indicate that while this type of learning assessment may be used, it is not the best option within the tutorial environment.[1]*

| KNOWLEDGE TYPE | EXAMPLE LEARNING VERBS | TYPES OF LEARNING-ASSESSMENT QUESTIONS | | | | | | |
|---|---|---|---|---|---|---|---|---|
| | | TRUE/FALSE | SHORT ANSWER/FILL IN THE BLANK | HOT SPOT | MATCHING | MULTIPLE CHOICE | SEQUENCE | SIMULATION |
| Declarative | Define | X | X | X | X | X | | |
| | Recognize | X | X | X | X | X | | |
| | Identify | X | X | X | X | X | | |
| Conceptual | Compare | X | X | X | X | X | * | |
| | Select | | X | X | X | X | | |
| | Locate | | X | X | X | X | | |
| Procedural | Organize | | | | X | X | X | * |
| | Modify | | | | | * | | * |
| | Implement | | | | | * | | * |
| Problem Solving | Diagnose | | | | | X | | * |
| | Predict | | | | | X | | * |
| | Assess | | | | | X | | * |

[1]Adapted from Dick, Carey, and Carey 2004, 155.

**Table 8.5.** Choosing Question Types and Writing Assessment Questions for Tutorials[1]

| QUESTION TYPE | WHEN TO USE THIS QUESTION TYPE | TIPS FOR USING THIS QUESTION TYPE |
|---|---|---|
| **True/False**<br>Learner picks one of two mutually exclusive choices. | • To assess the learner's ability to choose between two distinct categories<br>• To simulate decision making that has a yes/no response | • Include other question types as well in order to assess whether learners are just guessing<br>• Phrase the question in neutral, nonleading terms |
| **Short Answer/Fill in the Blank**<br>Learner provides limited, brief answers. | • To assess understanding of terminology within a defined context | • Provide sufficient, realistic context<br>• Use selection lists in order to eliminate synonym or spelling problems |
| **Hot Spot**<br>Learners click on the correct area on a provided image. | • To assess understanding of visual cues within a defined context | • Provide sufficient, realistic visual context<br>• Provide enough buffer space between hot spots to avoid accidental clicks |
| **Matching**<br>Learner matches items from one list to corresponding items in another list. | • To assess understanding of the relationships between concepts | • Keep the two lists short enough to avoid scrolling<br>• Include at least one item that does not match in order to eliminate guessing |
| **Multiple Choice**<br>Learner picks one (or occasionally multiple) item(s) from a list of written choices or pictures. | • To assess understanding of terminology, conceptual connections, the ability to organize information, or the ability to solve problems<br>• To simulate a wide range of scenarios textually | • Include realistic alternatives in order to reduce guessing<br>• Include almost right and almost wrong responses in order to encourage thinking<br>• Length of the item shouldn't give away the answer (e.g., the longest one shouldn't always be right) |
| **Sequence**<br>Learners arrange items in the correct sequence. | • To assess understanding of a process or procedure that has clearly defined steps | • Make sure there is only one, best way to order the steps |
| **Simulation**<br>Learners are given a realistic scenario and try to demonstrate a solution. | • To assess understanding of the ability to solve problems within a realistic context | • Use only if the software testing platform is simple enough for learners to use so that you can test the content not learners' ability to use the software |

[1]Adapted from Horton 2001, 25.

## Writing Learning Assessments (aka Quizzes or Tests)

Once you have determined how many questions to include throughout your tutorial to gather the assessment information you need and have chosen the appropriate question types for the type of knowledge you are covering, you can begin to write your learning-assessment questions. Here are some tips to help you get started writing questions regardless of the question type you choose:

- The importance of connecting your assessment questions to your learning objectives cannot be overemphasized. Consider printing out your learning objectives as a reminder and keeping them in front of you as you write your questions.
- Make sure that your writing is clear. Both the questions and the directions should be easy to read. A confusing question will not give your learners the chance to demonstrate what they have learned. Have other colleagues or a small group of learners try out your questions to make sure that your grammar makes sense and that your questions aren't unnecessarily convoluted or tricky.
- Make sure the questions are learner centered—think about your audience's vocabulary level, cultural backgrounds, and previous experiences, and then write questions that match those needs (Bozarth 2008; Dick, Carey, and Carey 2004). Including vocabulary or language that is too advanced for your learners won't help you measure the learning objectives that you intend to measure. By the same token, including culturally biased language or scenarios could be confusing or offensive and will skew your assessment information.
- Finally, make sure that the questions you write are realistic and connect to what the learner will actually be doing (Dick, Carey, and Carey 2004). If your tutorial showed nursing students how to use PubMed to find scholarly articles, don't ask these learners to demonstrate their knowledge using a scenario with a business database like Mintel Market Research Reports to find industry information.

Three sample learning objectives were introduced in chapter 4. Table 8.6 provides some learning-assessment activities that could be used to measure each of these three learning objectives. Note that the learning verbs are highlighted in order to emphasize their connection to the type of question that was chosen. Each question links back directly to the original learning objective and asks questions that match the context in which learners would apply the information. In addition, the directions are written as clearly as possible so that learners know what the guidelines are for making the best choice.

In addition to providing guidance for how to choose between each of the question types, table 8.5 also contains some tips for writing each of the types of questions. But as you likely noticed in table 8.4, multiple-choice questions can be used to address the widest variety of knowledge types if the questions are well written and link back to the learning objective. However, writing good multiple-choice questions is difficult

## LEARNING-ASSESSMENT QUESTION WRITING TIPS

- Link questions directly to learning objectives.
- Write clear directions and questions.
- Use learner-centered language and scenarios.
- Create realistic scenarios that match the learners' performance context.

**Table 8.6.** Assessment Activity Examples Linked to Learning Objectives

| LEARNING OBJECTIVE | SAMPLE OBJECTIVE REFERENCED ASSESSMENT ACTIVITY |
|---|---|
| Students will be able to **compare** different characteristics of primary and secondary sources in order to find appropriate sources for their research paper. | **Modified True/False:**<br>Indicate whether the following examples represent a characteristic of a primary or secondary source. Choose one best answer.<br><br>1. A recent journal article on immigration that used sources such as government documents, diaries, and other journal articles is a<br>  a. primary source<br>  b. secondary source<br>2. A scholarly article written 100 years ago about immigration that you read in order to understand the attitudes of that era is a<br>  a. primary source<br>  b. secondary source<br>3. A government document of a recent or historical congressional hearing on immigration reform is a<br>  a. primary source<br>  b. secondary source |
| Students will **recognize** the difference between sources available in the catalog and in databases in order to find books and articles for their research paper. | **Fill in the Blank:**<br>1. A _____ is a library resource for finding journal articles, newspaper articles, magazine articles, and conference proceedings.<br>2. A _____ is a library resource for finding books, journals, videos, and maps at this library.<br><br>Answer pool: catalog, database |
| Users will **recall** the steps of downloading an e-book using the vendor software in order to add e-books to their own personal e-reader device. | **Sequence:**<br>Drag and drop the following steps into the correct order to demonstrate that you know how to download an e-book from OverDrive using an Apple device.<br><br>• Download the book.<br>• Go to your account on Library2Go.<br>• Download the OverDrive app from the App Store.<br>• Go to Library2Go.<br>• Sign in to Library2Go.<br>• Sign up for an OverDrive account.<br>• Tap a book cover.<br>• Find Library2Go.<br>• Tap to borrow. |

and takes some practice. Here are some additional tips that especially apply to writing multiple-choice questions:

- The question portion of a multiple-choice question is sometimes called the *stem*. Make sure the stem is meaningful by itself so that learners don't have to constantly switch between the stem and the answers in order to understand what is being asked.
- Don't give away the answer by creating correct answers that are consistently very short or very long.
- Avoid stating your question or stem in negative terms as this is unnecessarily confusing (Gould 2010).

- Create alternative answers that are plausible so that learners are challenged.
- Try to write answers that require learners to think through the choices rather than just use the process of elimination (Horton 2001).

Multiple-choice questions can be extremely useful and versatile, but you need to write appropriately challenging questions if you use them for measuring learning for knowledge types such as problem solving. One way to do this is to include image-based multiple-choice questions in addition to text-based multiple-choice scenarios. Figure 8.2 shows a multiple-choice example based on information in a Zotero collection. Instead of writing out text-based answers describing the fields needed to create a complete APA citation, an image is used to more directly measure this skill.

Remember that the feedback you provide can be as helpful and instructive as the testing experience itself. Refer back to chapter 4 for tips on how to design feedback that is learner centered and constructive.

## Using Learning Assessments to Demonstrate Impact

Horton (2001) argues that evaluation of learning (Kirkpatrick's level 2) is often the only option for many instructors because conducting the higher levels of evaluation may not be practical or feasible. This is certainly the case when evaluating many online tutorials—determining exactly who the learners are and their connection to your program or institution may be difficult information to capture. While more robust evaluation of learning is recommended four to six weeks after engaging in training or instruction due to a natural drop in knowledge of up to 80 to 90 percent (Horton 2001, 23), waiting this long is not feasible for many librarians, especially those using tutorials at the point of need. As an alternative to measuring the knowledge and skills of each of your learners several weeks after using the tutorial, you could instead find a small group of learners to assess four to six weeks later in order to get a rough idea of how much information is retained over time. More options for evaluation sampling will be discussed in the next section of this chapter.

Another reality to keep in mind when evaluating the impact of your instruction on learning gains is that learning does not take place in a vacuum (Gagné et al. 2005). Motivation, prior knowledge, and learners' immediate environment are among the external factors that impact learners' ability to engage with your tutorial. Your learners are part of a larger system; this may be particularly clear in a higher-education setting where learners come with vastly different experience and are engaging in a wide variety of activities outside of their coursework. In addition, the specific learning objectives that you create are not stand-alone entities. These learning objectives are also tied to a larger system. For

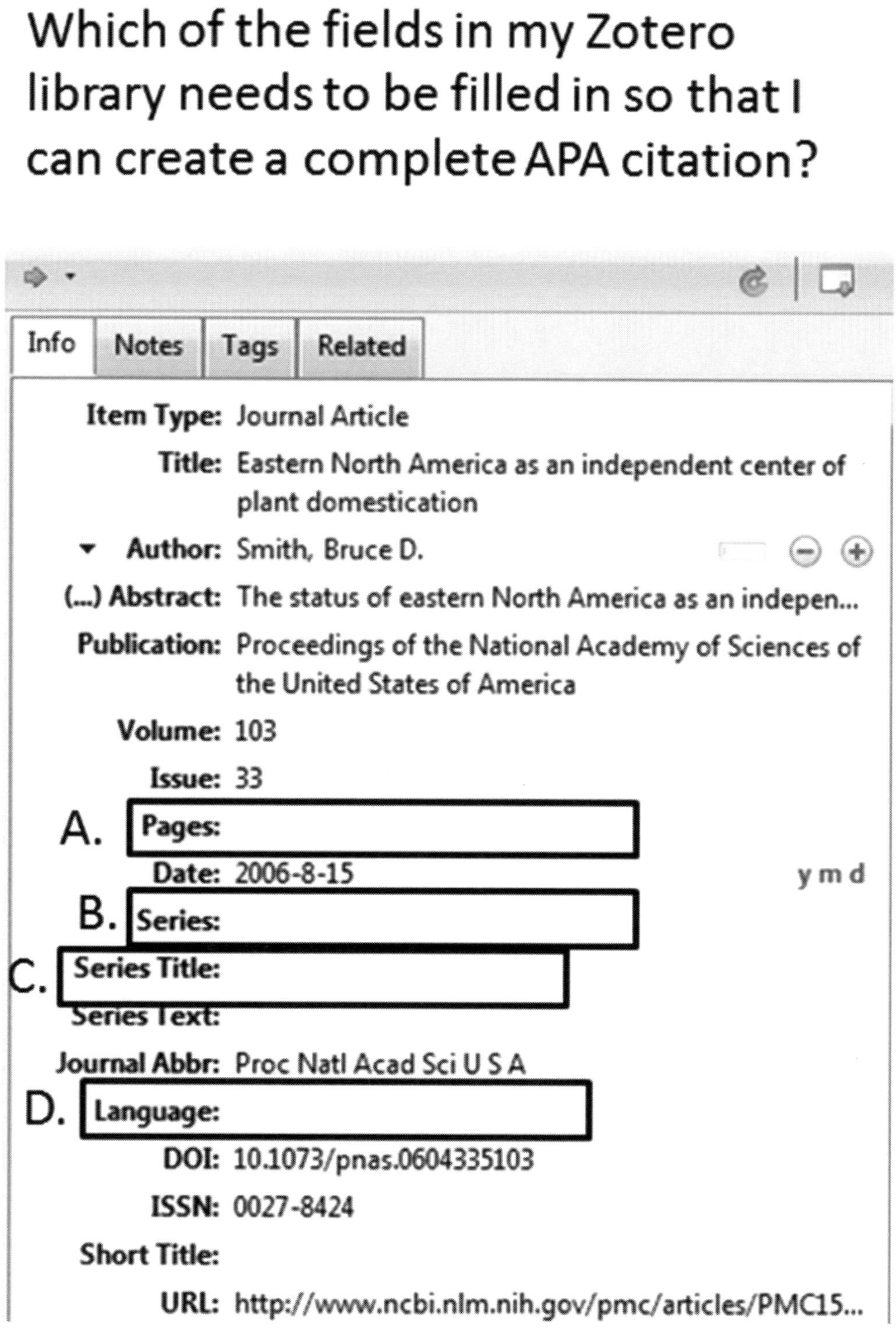

# Which of the fields in my Zotero library needs to be filled in so that I can create a complete APA citation?

**Figure 8.2.** Multiple-choice question using images instead of text

example, a learning objective that asks learners to identify a peer-reviewed article is not an end in itself. Rather, this is part of a learning experience that should be scaffolded throughout the educational system as learners begin to understand how an academic conversation works, how they can evaluate the evidence presented in that conversation, and how they can contribute to that conversation once they have the appropriate disciplinary grounding.

- Are the learning objectives for the tutorial met?
- Do content changes need to be made?
- Are more resources needed in order to redesign or expand the tutorial?

The evaluation data that you collect from learner assessments can be used to make content changes within your tutorial. You may realize that the language you use is unclear, that the information you cover is either too basic or too advanced, or that you need better examples in order to demonstrate your concepts. But if you see that learners increase their knowledge or skills after interacting with your tutorial, this indicates that the design you are using is effective. Demonstrating that learning gains are happening can be used to convince administrators that the resources dedicated to the tutorial were worthwhile and that the tutorial is showing a good return on investment. The next type of evaluation will help you show that learners are able to apply what they have learned, which can be used as even stronger evidence of the value of your tutorials.

## Measuring Application: Level 3

Kirkpatrick's (2006) level 3 evaluation measures whether or not learners have made behavioral changes and whether they can now apply the knowledge or skills that they learned in a realistic context. This type of evaluation contrasts with learning assessments that take place in a controlled but not particularly realistic environment, such as an on-line quiz. Learners who demonstrate that they can choose the correct multiple-choice response when asked to select a peer-reviewed journal article still might not be able to actually select a peer-reviewed journal article from a list of thousands of database results when they are performing their own research. Measuring learners' ability to apply or transfer what they have learned to a realistic setting provides a more accurate picture of deep learning. Moreover, the ability to evaluate the impacts of learning is improved if you can observe changes in behavior a significant time after taking the tutorial. Kirkpatrick (2006) recommends waiting between one to six months to observe application of learning in a realistic setting in order to get a true measure of behavioral change.

As noted earlier, measuring learning a significant amount of time after learners have engaged with the tutorial can range from difficult to impossible for many librarians depending on how much control the librarian has over the relationship with the learners. In addition, many librarians simply do not have the opportunity to observe application of learning within a realistic setting. If this is the case, remember that valuable evaluation information can be gathered from measurements of reaction and learning (Kirkpatrick's levels 1 and 2). However, there are some alternative methods of evaluation worth trying that can help provide a more realistic environment in which to observe knowledge transfer. If you are able to gather evaluation information measuring application several months after learners have engaged with your tutorial—great! If not, focus more on finding ways to observe or measure how learners apply their knowledge than on the timing issues.

Subjective assessments of learning (as opposed to objective assessments) like essays or live simulations are more likely to provide a realistic look at learners' ability to apply their knowledge. Subjective assessments take more time to score because an automatic response can't be given. Instead, tools like rubrics are often used in order to provide scoring consistency. In addition to the extra scoring time involved, another hurdle is that direct access to learners may be needed in order to evaluate their work. In the case of academic or school librarians, the types of work that could be evaluated to determine application of conceptual learning or cognitive strategies include presentations, term papers, annotated bibliographies, or class projects. These types of work could be particularly illuminating in regard to the effectiveness of the tutorial if the work is done a month or more after learners engaged with the tutorial.

Alternatively, to see whether learners can apply what they've learned in order to perform a particular process or demonstrate problem-solving skills, set up a simulation where learners conduct a realistic task, such as adding sources to a Zotero collection and creating a bibliography based on their research topic. This simulation could take place either in person or at a distance if screen-recording technology is available to the learner. Another option for observing how learners perform in an online simulated exercise is to use e-learning authoring tools like Camtasia, Captivate, or Articulate that allow the creation of scenarios with branching. The data gathered from these recorded simulations could provide a more authentic look at learners' application of knowledge but would not require you to be co-located with your learners.

If the tutorial you create is for a specific class or department, it will likely be easier for you to gain access to students' work or to observe students as they walk through a simulated problem. Perhaps you already have a good relationship with a classroom instructor or another stakeholder who has more access to your learners. If you can't gain access to all of the learners' work, an alternative would be to request a small sample of work or access to a small pool of learners in order to help you evaluate the effectiveness of the tutorial. Another option for gathering evaluation information if you can't gain direct access to learners is to talk to people who do interact with them frequently, particularly as they are applying their knowledge (Horton 2001). Usually, this will mean talking to classroom instructors in order to learn how well their students were able to put the ideas from the tutorials into practice.

If the tutorials you create are not tied to a specific class and you have few other options for interacting with your learners, you may need to solicit volunteers to help you measure learners' ability to apply what they've learned in much the same way that you would ask for usability testing volunteers. You could offer incentives for learners who

- Can learners apply what they have learned in realistic settings?
- Are larger curricular changes needed?
- Are tutorials needed in more or different contexts?

give you access to their final projects or who allow you to observe them demonstrating a particular task. While observing learners who have opted into this evaluation is not ideal since it can lead to a skewed set of results, sometimes this may be the only option if you don't have access through another stakeholder.

The evaluation data gathered from observing whether learners can apply what they have learned or whether they can transfer their skills to a different context are particularly helpful for making decisions about your tutorials at a broader level. Kirkpatrick's levels are meant to build on each other sequentially, so the information that you have gathered in the previous two levels should provide significant direction as you consider design and content changes at the individual tutorial level. If the evaluation information that you gather at the application level indicates that learners are not able to apply what they have learned, rather than tweaking the tutorial's navigation or the language, you may need to consider the larger context in which the tutorials are used. Perhaps the tutorials need to be introduced at a different time. Or several, shorter tutorials need to be used. Alternatively, tutorials may not be a good instructional fit for these learners. On the flip side, if learners can apply what they learn, this is good evidence that these tutorials or similar tutorials could be applied in other contexts. An argument could be made that more tutorials need to be developed and more resources dedicated to this work because a positive return on investment has been demonstrated.

## ⊚ Measuring Programmatic Results: Level 4

Kirkpatrick's (2006) level 4 evaluation examines whether or not your tutorial has led to real changes or results at the big-picture level. Typically, this evaluation level measures whether changes have happened that are impactful at a programmatic or even institutional level, and the measurements are used to guide high-level administrators. To evaluate impact at this level, the impact of the tutorial needs to be tied to specific programmatic or institutional goals. For example, perhaps your institution wants to increase student retention, graduation rates, and students' abilities to engage in lifelong learning. Of course, demonstrating the impact of library tutorials at this level is very difficult because the library is part of a much larger environment and is very rarely the sole factor influencing these big-picture outcomes. However, if you have gathered sufficient evaluation information from the previous three levels, and if you can tie some of the tutorial's learning objectives to the broader institutional outcomes, you can still present a compelling argument for the value of the tutorials.

In-depth institutional evaluations are rarely done because of the cost involved and the difficulty of gathering accurate and meaningful information at this level (Horton 2001).

One way to begin to gather evaluation information at this level is to map your learning objectives to larger standards. For example, you could reference the Association of College and Research Libraries (ACRL) information literacy standards or framework or the Association of American Colleges and Universities Liberal Education and America's Promise (LEAP) outcomes or other lifelong learning standards. Tying your objectives to standardized outcomes makes it easier for administrators to understand how the tutorials fit into the bigger picture as they communicate with accreditation agencies, donors, government officials, or other decision makers.

Institution-level evaluation measures may never be required for your tutorials. If that is the case, it may be more helpful to think of the ultimate level in your evaluation hierarchy as an evaluation of whether the tutorial is doing its job as a learning tool. Summative evaluations can help guide this type of decision making. One way of thinking of summative evaluation is as the test that happens at the end of the term. This kind of summative evaluation provides information to the instructor and the learner about how the learner did overall.

Entire courses or tutorials can be evaluated summatively as well. According to Walter Dick, Lou Carey, and James Carey, summative evaluation "is the process of collecting data and information in order to make decisions about the acquisition or continued use of some instruction" (2004, 339). When the focus of summative evaluation is turned on the instruction itself, the process of summative evaluation seeks to determine whether the tutorial is solving learners' knowledge or skill gaps and needs. Instructional designers use expert judgment and field testing in order to see whether learners as a group are meeting objectives and are able to transfer their knowledge. This level of evaluation can make use of the information gained in the previous levels of evaluation, but it is the most intentional in compiling what individual learners have learned into a comprehensive look at the effectiveness and overall impact of your tutorials.

The evaluation information that you gain from mapping your learning objectives to institutional-level standards and from taking a summative look at what has been learned can be used to determine whether or not you should continue using your tutorials or whether significant reworking of the tutorials is required. Programmatic evaluation can also be used in order to demonstrate the impact of library instruction to administrators. Administrators who understand the value of what the library does may not be conversant about the specific learning objectives of your tutorials, but they should understand how your tutorials connect to the overall learning experience.

## MEASURING PROGRAMMATIC RESULTS: LEVEL 4— EVALUATION QUESTIONS

- Do the tutorial learning-assessment results map to institutional or national standards?
- Does your tutorial contribute to a larger learning experience for a group of learners?
- Are curricular changes needed in order to connect the tutorial to a larger learning experience?

## ⊚ Key Points

Evaluating a tutorial helps provide both specific and general information about the impact of a tutorial. Measuring the effectiveness of your tutorial in terms of whether learners like your tutorial, have learned new skills, and are able to apply their knowledge can help determine the overall value of a tutorial programmatically. Here are some key points to take away:

- Beginning your evaluation process with a clear understanding of how you will use the information that you gather will help you to determine what combination of evaluation strategies will work best for you.
- Assessing learning is one of the most effective ways to evaluate the impact of a tutorial. Objective learning assessments directly tied to learning objectives help provide clear information about what has been learned based on what was covered in the tutorial.
- Objective learning assessments cover a wide array of knowledge types and provide evaluation information in order to help both the learner and the instructor make appropriate adjustments.
- Combining information from the four evaluation levels provides a complete picture to guide decision making about the future direction of a tutorial for both instructors and administrators.

Now that you understand the purpose of evaluation and what evaluation strategies will be most important for guiding decision making in your local context, you are ready to think about how you will maintain your tutorial. Chapter 9 will walk through the steps involved in creating sustainable tutorials, establishing a tutorial-maintenance workflow, and ways to maintain your own knowledge of how to create tutorials.

## ⊚ References

Anderson, Lorin W., and David R. Krathwohl, eds. 2001. *A Taxonomy for Learning, Teaching, and Assessing: A Revision of Bloom's Taxonomy of Educational Objectives.* New York: Longman.

Bozarth, Jane. 2008. *From Analysis to Evaluation: Tools, Tips, and Techniques for Trainers.* New York: Wiley.

Dick, Walter, Lou Carey, and James O. Carey. 2004. *The Systematic Design of Instruction.* 6th ed. Boston: Allyn & Bacon.

Gagné, Robert M., Walter W. Wager, Katharine C. Golas, and John M. Keller. 2005. *Principles of Instructional Design.* 5th ed. Belmont, CA: Thomson/Wadsworth.

Gould, Kevin. 2010. "Writing Questions Based on Bloom's Taxonomy." *Clicker Questions.* http://clickerquestions.pbworks.com/w/page/31115153/Writing-questions-based-on-Bloom%27s-taxonomy.

Horton, William. 2001. *Evaluating E-learning.* Alexandria, VA: American Society for Training & Development.

Kirkpatrick, Donald. 2006. *Evaluating Training Programs: The Four Levels.* San Francisco, CA: Berrett-Koehler Publishers.

Mager, Robert Frank. 1997. *Measuring Instructional Results or Got a Match? How to Find Out If Your Instructional Objectives Have Been Achieved.* 3rd ed. Atlanta, GA: Center for Effective Performance.

Means, Barbara, Yukie Toyama, Robert Murphy, Marianne Bakia, and Karla Jones. 2009. "Evaluation of Evidence-Based Practices in Online Learning: A Meta-Analysis and Review of Online Learning Studies." U.S. Department of Education. http://eric.ed.gov/?id=ED505824.

Smith, Susan Sharpless. 2010. *Web-Based Instruction: A Guide for Libraries*. 7th ed. Chicago: ALA Editions.

# CHAPTER 9

# Maintenance
## *Sustainable Approaches for Revising*

▷ Revisiting the main takeaways from using the ADDIE process to design tutorials

▷ Exploring the value of creating modular tutorials that can be sustainably maintained

▷ Choosing a method for establishing a tutorial-maintenance workflow

▷ Considering options for learning more tutorial-creation skills

ONLINE TUTORIALS ARE VALUABLE instructional tools for reaching diverse groups of learners. Throughout this book you have seen examples of different contexts in which tutorials can be used. You have read about how tutorials can effectively deliver a variety of types of content. And you have learned that simple, accessible tutorials tied to specific learning outcomes provide the best learning experience. In other words, for most audiences flashy does not equal better! Paying careful attention to your learners' needs, using proven instructional design strategies to minimize cognitive overload, focusing on providing meaningful feedback and assessment, and learning how to use the tools that help you do those things will provide better return on your investment than struggling to build a technologically complicated but pedagogically weak tutorial.

This book has used the ADDIE principles of design to help provide you with the strategies you need to create your own tutorials. The ADDIE model was chosen because of the flexibility it provides and because its principles translate well to a wide variety of instructional settings. This final chapter will begin with a review of some of the main takeaways from the ADDIE model. Later in the chapter, strategies for moving forward with the important work of maintaining the tutorials you have created will be discussed.

The chapter will conclude with some suggestions for continuing to develop your tutorial-creation skills.

## ⊚ ADDIE Takeaways

The five steps of the ADDIE model were used throughout this book to help provide guidance and structure to the process of creating a learner-centered tutorial. One of the reasons that the ADDIE model is so effective is because it is meant to be iterative. As you create your own tutorials, keep revisiting the main principles of the model, especially the principle of evaluation. The ADDIE model was created as a way to approach many instructional situations—from workplace training to higher education to informal learning settings. Hopefully, you are now able to think specifically about how the ADDIE model translates to the process of creating online tutorials, especially tutorials intended for library instruction. This section summarizes key points about how ADDIE can be used to help guide librarians through the process of creating tutorials (see table 9.1).

### Analysis

The ADDIE model suggests several types of analysis to help prepare instruction that is learner centered. As you start to create your own tutorials, the key analysis steps to include are

- determining your instructional task,
- knowing who your learners are, and
- finding out what resources you have and what resources you need.

Remembering to begin the tutorial-planning process focused on a specific instructional task that meets the needs of your particular learners will keep you from the temptation to include nonessential content. An analysis of your specific learners will prepare you to create tutorials that assume an appropriate level of prior knowledge and that use relevant language and examples. As you map out what content you will deliver, determining what people and technology resources you will need to gather is a crucial analysis step. Researching and purchasing or borrowing the necessary tools early on will help you from being delayed at later points. Gathering the teammates or support personnel who have skills that you can draw on as you create your tutorials will also help your task feel less daunting.

Some example tasks that you might start during the analysis phase are

- writing instructional goals,
- surveying your learners,
- talking to colleagues who know your learner population,
- conducting a skills inventory, and
- purchasing necessary software or hardware.

These tasks can either be divided out among your tutorial team or scheduled far enough in advance of your tutorial-production process to help spread out the work. When drafting your project timeline, be sure to include sufficient time for these analysis steps (see

**Table 9.1.** Summary of ADDIE Principles for Creating Tutorials

| | KEY POINTS | EXAMPLE TASKS |
|---|---|---|
| **Analysis** | • Determine your instructional task.<br>• Know who your learners are.<br>• Find out what resources you have and what resources you need. | • Write instructional goals.<br>• Survey your learners; talk to others who know your learner population.<br>• Conduct a skills inventory; purchase needed software or hardware. |
| **Design** | • Divide your overall learning goals into smaller components.<br>• Plan an assessment strategy.<br>• Choose instructional strategies based on your content.<br>• Organize the tutorial with a logical flow. | • Write learning objectives.<br>• Brainstorm assessment strategies for your learning objectives; create active learning opportunities based on those strategies.<br>• Map your content to the appropriate knowledge type; create graphics or simulations based on your objectives.<br>• Create a storyboard to visualize the tutorial flow; create learner-controlled navigational choices. |
| **Development** | • Plan your narrative.<br>• Use the right tools for your task.<br>• Make the tutorials universally accessible. | • Write scripts based on your learning objectives.<br>• Find e-learning authoring tools that match your budget, timeline, expertise, and tutorial content type; decide if you need dedicated audio or visual creation and editing tools.<br>• Consult accessibility standards and follow accessibility guidelines. |
| **Implementation** | • Conduct usability testing to get learner feedback.<br>• Plan a promotional strategy.<br>• Determine whether other colleagues could use your tutorial. | • Set up at least one round of usability testing; make revisions.<br>• Create a promotions calendar.<br>• Develop a professional development event to let other librarians explore ways to use the tutorial. |
| **Evaluation** | • Make an evaluation plan.<br>• Create formative learning assessments.<br>• Use evaluation data to demonstrate the tutorial's value. | • Create objective learning assessments based on your learning objectives.<br>• Test your learning assessments for clarity.<br>• Find ways to evaluate learners' ability to apply what they've learned.<br>• Discuss the tutorial's impact with administrators. |

chapter 2 for time suggestions). Time spent writing targeted instructional goals and performing an environmental scan will result in a tutorial that matches the needs of your learner audience.

## Design

The ADDIE principle of design helps you begin to transition to the nuts-and-bolts work that happens during the development phase. The key points to focus on during the design phase are

- dividing your overall learning goals into smaller components,
- planning an assessment strategy,
- choosing instructional strategies based on your content, and
- organizing the tutorial with a logical flow.

Taking the larger instructional goals developed in the analysis phase and turning them into smaller components prepares you for the modular work of creating online tutorials. You can then realistically start to think about how you will assess the smaller modules of your tutorial as well as the tutorial as a whole. Before starting the production process, specifically designing your tutorial with appropriate strategies such as building in learner control and using visual examples relevant to the knowledge type addressed in the tutorial will make the work of creating that content more straightforward. Creating a storyboard or map of your entire tutorial and letting other people provide feedback will help you to more clearly see a logical navigational path through your tutorial.

Some example tasks you might work on during the design phase are

- writing learning objectives,
- brainstorming assessment strategies for your learning objectives,
- creating active learning opportunities based on those strategies,
- mapping your content to the appropriate knowledge type,
- creating graphics or simulations based on your objectives,
- making a storyboard to visualize the tutorial flow, and
- creating learner-controlled navigational choices.

While these tasks can be divided among a team, each task is critical enough that it would be wise to solicit feedback on all of them, even if you are not working on this project as part of a team. Having clear learning objectives and an assessment plan will not only help you as you move to the development phase but will also communicate the main focus of your tutorial to other stakeholders or future colleagues who may be working on updates.

## Development

The ADDIE principle of development includes much of the nitty-gritty work of creating the actual tutorial product. The key points to focus on during the development phase are

- planning your narrative,
- using the right tools for your task, and
- making tutorials universally accessible.

If you have laid the groundwork for your tutorial content and its learning objectives in the earlier phases, creating a script or narrative for your tutorial that matches the audience level should be more straightforward. The work done in the design phase will have prepared you for tool decisions during the development phase as you should already know where you will need images, videos, audio, or text throughout the tutorial. Paying careful attention to the production tools you use and the accessibility support you build in will make your tutorial usable for a wider range of learners.

Some example tasks you might work on during the development phase are

- writing scripts based on your learning objectives;
- finding e-learning authoring tools that match your budget, timeline, expertise, and tutorial content type;

- deciding whether you need dedicated audio or visual creation and editing tools;
- consulting accessibility standards and following accessibility guidelines.

The development phase is often the stage where many librarians need outside help. If you don't have any previous experience using e-learning authoring tools or working with accessibility standards, you are not alone. Don't feel shy about admitting that you need to take a course, spend some extra time reading online help forums, or consult with more experienced e-learning colleagues at a neighboring school, in another department, or get a freelancer's assistance.

## Implementation

The ADDIE principle of implementation is the reality-check phase when you learn whether or not your learners can actually use your tutorial. This phase is also when you determine the best ways to deliver your tutorial to your intended audience. The key points to focus on during the implementation phase are

- conducting usability testing to get learner feedback,
- planning a promotional strategy, and
- determining whether other colleagues could use your tutorial.

Your usability testing strategies can range from fairly simple techniques like asking a handful of people for feedback on a prototype to more involved trials in a classroom setting. Building in the time for at least some usability testing is crucial to the success of your tutorial—even if it does mean that you need to undertake some revisions! Some tutorials come with a built-in audience; other tutorials must be promoted in order to reach an audience. Depending on your situation, dedicate some time to making sure your tutorial reaches your intended learner group. If you would like other colleagues to be able to use and possibly adapt your tutorial for their instructional needs, make sure to get their feedback and work with them to come up with strategies for incorporating your tutorial into their instructional workflow.

Some example tasks you might work on during the implementation phase are

- setting up at least one round of usability testing,
- making revisions,
- creating a promotions calendar, and
- developing a professional development event to let other librarians explore ways to use the tutorial.

While one person or a small group from your tutorial team may be responsible for the implementation phase, the key to successfully implementing your tutorial is collaboration. Learn from the input that you gather and make sure that you tap into the expertise of others, whether that is in the form of proofreading while making revisions or generating promotional ideas that will be meaningful in your environment.

## Evaluation

The last ADDIE principle is evaluation and is actually an iterative step because you will be evaluating the tutorial at multiple phases of your project. As you formulate your own evaluation plan, the key points to focus on are

- finding the right combination of evaluation strategies,
- creating learning-assessment opportunities to help both the instructor and the learner, and
- using the evaluation information gathered to demonstrate the tutorial's value.

Recognize that not all evaluation methods work equally well for all projects. Think about the audiences who will be interested in the impact of your tutorial and choose evaluation strategies that will help guide their decisions. Developing learning-assessment activities that relate directly back to specific learning objectives helps keep both the learner and the instructor on track. The feedback received from these formative assessments will also allow both the instructor and the learner to make needed changes. Evaluation information can be gathered that helps you adjust the tutorial's look and feel, the information covered, or the curricular placement. Learning how to communicate the right evaluation information to the appropriate stakeholders will help you make the best decisions about how to move forward with your tutorials.

Some example tasks that you might start on during the evaluation phase are

- creating an evaluation plan,
- compiling data documenting learners' reactions to the tutorial's look and feel,
- creating a learning-assessment plan,
- drafting formative assessment tools such as pretests or quizzes based on your learning objectives,
- looking for partners to help you evaluate learners' ability to apply what they have learned,
- investigating whether your learning objectives can be mapped to larger institutional objectives, and
- discussing the tutorial's impact with administrators.

These tasks can be divided among your tutorial team members. If you are not working with a team, run your evaluation and learning-assessment plan by other colleagues to get some additional feedback. Also, try out your learning-assessment quiz questions on a few sample learners to make sure that your questions are clear. Getting evaluation feedback throughout the tutorial-creation process will help you build a tutorial that meets learners' needs as well as the needs of your instruction program.

## ⊚ Design Modularly to Enhance Sustainability

While using the ADDIE model to tackle the various components of your tutorial projects can help you plan and conceptualize your tutorial project so that it feels more manageable, creating a tutorial still takes a lot of work. Unfortunately, the need for changes and edits are unavoidable—databases, websites, and procedures all change over time—

**Figure 9.1.** Using YouTube statistics to gather modular data

and these changes often are not under your control. Building a tutorial that is able to be maintained and reused without reinvesting an equivalent amount of effort on a regular basis takes careful planning. One of the most common and successful methods of creating more sustainable and repurposable tutorials is through modular design.

Fortunately, creating modular tutorials is both user centered and designer centered. Creating modular tutorials benefits learners because shorter modules help reduce cognitive load and give learners more control as they navigate through the tutorial (see this discussion in chapter 4). Creating modular tutorials benefits tutorial designers because modules are more flexible and can be moved around or edited as needed in small chunks rather than on a global scale.

Modular tutorials also allow the tutorial designer to clearly evaluate the separate components of the tutorial. Librarians at Wayne State University created a tutorial with six modules. They were able to ask evaluative questions about each separate module and make targeted changes accordingly (Befus and Byrne 2011). In addition to directly surveying users about individual modules in your tutorial, you may also be able to use web analytics to gather modular-level data. For example, if you store videos for your tutorial in YouTube, you will be able to see how many people have viewed each of those videos (see figure 9.1 for an example). Or if you use LibGuides as the platform for hosting your tutorial, you will be able to see how many times each of the tabs or pages within your LibGuide have been viewed (see figure 9.2). Gathering modular statistics can help you determine how to most efficiently spend your time—a video that has been viewed fifteen times may not deserve the same maintenance priority as a video that has been viewed 1,500 times. Alternatively, evaluating the statistics for your tutorial at a modular level can notify you that a particular module isn't being used, and you can then take steps to solve that problem.

Not only can modularly designed tutorials help you prioritize maintenance decisions and more easily make those necessary changes, but modularly designed tutorials encourage sharing and borrowing from other tutorials. In chapter 1, several tutorial repositories, including MERLOT II and PRIMO, were suggested as excellent places to look for inspiration for your own tutorial. However, you can also use some of the open, modularly designed tutorials in these repositories as a resource for finding modules that you can incorporate into your own tutorials. Librarians work within an amazingly collaborative and open community—take advantage of the work that your colleagues have done and

| | ID | Page Name | Jan | Feb | Mar | Apr | May | Jun | Jul | Aug | Sep | Oct | Nov | Dec | Total ▾ |
|---|---|---|---|---|---|---|---|---|---|---|---|---|---|---|---|
| 1. | 3619551 | 1. Get Started | 112 | 129 | 42 | 104 | 57 | 40 | 54 | 36 | 70 | 114 | 69 | 99 | 926 |
| 2. | 3836246 | Annotating & Highlighting | 68 | 24 | 32 | 62 | 72 | 142 | 123 | 135 | 24 | 0 | 2 | 4 | 688 |
| 3. | 3830634 | Install Zotero | 27 | 13 | 6 | 14 | 9 | 13 | 14 | 14 | 3 | 25 | 24 | 26 | 188 |

All Guides | **Page Views** | Links    Hit source: **All** | Standard | Mobile | API | Widget    Export to: Excel | Plain view

**Figure 9.2.** Using LibGuides statistics to gather modular data

**Table 9.2.** Repository Examples for Storing Different Learning-Object Types

| LEARNING-OBJECT TYPE | REPOSITORY EXAMPLES |
| --- | --- |
| Images | Flickr, wiki, LibGuide, Dropbox, Tumblr, Pinterest, DSpace |
| Videos | YouTube, wiki, LibGuide, Dropbox, Tumblr, Pinterest |
| Quizzes | Quia, SurveyMonkey, Qualtrics |

borrow the modules, videos, or infographics that fit within your tutorial's theme. Much of the content in these repositories is openly available to use or adapt, but it is a good practice to always check first. Also, in most cases, attributing the original author is both the correct and the collegial thing to do!

As your own tutorial grows, you and your colleagues will be creating your own repository of modules—the learning objects or components that make up your tutorial. Rather than just letting these modules accumulate in a haphazard fashion, begin thinking about the benefits of creating a separate repository for your tutorial's modules that can be accessed when another colleague at your institution wants to create a tutorial for their instructional needs. Depending on your context, it might be helpful to create a repository of images using a tool like Flickr, a repository of videos using a tool like YouTube, or a repository of quizzes using a tool like Quia (see table 9.2 for more repository examples). Creating a repository of learning objects or tutorial modules makes the tutorial-sharing process more transparent, which can make it simpler for new colleagues to incorporate these learning objects into their projects. Don't let the work of setting up and maintaining a learning-objects repository consume all of your time. Content will change, and you won't always be able to reuse images or videos; however, establishing a culture of modular sharing can help create more consistent tutorials and can reduce the amount of time it takes to build new tutorials.

## ⑥ Maintenance: The Practice of Constant Revision

Tutorial maintenance is often internally driven, either as part of a continuous maintenance workflow, by your library's decision to switch to a new database vendor, or by the gentle nudging of a colleague who notices information that is out of date. The need for tutorial changes may also be driven by external factors such as changes in curriculum, vendor interface changes, updates to accessibility norms, and changes in technology such as the move toward responsive sites that work equally well on desktop computers and mobile devices. Or you may base the need for change on feedback that you actively solicit from your learners. Regardless of what prompts the need for tutorial maintenance, developing a plan for maintaining your tutorials will ensure that your tutorials remain relevant and useful.

Creating a modularly designed tutorial prepares you to make changes to certain aspects of your tutorial without re-creating the whole tutorial. However, even with a modular design, your tutorials won't maintain themselves. Keeping your tutorials up to date will require establishing a maintenance workflow and budgeting the time to actually perform the needed maintenance. Start by finding a reoccurring time that hopefully isn't as busy and when making adjustments won't negatively impact your learners. For academic librarians, this time slot is often during the summer or during winter break (Scales, Nicol, and Johnson 2014). Put that maintenance time onto your calendar each year. If you have a team available to work on maintenance projects, schedule a yearly maintenance kickoff party or gathering to make the work more collaborative and fun.

Establishing a routine time for maintenance is only one piece of the maintenance puzzle. Developing a process or workflow for evaluating, editing, and potentially weeding out old tutorials will help provide systematic guidance to your regular maintenance activities. One way to evaluate your tutorials is through the use of a rubric, as the scores you assign can help you decide which tutorials to keep, revise, or discard (see table 9.3 for an

**Table 9.3.** Tutorial Evaluation Rubric Based on Best Practices[1]

| | 2 (KEEP) | 1 (NEEDS SOME REVISION) | 0 (NEEDS SIGNIFICANT REVISION/DISCARD) | DOESN'T APPLY |
|---|---|---|---|---|
| Design | The design used matches the content presented. | Some design elements match the content presented. | The design does not match the content presented. | |
| Learning Objectives | The tutorial is focused on a single learning objective. | The topic is focused on several connected learning objectives. | The tutorial does not connect to any learning objectives. | |
| Logical Flow | The tutorial is logically structured. | Sometimes the tutorial flow is hard to follow. | The tutorial lacks a logical flow. | |
| Length | Videos in the tutorial are under 2 minutes. | Videos in the tutorial are between 2 and 4 minutes. | Videos in the tutorial are 5 minutes or longer. | |
| Interactive | The tutorial includes interactive elements tied to the learning objectives. | The tutorial includes interactive elements, but they are not tied to learning objectives. | The tutorial does not include interactivity. | |
| Ease of Navigation | The tutorial has clear navigation options. | The tutorial sometimes provides navigational options. | The tutorial lacks navigational options. | |
| Accessible | The tutorial includes captions, does not include Flash, and works with a screen reader. | The tutorial is lacking either captions or the ability to work with a screen reader. | The tutorial lacks captions and the ability to work with a screen reader. | |
| Modifiable Format | The tutorial can be easily modified. | Modifying the tutorial would take some work. | Modifying the tutorial would take a lot of work. | |
| Relevant and Up to Date | The information is relevant, currently up to date, and not easily dated. | The information is relevant and currently up to date but will soon become dated. | The information is no longer relevant, is out of date, and is hard to maintain. | |
| Branding and Styling | The tutorial follows institutional branding and style guides. | The tutorial sometimes follows institutional branding and style guides. | The tutorial does not follow institutional branding or style guides. | |
| Total Score | | | | |

[1]Adapted from Amanda Hess's (2014) MAGIC rubric.

example rubric). Your rubric should reflect your tutorial design and development values. For example, if easily modifiable tutorials are a priority, make sure to include that criteria in your rubric and then be on the lookout for elements in your tutorials that are not easily modifiable, such as Flash. Or if tutorials that are branded with your institution's logo or that use your institution's style guides are important, then make sure to include that criteria in your rubric. The example rubric provided in table 9.3 is just a starting point. Consider your local context and values and feel free to add other evaluation criteria such as image quality, audio quality, or modularity.

Once you establish the criteria for evaluating your tutorials, you can then use the scoring system to help you decide whether to keep, revise, or discard your tutorials. You may also realize that you need some new tutorials. At Oakland University, Amanda Hess made a tutorial-creation decision-making matrix in order to help librarians decide whether or not to make new tutorials or modules. The matrix uses the foundations of tutorial design to walk through questions related to the knowledge type of the tutorial, as well as through such practical (but often ignored!) questions such as "Do we already have a tutorial about this?" or "Will a vendor-based tutorial serve us equally well?" (2014, 95).

Technology-driven maintenance questions might also include regular assessments of whether or not your graphics are too resource intensive. If an analysis of your learner community reveals that they use your tutorial via relatively low bandwidth, you may need to revise your tutorial using less resource-intensive graphics. Or you may discover that bandwidth is no longer a constraint for your learner population and revise your tutorial to have higher-quality graphics.

Another area for regular review is the incorporation of social media elements. If social media tools are used as a way for your learners to communicate with each other or can be used as a way to provide formative assessment activities, consider updating your tutorial to include some of these tools. Options for user-generated content may be another future technological avenue to consider including in certain types of tutorials. For example, processes that change considerably depending on the device used, such as the process of downloading an e-book, might be enhanced by allowing users to create content such as a YouTube video and then share how to download e-books based on their device.

Web analytics can also help guide your maintenance decisions. As described in the previous section on the value of creating modular tutorials, information from YouTube and LibGuides can help you target the portions of your tutorial that need to be updated or revised. Tools like Google Analytics may help you discover whether and how much your tutorial is being used (Betty 2008). If your usage statistics are low, digging into how findable your tutorials are may become increasingly important. Many learners don't come directly to the library's website to look for tutorial information, so placing your tutorials in a variety of locations may make them more findable. Hess (2014) suggests placing library tutorials on YouTube because this is where many of her college student learners search for information already.

Gathering feedback from your learners can be a valuable source of information to help guide your maintenance decisions. Hopefully, you performed some type of usability testing when you were rolling out the initial iteration of your tutorial, but checking in with your learners after your tutorial has been in place for a little while is also a good practice. Many libraries put assessment forms directly on their tutorials in order to gather feedback on a continuous basis. However, you may need to reach out to your learners directly in order to get more targeted feedback. Consider selecting a class or two to gather feedback from. At Washington State University, an online information literacy class was asked a few open-ended questions in order to help guide a tutorial redesign project (Scales, Nicol, and Johnson 2014). The designers learned that these students found the audiovisual components of the existing tutorial to be the most valuable. This information then helped the designers prioritize how content was delivered in the redesign. Evaluation of student work can be another way to determine the maintenance and redesign priorities. At Florida Gulf Coast University, designers reviewed how well students communicated what they learned, and then revised the tutorials based on the gaps in knowledge that their learners displayed (McClure, Cooke, and Carlin 2011).

Finally, consider asking for feedback from your peers (Hess 2014). Check in with your fellow librarians or instructors to see how they have observed learners using the tutorial, what gaps they may have noticed in the content, or what changes they might like to see. Creating a space for honest and open feedback or criticism isn't always easy. Start by demonstrating that you are willing to make changes and aren't offended by constructive feedback. It is likely that your colleagues will also be invested in creating the best experience for your learners.

## ⓖ Suggestions for Continuing Your Tutorial-Creation Education

Now that you've whetted your appetite for tutorial creation, you might be excited to create tutorials for and about everything in your life! Alternatively, you may be very relieved that your big tutorial project is over and that you can catch your breath again. Either way, hopefully the process of creating tutorials is one that you are willing to return to as future opportunities arise. This section will cover some suggestions for how to progressively build up your tutorial-creation skill set.

If you were involved in creating tutorials as part of a team for your first tutorial-creation experience, perhaps you were involved with some but not all of the tasks. For your next tutorial project, consider taking on some new tasks. Table 9.4 walks through some suggestions of how to progressively tackle new design and development skills. For your first tutorial, a good goal might be to work on creating clear, simple screenshots that minimize cognitive load. A progressively difficult design and development task would be to include some assessment activities along with those clear screenshots. Your next design and development challenge could be to produce screencasts in addition to screenshots when appropriate. Once you master the recording and web-publishing techniques, you might consider learning how to include branching elements or problem-based scenarios in order to engage your learners in more deep learning exercises.

If you started with a strong set of design and development skills, consider stretching yourself in other ways. Take on more project management tasks. Learn more about creating measurable learning objectives. Read more about writing meaningful multiple-choice questions. See whether there is more that you could learn about usability testing. Find new promotional techniques that you could try out. Advice for learning about tutorial creation often fixates on the technical aspects, but there are other skills involved in creating successful tutorials that are important to acquire and practice. The framework that is included in this book is meant to provide you with more confidence so that you can progressively apply what you have learned to new projects.

There are a variety of learning resources available both online and in person to help you continue to hone your tutorial-creation skills. Lynda.com is a valuable resource for increasing your technical skills and is worth the subscription fee. Monitoring instructional

**Table 9.4.** Example of a Progressive Tutorial Learning Plan

| PROGRESSIVELY MORE COMPLICATED TASKS | SKILLS | TOOLS |
|---|---|---|
| Create screenshots that include simple text both on the image and next to the image in order to teach a single concept. | • Identifying appropriate example content for screenshots<br>• Editing the screenshot<br>• Including text on a screenshot<br>• Incorporating screenshots into a content management system (CMS)<br>• Writing for the web | • Screen-capture tools like Jing or Print Screen<br>• Editing tools like Microsoft Office tools<br>• CMS like LibGuides |
| Connect screenshots in order to demonstrate multiple concepts. Include assessment activities. | • Scaffolding the flow for multiple concepts<br>• Creating a navigation system<br>• Designing formative assessment activities<br>• Collecting assessment data | • Storyboarding tools<br>• Survey or polling tools like Google Forms, Qualtrics, or LibGuides<br>• CMS choices for hosting and navigation like LibGuides or Drupal |
| Record screencasts with audio and video components. | • Writing scripts<br>• Choosing appropriate amount of content so videos aren't too long<br>• Editing audio and video<br>• Web-publishing experience<br>• Video-hosting experience | • Screencast tools like Camtasia, Captivate, or Screencast-O-Matic<br>• Server space<br>• Video storage space like YouTube |
| Include branching elements in order to accommodate different learners. Incorporate problem-based learning scenarios for deeper learning. | • Advanced storyboarding<br>• Advanced use of e-learning authoring tools to include branching<br>• Scenario-writing skills<br>• Creating graphics to use in the scenarios | • Online storyboarding tools<br>• E-learning authoring tools like Camtasia, Captivate, Storyline, or Articulate |

design sites, like the eLearning Guild, can provide learning opportunities and information about current trends. The Association of College and Research Libraries' (ACRL) Immersion program is an in-person training opportunity specifically tailored to help librarians enhance their assessment and design skills. Increasingly, massive open online courses (MOOCs) are an option for gaining new skills, particularly in areas like instructional design. Many campuses offer periodic continuing education or professional development activities for their staff. Check to see whether any upcoming training is about issues related to tutorial creation, and if they aren't, suggest some training topics to the organizers. The more you make use of the training opportunities around you and gradually gain new skills, the less daunting your next tutorial project will be.

## Key Points

Creating a tutorial is just the first step in delivering quality instructional content via the web. Continual maintenance of your tutorials and regular practice with the techniques involved in creating tutorials will help your tutorials remain useful and relevant for your learners. Here are some key points to take away:

- Use the principles of the ADDIE model to guide your tutorial-creation process. This iterative framework provides flexible guidance that can be transferred to a wide variety of instructional contexts.
- Designing modular tutorials helps both the learner and the tutorial designer. Set yourself up for more sustainable tutorial-maintenance practices by building a tutorial that can be assessed and changed in smaller sections.
- Develop a maintenance plan. The need to make changes to your tutorial is inevitable. Establish practices for reviewing and evaluating your tutorials so that your content remains relevant and effective.
- Find ways to keep learning. Progressively challenge yourself to learn more about the various elements of the tutorial-creation process and use the resources around you to continue to build up your tutorial-creation skill set.

## References

Befus, Rebeca, and Katrina Byrne. 2011. "Redesigned with Them in Mind: Evaluating an Online Library Information Literacy Tutorial." *Urban Library Journal* 17, no. 1. http://ojs.gc.cuny.edu/index.php/urbanlibrary/article/view/1245.

Betty, Paul. 2008. "Creation, Management, and Assessment of Library Screencasts: The Regis Libraries Animated Tutorials Project." *Journal of Library Administration* 48, no. 3/4: 295–315.

Hess, Amanda Kathryn Nichols. 2014. "Web Tutorials Workflows: How Scholarship, Institutional Experiences, and Peer Institutions' Practices Shaped One Academic Library's Online Learning Offerings." *New Library World* 115, no. 3/4: 87–101.

McClure, Randall, Rachel Cooke, and Anna Carlin. 2011. "The Search for the Skunk Ape: Studying the Impact of an Online Information Literacy Tutorial on Student Writing." *Journal of Information Literacy* 5, no. 2: 26–45.

Scales, B. Jane, Erica Nicol, and Corey M. Johnson. 2014. "Redesigning Comprehensive Library Tutorials." *Reference & User Services Quarterly* 53, no. 3: 242–52.

## More Resources

ACRL's Immersion Program. http://www.ala.org/acrl/immersionprogram.

ACRL's PRIMO (Peer-Reviewed Instructional Materials Online Database). http://www.ala.org/CFApps/Primo/public/search2.cfm.

eLearning Guild. http://www.elearningguild.com/.

Lynda.com. http://www.lynda.com/.

MERLOT II (Multimedia Educational Resource for Learning and Online Teaching). www.merlot.org.

# Appendix:
# Tutorial Analysis
## *Learning Task, Learner, Learning Environment, Resource*

## Learning-Task Analysis

| Describe the initial condition that requires instruction | Is it a: <br> ☐ Problem <br> ☐ Innovation <br> ☐ Discrepancy | Short description of condition: |
|---|---|---|

**Is instruction the best method to address this condition, or are there other factors causing the problem/innovation/discrepancy?**

**Write the elements of the instructional goal below:**

**Content** (what will be learned):

**Context** (how knowledge will be used):

**Assessment** (how attainment of knowledge/skill will be measured):

**Combine the goal elements into an instructional goal statement:**

**What type of knowledge will learners be expected to gain after interacting with this tutorial? Check all that apply:**

☐ Declarative                 ☐ Cognitive
☐ Conceptual               ☐ Attitude
☐ Procedural                ☐ Psychomotor
☐ Problem solving

**Use the concepts or steps of the instructional goal plus likely prior knowledge and prerequisite knowledge to write instructional objectives.**

**Learning Goal:**

**Steps/concepts of the instructional goal:**

| Prerequisite knowledge needed (and if it will be addressed in coursework or another tutorial): | Prior knowledge likely (and if it has been addressed in coursework or another tutorial): |
|---|---|

**Learning Objectives:**

**Learner Analysis**

**What do you know about the characteristics of your target population?**

**Target population:**

**Age:**

**Developmental stage/reading level/academic attainment:**

**Motivation for learning:**

**Cultural background:**

**Learning/cognitive style or preference:**

**Technological expertise/comfort:**

**Language:**

**Prior knowledge of topic:**

**What additional information about target learners should be gathered before proceeding?**

**Learning-Environment Analysis**

**Describe the educational context for which learning will be designed.**

**What are the mission, philosophy, and taboos of the larger organization?**

**What is the curriculum into which this instruction must fit?**

**What knowledge and skills are learners likely to possess about this topic from prerequisite courses?**

**What is the general level of technological skill and comfort of the learners?**

**What type of technology is available to learners? Where will learning take place?**

**What characterizes the instructors who will use this tutorial?**

**What additional information about the learning environment should be gathered?**

**Resource Analysis**

## Personnel/skills

| Need | Have | | Need | Have | |
|---|---|---|---|---|---|
| ☐ | ☐ | Content knowledge | ☐ | ☐ | Writing |
| ☐ | ☐ | Tutorial-creation technology | ☐ | ☐ | Acting |
| ☐ | ☐ | Programming | ☐ | ☐ | Narration |
| ☐ | ☐ | Graphic design | ☐ | ☐ | Video/audio production |
| ☐ | ☐ | Still photography | ☐ | ☐ | Usability testing |
| ☐ | ☐ | Video photography | ☐ | ☐ | Project management |
| ☐ | ☐ | Collaboration tools | ☐ | ☐ | Other _____ |

**What personnel or skills are needed and not currently available?  How will you meet that need?**

## Equipment

| Need | Have | | Need | Have | |
|---|---|---|---|---|---|
| ☐ | ☐ | Screen-capture software | ☐ | ☐ | Still camera |
| ☐ | ☐ | E-learning/tutorial software | ☐ | ☐ | Video camera |
| ☐ | ☐ | Audio recorder | ☐ | ☐ | Soundproof area—audio capture |
| ☐ | ☐ | Microphone | ☐ | ☐ | Video-recording studio |
| ☐ | ☐ | Stock photography | ☐ | ☐ | Audio/video editing |
| ☐ | ☐ | Other _____ | ☐ | ☐ | Other _____ |

**What equipment or software is needed and is not currently available? How will you meet that need?**

**Network Resources**

**Will tutorial video and image files be locally hosted or stored on the Internet/in the cloud?**

**Are there limits to this storage space?**

**Are the files easily accessed for revision and updating?**

**If there are access options, how can they best be resolved?**

**Are there storage costs involved for local or remote file storage?**

**Who is the key resource person for local/remote storage issues?**

**Time**

**When is this tutorial needed? How much time do you have before the deadline?**

**Are key personnel available to work on this project in order to meet the deadline?**

**If key personnel are not available, how will that affect the design/production/implementation portions of the process?**

# Index

SurveyMonkey, 58, 156, *176*
Synfig, *87*, 90

text-based tutorials, 88
time estimates, for tutorial creation, 30
timeline construction, 25–30
timeline tools: Office templates, 26–27; project
    management software, 27–28
tutorial authoring tools. *See* e-learning authoring tools
tutorial length recommendation, 59
Twine, *79*, *80*

universal design, 104–5, *109*
usability testing: asynchronous testing, *130*, 132–33;
    best practices, 132; beta testing (*see* trials); formative
    usability testing, 128–34; rapid prototyping, 126–28;
    trials, 134–36

video storage, 50, *51*
video tools, 94–95
video-based tutorials, 89

visual disabilities, tutorial solutions, 107–8, *109*
visual examples: animations, *61*, 65–66; infographics, *61*,
    64–65; real-world scenarios, *61*, 68; worked examples,
    *61*, 66–67. *See also* graphics

WAVE accessibility checker, 105, 115
web accessibility initiative, 104
WebAIM, 105, 107
web analytics, 16, 29, 150, 175, 178
web-based tutorials, 88
Web Content Accessibility Guidelines (WCAG), 104,
    106
Windows Movie Maker, *87*, 89

Xmind, *79*, *80*

YouTube: editing videos, *87*, 89; finding videos to use, 95;
    professional development source, 25; video storage, 50,
    175–76, 178, *180*

Zoho, 27–28

# About the Authors

**Hannah Gascho Rempel** is an associate professor at Oregon State University (OSU) Libraries in the Teaching and Engagement Department. Since joining OSU in 2007, she has spearheaded the development of OSU Libraries' services for graduate students and has been deeply involved in the Teaching and Engagement Department's transition to a more strategic focus on instruction activities. She earned her bachelor of science in biology from Eastern Mennonite University, her master of science in horticulture at Oregon State University, and her master of library and information science at the University of Washington. Prior to working at OSU, she served as an adult reference librarian at the Corvallis-Benton County Public Library.

As an instruction and science librarian, Hannah has created a variety of tutorials for a range of audiences. Her Zotero tutorials are widely used by members of the OSU research community, as well as researchers beyond OSU. More recently she has been involved in creating do-it-yourself tutorials for first-year students. She has written and presented on the barriers to creating and managing tutorials. In addition, she writes frequently on providing library services targeted at graduate students' needs, as well as on how to strengthen the library's mobile presence. She helps shape the conversation about technology and web use in libraries by editing the peer-reviewed publication the *Journal of Web Librarianship*. She lives in Corvallis, Oregon, where she is involved in raising two fine daughters.

**Maribeth Slebodnik** is an associate librarian in the Arizona Health Sciences Library at the University of Arizona, where she is an embedded librarian in the College of Nursing. She was the biomedical sciences information specialist and an associate professor in the Purdue University Libraries from 2006–2015. She has created tutorials for a variety of students, including beginning biology and graduate nursing and nutrition science students. Her research focus is on improving library instruction and course transformation, and she participates in the publication of systematic reviews and meta-analyses. She is a member of the Association of College and Research Libraries division of the American Library Association, for which she has served on the Information Literacy Standards Committee, the Instruction Section PRIMO Committee, and as chair of the Science and Technology Section.

Maribeth earned a bachelor of science degree in nursing and a master of library science degree from Indiana University. After twelve years as a neonatal intensive care nurse, she returned to school to retool as a medical librarian. She was a corporate librarian at Mallinckrodt Medical and the Donald Danforth Plant Science Center in St. Louis, Missouri, and an academic librarian at Indiana State University and Purdue University. She currently lives in Tucson, Arizona, where she is a master gardener, knitter, and enthusiastic cook.